Return to the Parish

Return to the Parish

The Pastor in the Public Square

Edited by
David Horn *and*
Jason R. McConnell

CASCADE *Books* • Eugene, Oregon

RETURN TO THE PARISH
The Pastor in the Public Square

Copyright © 2022 Wipf and Stock Publishers. All rights reserved. Except for brief quotations in critical publications or reviews, no part of this book may be reproduced in any manner without prior written permission from the publisher. Write: Permissions, Wipf and Stock Publishers, 199 W. 8th Ave., Suite 3, Eugene, OR 97401.

Cascade Books
An Imprint of Wipf and Stock Publishers
199 W. 8th Ave., Suite 3
Eugene, OR 97401

www.wipfandstock.com

PAPERBACK ISBN: 978-1-6667-3524-6
HARDCOVER ISBN: 978-1-6667-9212-6
EBOOK ISBN: 978-1-6667-9213-3

Cataloguing-in-Publication data:

Names: Horn, David, editor. | McConnell, Jason R., editor.

Title: Return to the parish : the pastor in the public square / Edited by David Horn and Jason R. McConnell.

Description: Eugene, OR: Cascade Books, 2022 | Includes bibliographical references.

Identifiers: ISBN 978-1-6667-3524-6 (paperback) | ISBN 978-1-6667-9212-6 (hardcover) | ISBN 978-1-6667-9213-3 (ebook)

Subjects: LCSH: Pastoral theology. | Christianity and culture. | Church and the world.

Classification: BR517 .R57 2022 (print) | BR517 (ebook)

11/02/22

Unless otherwise indicated, Scripture quotations are from the Holy Bible, New International Version, NIV. Copyright 1973, 1984, 2011 by Biblica, Inc. Used by permission of Zondervan and Biblica. All rights reserved worldwide. www.zondervan.com; Biblica.com. Italics in the NIV text have been added by the author for emphasis.

To all pastors who have already caught a vision for new parish ministry and have modeled faithful service to their local communities beyond their own congregations.

Contents

List of Contributors | ix
Preface | xi
Acknowledgments | xv

Introduction: Return to the Parish | xvii
DAVID HORN

1   **Engaging the Business and Workplace Parish** | 1
    JASON R. MCCONNELL

    Engaging the Business and Workplace Parish: Interview | 18

2   **Engaging the Science and Technology Parish** | 22
    JON PAUL

    Engaging the Science and Technology Parish: Interview | 39

3   **Engaging the Healthcare Parish** | 42
    JUSTIN FRANK

    Engaging the Healthcare Parish: Interview | 58

4   **Engaging the Political Parish** | 61
    MATTHEW WIGTON

    Engaging the Political Parish: Interview | 78

5   **Engaging the Education Parish** | 81
    CHRIS DUNAWAY

    Engaging the Education Parish: Interview | 104

6   **Engaging the Arts Parish** | 108
       SETH ANDERSON

       Engaging the Arts Parish: Interview | 128

7   **Engaging the Multiethnic Parish** | 132
       KENNETH LIU

       Engaging the Multiethnic Parish: Interview | 152

8   **A Passionate Plea for New Parish Ministry** | 155
       JASON R. MCCONNELL

       Epilogue: The Making of Pastoral Learning Communities | 173
       DAVID HORN AND JASON MCCONNELL

       Bibliography | 183

List of Contributors

Dr. David Horn was the director of the Ockenga Institute at Gordon-Conwell Theological Seminary for over twenty years. He is currently the executive director of the Ockenga Fellows Program and a mentor in the Doctor of Ministry program at GCTS. He is also the director of Theology Matters InterVarsity New England.

Dr. Jason R. McConnell is the senior pastor of the East Franklin Union Church and Franklin United Church in Franklin, Vermont. He also serves as adjunct professor of pastoral ministry and co-director of the Ockenga Fellows program and a mentor in the Doctor of Ministry program at GCTS.

Rev. Seth Anderson is the senior pastor of Trinity Presbyterian Church in St. Albans, Vermont.

Rev. Chris Dunaway is the senior pastor of Middle Street Baptist Church in Portsmouth, New Hampshire.

Rev. Justin Frank is the senior pastor of Penny Memorial United Baptist Church in Augusta, Maine.

Rev. Kenneth Liu is the assistant pastor at Boston Chinese Evangelical Church in Newton and Boston, Massachusetts.

Rev. Jon Paul is the senior pastor of Free Christian Church in Andover, Massachusetts.

Rev. Matthew Wigton is the senior pastor of First Baptist Church in Rockport, Massachusetts.

Preface

THIS BOOK HAS ITS origins somewhere. If you want to know the true nature of a river—perhaps its water quality or the character of its flow—all you have to do is go to its source. The headwaters of this book began upstream over twenty-five years ago when fifteen pastors serving seemingly "flourishing" churches from around New England met together under the auspices of the Ockenga Institute, at Gordon-Conwell Theological Seminary. It is not an easy task to identify such churches given the rocky shoals of church life in a geographical region like New England.

Nevertheless, we met together in the same room on a monthly basis for fifteen months to discuss our understanding of what makes churches flourish in such an environment. We talked about the normal sources of church vitality—visionary leadership, good preaching, healthy community life, and the like—and, although all these areas contribute, the one persistent theme that kept rising to the surface was: healthy, flourishing churches always, always have an outward focus.

This is not a natural impulse. Physiologically, we all know that our most natural impulse is to clutch tightly to something lest it fall to the ground. See our strained fingers and forearms. We grab hold most firmly to those things most dear to us. Small struggling churches that fill much of the American landscape tend to have this impulse to the max. Sometime along their life cycles, small, perhaps once-growing but now struggling churches, become "grasping" churches. They grasp onto their God-given resources in the same way that housebound hoarders grasp their goods for themselves. All their attention goes inward, and all their energy begins to be focused in on the inner needs of members of their congregation.

This inward focus for churches has the residual effect of detaching themselves from the larger world around them. In a way, small, dying churches become "decontextualized." They become disconnected from their own communities. And, without a sense of the larger context surrounding them, they lose their mission, and when churches lose their mission, they ultimately lose their purpose for existence.

With these preliminary ruminations in mind, it did not take much to accept an invitation from Chris Coble, director of the Lilly Endowment's Division of Religion, who invited me to consider applying for a grant that addresses many of the observations mentioned above. We applied and received an Early Career Pastoral Leadership Development Initiative grant. At the core of the grant is a hunch initiated by the endowment that congregations grow and flourish to the extent that the pastors and their congregations are engaged meaningfully in the public square outside the church edifice.

Briefly, the program that we proposed and that was accepted by the Lilly Endowment is called the Ockenga Fellows Program and is run through the Ockenga Institute of Gordon-Conwell Theological Seminary. Every other year, fourteen young pastors are selected to participate in seven three-day retreats within a two-year cycle. Each retreat focuses on one area of the public square: New England: A Unique Ministry Context, Business and Work, Science and Technology, Healthcare and Bioethics, Government and Society, Education and Information, and Arts and Media. In addition, the program has allowed for these pastors and directors to engage in a ten-day trip where they have an opportunity to interact with key young pastors in the church in China, both from underground and Three-Self Church movements.

Taken from the grant proposal, the stated goals of the program include the following:

1. To explore effective ways for early career pastors to lead their churches with a deeper understanding of its unique culture and ethos.

2. Engage early career pastors with the broader community, requiring in them the ability to interact meaningfully with the community surrounding the church: its civic, governmental, economic, scientific, educational, and artistic contexts. What are the most pressing challenges facing the community that the pastor and her or his congregation hope to impact? This will help them as they seek to impact

the larger world around them in order to proclaim the gospel in the contemporary world in which they live.

3. Equip early career pastors to understand local church idiosyncrasies. Pastors must develop the ability to observe and understand the inner workings of church culture.

4. Develop a diverse community of early career pastors committed to serving in long-term ministry. Special emphasis will be placed upon creating an environment where these early career pastors can grow together interpersonally and spiritually.

5. Stimulate conversations between leaders in the church and leaders outside the church (in business, civic realms, educational institutions, etc.). Toward that end, a key component of the program will be to strategize specific ways in which what is learned by these early career pastors from these outside voices will translate back to their ministry contexts. The church leaders who have the biggest impact are those who can exegete the cultures around them. This program will help fellows learn to exegete their region, communities, and local churches via a dialogue with peers, who will hopefully become lifelong conversation partners. As a result, these fellows will be better prepared for greater leadership in the future.

The Ockenga Fellows program has proven to meet these goals in amazing ways through eight years of conversations with our early career pastors. Which brings us to the doorsteps of this book. Once again turning to the Lilly Endowment, we requested additional grant funding to explore in greater depth the subject of how churches might better engage with the communities around them. Six exemplary pastors from our first two cohorts of the Ockenga Fellows Program were selected to join my colleague, Jason McConnell, and I in the writing of the book that is now before you.

With a Lilly Endowment grant in hand, what followed was two years of collaboration that included two writers retreats filled with the hard work of theological and pastoral reflection, writing, critiquing, and editing, and the more delightful aspects of growing in friendship and pastoral collegiality. Indeed, even if no one was ever to read the product of our labor, the value of our pastoral kinship together has proven to be immeasurable (see Epilogue). Pastors desperately need to be in community with each other.

Our names are Ken, Seth, Jon, Justin, Chris, Matt, Jason, and me, David. We are the authors of this book. We do not share as much diversity, as a group, as some would like—we are all male and we only have one person who is ethnically different than the rest—and we readily acknowledge this weakness in our perspective. If this lack of diversity is a nonstarter for you, we thank you for your short read of the book thus far, and we respect your suspicions of our shortcomings and the limitations of the book.

For those who continue, we are seven relatively young pastors (thirty-five to forty-five years old), and one pastor at the end of his life of ministry. All but the latter are in either the first or second way stations in their lives of ministry. I suppose you can say we are ambitious, or, perhaps, better stated, we are young enough to still be idealistic in the ways we do ministry. We represent three separate denominations, both in the mainline and evangelical Protestant traditions. And we are all married and have families.

What binds us together as a group is our passionate desire to see our congregations flourish, flourish for the sake of Christ and his kingdom, and flourish for the sake of the individuals we face every Sunday as we preach. In part because of our combined exploration as Ockenga Fellows, I would add there is a growing desire in all of us to see the communities around our churches flourish as well. We desire these communities to thrive, both for their sake and, as has already been mentioned, for the sake of our congregations.

One final characteristic of our merry group of authors is that all of our churches unapologetically reside in New England, in four of the six New England states to be exact. Does this provide a limitation in our perspective? Perhaps, but, as will be stated in the next chapter, we feel "place" matters. We are confident that the real issues that are part of everyday life in New England are not too different from your "place" of ministry, wherever that may be. All this being said, we want to welcome you now to our parish!

David Horn

Acknowledgments

WE (THE CONTRIBUTING AUTHORS) would like to thank Dr. Chris Coble, vice president for Religion and Dr. Jessica Duckworth, program director, at the Lilly Endowment Inc., and Rev. Libby Manning and Dr. Derek Nelson at the Wabash Pastoral Leadership Program. Your vision for pastors in the public square during the Early Career Pastoral Development Initiative inspired this book project and your generous support made it possible.

We also express our gratitude to Gordon-Conwell Theological Seminary, which graciously hosts the Ockenga Fellows Program. We have all immensely benefitted from this program and continue to reap its rich blessings.

And last, but certainly not least, we would like to thank our families and the church communities we serve. Your constant love and encouragement enable us to lead God's people inside the church and provide a pastoral presence to the broader parish.

Introduction

Return to the Parish

David Horn

The country parson desires to be all to his parish, and not only a pastor, but a lawyer also, and a physician.

—GEORGE HERBERT, IN *THE COUNTRY PARSON* (1632)

Seventeenth- and Eighteenth-Century Parish Life

THE OLD MEETING HOUSE stood right there in the center of the village, occupying the whole south side of the village green. Certainly, no one would describe it as stately. Until 1762 when the first meeting house was torn down and replaced by a second, it could easily be confused for a barn, looked upon more for its utility than its transcendence. The rafters were bare. Consequently, it is rumored that the meetinghouse of the Hamlet village was actually occupied by swallows, which one can imagine, made for quite a distraction during early Puritan worship.[1]

Follow the imprint of matted grass laid bare by old man Whipple's team of oxen and the horse carts of several others in the village, and it

---

1. Horn, *Story of God's Faithfulness*, 8.

would be plain to see that every walking path, every dust-filled road within the community, led to the front door of this sacred little barn in the village first called the Hamlet. The meetinghouse was the epicenter of village life in every way. Everything—every aspect of the Hamlet's life—occurred under its roof. On Sunday, the swallow-filled rafters rang with worship and the Word. But on Monday through Saturday, the rest of the business of the Hamlet happened—all civic activity, all commerce happened, all discussion of rumors of new great spiritual awakenings and rising conflicts with Mother England, even the entertainment of the village centered within.

The multifaceted functions of this early seventeenth- and eighteenth-century meetinghouse bore witness to something far deeper than its physical structure. The meetinghouse of the Hamlet was the "parish" meetinghouse for the village and surrounding area. The Hamlet, like every other locality in the Commonwealth of Massachusetts, was mandated by law to provide support to pay a minister and finance a meetinghouse to encourage public morality and worship attendance. This meant that, from the fall of 1713 when the petition was made in the Massachusetts General Court and approved to break off from the Ipswich parish, well into the nineteenth century, every citizen of the parish village of the Hamlet and surrounding area was technically a member of the church. For a brief time at least, the worship of God and all civic life were the shared domain of the parish and existed under one roof.

Undergirding this parish structure was the ideal of a Christian society envisioned foremost by a deep, abiding commitment to the common good. The goal was, in the words of the title of a book by the great Puritan pastor, Richard Baxter, to establish a "holy commonwealth." Thomas Cartwright, the English Puritan, declared: "The commonwealth must be made to agree with the church [that is, with Christian principles]. . . . As it is the foundation of the world, it is meet with the commonwealth, which is builded upon that foundation, should be framed according to the church."[2] This grand Puritan experiment in America was, in John Winthrop's words, to be nothing less than a beacon of light for all to see: "For we must consider that we shall be a city upon a hill, the eyes of all people are upon us."[3]

---

2. Walzer, *Revolution of the Saints*, 182.
3. Ryken, *Worldly Saints*, 174.

Introduction

As it was, even as the meetinghouse was at the center of the parish village, so were its ministers. Samuel Wigglesworth was the first minister of the Hamlet, followed fifty-four years later by one even more renowned than the first, the honorable Dr. Manasseh Cutler. Both men served their parish faithfully, and in doing so, were first among equals within the community. Although neither played official roles in town or colony government, they were often called to advise the civic magistrates. As with their fellow ministers, they were perhaps the most public and respected individuals within the community. In truth, they were pastors not only of their churches, but also of the entire town in which they served.

So, it was not unnatural, for example, that, before school boards ever existed, Rev. Cutler was viewed as the central educational force in the community. His commitment to education began early within the context of the church with the catechizing of children on Sunday afternoons right after the Sunday service. After the Revolutionary War, in 1782, his commitment to education for the community expanded further when he started a boarding school on the third floor of his own house to educate young boys from the community. When public schools were finally instituted in the community now called Hamilton, as head of the parish, it was Rev. Cutler who annually inspected the four schools of the parish, aptly, if unimaginatively called the East, West, North, and South schools.

Both ministers also were central players in caring for the physical and medical needs of the community. Rev. Wigglesworth, in fact, was trained at Harvard as a doctor prior to his training as a minister. And Dr. Cutler trained as a doctor in the midst of the Revolutionary War, in part because cash was scarce and further income was required to offset what could not be paid by the parish. During and after the war, records show that he inoculated at least forty people for smallpox from his parish and a surrounding parish. Much care was taken by both of these ministers during their long lifetimes in terms of the physical and emotional care of the people of their parish.

In addition, these ministers led in other ways that tied their sacred responsibilities of the parish to the more profane functions of community life. In one small example, in 1719, it befell upon the Rev. Wigglesworth to discipline one Edward Bishop who lied before the justice of the peace in a quarrel with another village member, Robert Symonds. The good reverend declared that he was not going to "lie still for the sake of being applauded by those who advocated false peace as a covering for their own faults."[4] The discipline for such a civil offense—that otherwise rested outside the walls of the church—reflected the blurred line that existed between the role that the minister played in his church and the role he played in the larger community. Religious discipline was social discipline for the pastor, and when he tended to the spiritual needs of his flock, he was simultaneously tending to the social needs of the community. So it was, Wigglesworth demanded that Edward Bishop's punishment was to absent himself from the Lord's Table until he acknowledged his folly and confessed his guilt. Only then could he enter back into the graces of the community life of the village.

Further, lacking any other social networks outside the church, it was the pastor and his flock that bore direct responsibility for the indigent and the poor of the community. The physical needs of widows in the parish and wayfarers from without were watched carefully and cared for by these two pastors and the parish church.[5] Incidents of drunkenness, and what would now be considered domestic abuse and violence, were addressed within the confines of the parish, not only as moral issues, but as issues affecting the social fabric of the community.

Drs. Wigglesworth and Cutler are presented here as only two examples of the role ministers of the seventeenth and eighteenth centuries played in parish life. They were extraordinary, indeed, but not necessarily unique. Almost all ministers of that period were called to live out similar callings within their individual parishes. If their leadership seems foreign by modern standards, it is that they led their communities by force of their personal character rather than as a matter of career. Ministry in the parish was viewed as a calling and an office rather than a profession as we know it today. As a result, ministers' status in the community and the church rested not so much in functional terms but, rather, on the backs of the moral authority they possessed as individuals. Parishes selected their ministers for "who" they were rather than "what" they did in a prior life, and their effectiveness within the parish was measured by how much they were able to maintain order within their community.

4. Horn, *Story of God's Faithfulness*, 12.

5. A fine example of this commitment to the poor is the words of Increase Mather: "A poor man cometh amongst you and he must have a commodity whatever it cost him, and you will make him give whatever you please, and put what price you please upon what he hath to give . . . , without respecting the just value of the thing." This commitment to the poor began with ministers themselves, even though they too were often poor. Of the minister John Hooker's house, it was said: "a table spread with good store of meat and beset full of beggars and poor folk . . ." Ryken, *Worldly Saints*, 177–78.

Furthermore, parishes assumed that their pastoral leaders would lead for a lifetime rather than as a stepping stone to a more desirable location. Of the 550 graduates from Yale entering into Congregationalist churches from 1702 to 1794, 392, or 71 percent, ministered in the same congregation in which they were ordained.[6] Wigglesworth and Cutler were prime examples of what was typical: Wigglesworth ministered in the Hamlet for fifty-four years, followed by Cutler's fifty-two years. Longevity mattered for seventeenth- and eighteenth-century parish life, in large measure because pastors saw ministry not in terms of a trajectory toward vocational advancement, but as radical commitment to a place of service and community.

In a word, they committed themselves to a "place." If the idea of "parish" lacked the hard-and-fast boundary between sacred and secular so common to today's culture, it was otherwise defined by another boundary in the most radical terms. The idea of parish was defined fundamentally as a matter of physical space. For the Hamlet parish, it was defined by the fifteen square miles of farmland bounded by Salem on the south, Ipswich on the north, Topsfield on the west, and Essex and Manchester on the east. Every parish was defined similarly. In this sense, parishes had a deep commitment to a location. It is not that individuals from one parish could not wander into another, but it was the case that people of the parish had a deep, abiding commitment to their community. Physical space mattered, both literally and within their own consciousness.

"We're Not in Kansas Anymore"

Of course, much has changed since precolonial New England that mitigates against fully exporting the parish principle as it was represented then. We live in a different world from early Puritans in so many ways and much water has gone under the bridge, as it were, both culturally and historically. Perhaps most obviously, the early concept of parish assumed a cultural and religious homogeneity that no longer exists today.[7]

---

6. Scott, *From the Office to Profession*, 3.

7. From almost the start, the sweep of history and culture has been set against the vision and reality of the early parish understanding. Indeed, some have even observed that the idea of geographical and spiritual parish may very well have broken down at all levels—certainly at an institutional level and from within—even as it was being formed. The early Puritan vision of "a City on a Hill" was dimming even as it was being formed.

Starting after the Revolutionary War and particularly in the 1790s, the blurred lines between the church and state began to harden into a growing separation between the sacred and secular. The American Constitution explicitly separated church from state, under the influence of such men as Thomas Paine, in *The Age of Man*, and our other political forefathers. By the end of the nineteenth century, this separation between the two was codified into law and has expanded exponentially ever since until today, from a legal, political, and social perspective, the religious and the secular spheres now exist wholly independent from one another.

Further, starting after the Revolutionary War, a whole new set of cultural values were being accentuated, replacing an earlier communalism so fundamental to the underpinnings of parish community life. Values like independence and human progress began to drive the human imagination in America, replacing the notion of a commonwealth of like-minded people so central to the idea of parish life. Even as it was being written into the founding documents of a new nation, the notion of the independent "individual" was replacing the notion of community at large.

It goes without saying that our culture has become increasingly pluralistic. We have become elastic in every way, expanding outward into a nation that values its diversity, perhaps above all else: ethnically, socially, politically, economically, and in terms of our sexual expression. (Might this not be the central doctrine that binds us together under our current notion of civil religion?) Of course, this diversity has its strengths, but it has its weaknesses as well, what James Davidson Hunter identifies as the "challenges of difference."[8] No longer does our country possess what our early seventeenth- and eighteenth-century forefathers possessed. No longer does our nation possess a "dominant culture" that gives a central coherence and predictability to thought and action.

Finally, this pluralism that runs crosscurrent to the notion of parish is most dramatically found within the church itself. From as early as the late seventeenth century, it did not take long before the likes of Roger Williams and Ann Hutchinson expanded the boundaries beyond the coherent notion of a singular Puritan commonwealth and into new religious landscape populated with the religious entities we now call denominations. The concept of geographical "place" so central to the idea of parish, broke down quickly, not only as a legal entity, but as a result of religious bodies invading and competing with the religious affections of

---

8. Hunter, *To Change the World*, 200.

members within the parish. What has been the result? The idea of parish has been broken up into a marketplace of church life. Currently, the church in the United States is made up of approximately five thousand denominations, all competing for a market share of the religious faithful.

How has the role of the pastor fared in the midst of these cultural changes? We have only to contrast the picture of the role of the minister from the past—who held together his parish through force of personal character and was based upon the trust of the community he served—with the current highly professionalized role of the pastor today. How did we get from there to here? Donald Scott, in his *From Office to Profession*, identifies a seemingly subtle cultural shift surrounding the time of the Revolutionary War that had a significant impact upon how the clergy in America began to perceive themselves in new ways, and, in turn, how they were perceived in new ways by the community at large.

The wake of the war kicked up a highly charged political dust storm that ultimately settled into what, heretofore, was a new American institution, the political party. The country became politicized, namely, between the Federalist and the Democratic parties. As central cultural players at this time, pastors were especially not immune to this influence. In short, pastors themselves became highly politicized, which, in turn, changed entirely the basis upon which they perceived their authority as ministers. No longer was the source of pastoral authority based upon the pastor's personal calling to care for his geographical parish. Sacred calling subtly shifted to his role as public figure. He became an office holder that gained his position within the church like other public figures. He became elected.

Calling pastors public figures is one step removed from seeing them in professional terms. Pastors may very well still see themselves against the backdrop of personal calling, but their calling is invariably realized in vocational terms. Pastors are educated and accredited according to professional standards. They are selected on the basis of vocational criteria. They progress upward or downward, based upon professional criteria. They are ever mindful of the marketplace surrounding them, which assesses them vocationally. Vocationalism has settled into their bones, and they are shaped by their profession in ways they may not even realize. All of this vocational infrastructure stands in stark contrast to the parish minister from a different era.

A Fresh Look at an Old Concept: Call for a "New Parish"

The old meetinghouse in the Hamlet, now Hamilton, still stands prominently where it has always stood, on the south end of the town green. Travelers can't help but notice it as they travel past on the Old Bay Road, from Salem to Ipswich. It is a beautiful, old colonial building that attracts lots of pointed cameras. But, as the town has grown in population and stature through the years, it has also grown farther away from the old meetinghouse that once occupied its center. The meetinghouse now exists on the town outskirts. Most of the real life of the town has since migrated south next to the commuter rail and the high volume of commercial and residential life of South Hamilton.

The old church that was once at the epicenter of the parish now exists on the outer edge of town. Writ large, many would say this is an apt picture of the current state of the church in America today. No longer does the church exist center stage in the consciousness of the public square. Some of this may be because of what has been abdicated from within our churches, but more probably, the church has become marginalized from without by the increasingly secular cultural life and institutions of our society. It begs the question, aside from being an aesthetically pleasing relic of an age gone by, could the church become more than this for our culture today?

Here perhaps, the idea of "parish" can help. Is there something of the parish principle worth saving for today? Although threadbare, if scrubbed of its sentimentality, and even given the new realities of a changing and highly complex cultural context, what might we reclaim of this vision of church and community life that could be helpful, even revolutionary, in the way churches currently engage their communities?

This is the question being asked by the seven young pastors (and one old one) who have contributed to this book. We are grappling with the question of "new parish" thinking. How might our churches reassert ourselves morally and spiritually back into the public square of our various communities? Just like the current physical posture of the Hamilton meetinghouse mentioned above, we acknowledge this may require a new understanding of the role of the church and its minister. But what might a "new parish" understanding of our churches look like?

First, quite obviously, the new parishes of today are significantly more diverse than in yesteryear. The breadth of parish life illustrated by the seven churches whose pastors are participating in this book, in fact, is a wonderful mosaic of what we see throughout the entire country. In addition to the creaky three-hundred-year-old historic church that now serves as a bedroom community north of Boston and that has served as an illustrative backdrop to this chapter, our churches include a thriving yoked parish in rural Vermont just a few miles from the Canadian border, where farm fields stop at the doorsteps of the church, literally. They include a big steeple church that once served the political and social elite in the largest city in Maine. The social and political elites have long since gone, leaving a church of good-hearted people who are seeking to reclaim a place in their community. One of our churches is located in the ideal spot, at the very center of a picturesque little seaport town that attracts vacationers from around the globe. And there is a thriving multi-staff suburban church that is best known for being one of the very first abolitionist churches in America.

In addition, our churches include another prominent big steeple church in neighboring New Hampshire that is no longer at its prime numerically but is showing great promise in re-energizing the center of its medium-sized city. There is a thriving ethnic church at the very heart of urban Boston that serves Chinese throughout the city and region. And finally, there is a healthy small-town Presbyterian church serving in a state with entirely opposite political and social instincts than its own, but is thriving, nevertheless. Rural, suburban, urban, historic, relatively young, big steeple, small steeple, church plant, storefront, thriving, threadbare, progressive, conservative, denominations of all sorts: this is the face of the new parish of today.

For those that are beginning to reimagine the idea of parish, the common denominator in this diverse group of churches is a growing commitment to geographical "place" at the center of their missions. Taking our cues from our forefathers, we are seeking to reclaim the sacred tie between the church and the community surrounding it. How has this tie been lost through the years? Perhaps it has been lost in part because we live in a media-saturated society whose centrifugal force has been casting our attention ever outward to expanding national and global foci at the expense of focusing on our local communities. Or perhaps the opposite has been the case; perhaps churches have been so engrossed within their sacred communities, they have lost sight of what is around them. Either way, the new parish thinking we are proposing focuses our attention back on the communities surrounding our churches.

To do this, we are purposefully seeking to do the hard work of reintroducing ourselves to these communities that have surrounded our churches. With fresh eyes, we are asking lots of questions: What do our communities look like? How do they work? What are their histories and how do their pasts inform the present? What are the cultural patterns that make them unique? Who are their community leaders? That is, who leads them in formal, institutional ways—community officials—but even more so, where are the *real* centers of power within these communities?

Further, communities are never flat plains. They always exist with high points and low points. What are the low valleys in our communities? Every community has "the other side of the tracks." Where are they in our communities? This may involve not only a deeper understanding of the pockets of the unchurched, but also where are the pockets of greatest physical and emotional needs. Where does poverty exist, and where are the potential places of conflict? Conversely, where are communities flourishing, and what are the more silent needs of the more prosperous in our communities? How does commerce work—or not work—in our cities and towns, and what would make our communities flourish?

But asking these questions is not enough. A renewed understanding of parish life blurs the line between the church and the community it has the potential of serving. Toward that end, new parish thinking requires a renewed commitment to and identification with the communities surrounding our churches. Fundamentally, it requires that our churches be willing to be shaped by what is around them in ways that, on the one hand, certainly does not compromise their message in any way, but, on the other hand, makes them open and vulnerable to the needs immediately at their doorsteps. In a sense, it requires taking on the character of our communities—their identity—and this requires that our churches get involved. This involvement certainly may include being a moral voice, but it must extend beyond what has been their typical role. Perhaps for too long, our churches have tended to be oases that have made pronouncements from afar but not actually been engaged in the life of the communities around them. This involvement includes actual interest in and participation in the social, political, and educational missions of our cities and towns.

Taking on the character of our communities does not come without costs. New parish thinking comes with the realization that churches may need to expand their focus beyond the needs of the faithful within the church. Not only does this require hard work in seeing "with new parish eyes," but it may require rethinking its mission and priorities in very concrete ways. It may even require reallocation of resources away from the church and in service to the community it now seeks to serve. One concrete example of this may be that churches become willing to resist the temptation to keep their minister strictly for themselves—there is always another administrative detail to fulfill, another funeral to perform, another person to visit, another sermon to preach—in order to free their minister for the task of ministering to the community at large.

What might this parish commitment to community look like in today's modern culture? As has already been stated, in terms of our present situation, "we're not in Kansas anymore!" Complicating this vision of establishing a new parish mentality for our churches is that we now live in a highly divided, pluralistic, secularized, and even antagonistic society that has marginalized the church. This marginalization reaches down to even the local level in so many ways. The reality is that our communities may very well not be sympathetic partners to the overtures of our churches, as sincerely offered as they may be. Did I mention "we're not in Kansas anymore"? The parish life of the early Puritans breaks down in so many ways for us today.

This requires that our churches may very well have to be willing to live on the edge of our parishes. And this, in turn, may require that we serve our communities without power and power's younger sibling, entitlement. James Davison Hunter, in his book, *To Change the World*, provides a particularly scathing critique of where the notion of power has taken the American church, particularly political power exercised on both sides of the political spectrum. His critique suggests that the way the church has attempted to effect change politically has compromised the church and, ultimately, its moral authority. In the end, he describes a situation where the road to power has led to a cul-de-sac where the church has lost its religious compass and, consequently, has found itself driving around and around endlessly without true direction.

Rather than seeking political power, Hunter paints an altogether different center for the church, what he calls, "faithful presence."[9] Reaching back to the prophet Jeremiah, he calls the religious faithful, exiled and living in pagan Babylon, to seek the welfare of the culture in which they live:

---

9. Hunter, *To Change the World*, 276.

> Take wives and have sons and daughters; take wives for your sons, and give your daughters in marriage, that they may bear sons and daughters; multiply there and do not decrease. But seek the welfare of the city where I have sent you into exile, and pray for the Lord on its behalf, for in its welfare you will find your welfare." (Jer 29:6–7)

What a wonderful picture is being described here as a backdrop to our concept of building a new parish church for today. Rather than seeking power at the center of our modern-day cultural parish, perhaps the church is most powerful exerting itself on the outer edges.

What would this church look like on the outer edges of the parish? What would it look like without the power and the kind of influence that we often covet? How could our parishes survive without our confident intrusiveness into our communities? At first blush, this concept of Hunter's "faithful presence" has the appearance of weakness. It might initially feel like passivity on the part of our congregations. But that would be wrong.

The influence for a new parish church living on the edges of culture is the influence we see time and time again displayed in the Gospels. It is the power of the gospel displayed by Jesus in his radical service to others without any thought of reciprocation. We see it breathed into us in his very blessings in Matthew 5, blessings that come with a promise: The parish churches that are poor in spirit and mourn easily, who are meek and thirsty for righteousness, who are merciful and pure of heart, and who seek radical peace and are even willing to live with the humiliation of suffering and persecution; it is these, Jesus says, who will inherit the kingdom of heaven.

This church living on the outer edges is further displayed by the apostle Paul's admonition to the church at Corinth, a church that, perhaps more than any other of his churches, mimics our own. To this self-confident parish at Corinth, he reminds them:

> Brothers, think of what you were when you were called. Not many of you were wise by human standards; not many were influential; not many were of noble birth. But God chose the foolish things of the world to shame the wise; God chose the weak things of the world to shame the strong. He chose the lowly things of this world and the despised things—and the things that are not—to nullify the things that are, so that no one may boast before him. (1 Cor 1:26–29)

Uninfluential, seemingly foolish by outward standards, weak, lowly, even despised: these are the characteristics that we are being called to reflect in the midst of the communities around us. We are called to live on the edges of our parishes.

Is there a new parish model for us today, a model built on sincere yet humble service by congregations and their pastors to the communities around them for their own human flourishing? Can pastors reclaim a moral voice for their communities built, not on external pronouncements pitched at arm's length but rather on actual understanding and participation within their communities? Following are seven snapshots of young pastors seeking to do just that, as they lead their congregations to make an impact on the communities around them.

Although all of us have sought to foster a broad approach of engagement in our various communities, we have asked each young pastor to focus on one area of the public square that make up the surroundings around their congregations. Consequently, you will find chapters laid out before you in the following manner: "Engaging the Workplace and Business Community Business and Workplace Parish" (Dr. Jason McConnell), "Engaging the Science and Technology Parish" (Rev. Jon Paul), "Engaging the Healthcare Parish" (Rev. Justin Frank), "Engaging the Political Parish" (Rev. Matt Wigton), "Engaging the Education Parish" (Rev. Chris Dunaway), "Engaging the Arts Parish" (Rev. Seth Anderson), and "Engaging the Multiethnic Parish" (Rev. Ken Liu).

1

Engaging the Business and Workplace Parish

Jason R. McConnell

> *Business! Mankind was my business. The common welfare was my business; charity, mercy, forbearance, and benevolence, were, all, my business. The dealings of my trade were but a drop of water in the comprehensive ocean of my business!*
>
> —Jacob Marley, in Charles Dickens's *A Christmas Carol*

The sounds of Armageddon shot across the Merrimack Valley at 4:15 pm on September 13, 2018. Excessive pressure in natural gas lines caused a series of massive explosions and fires to erupt throughout the neighboring towns of Lawrence, Andover, and North Andover in northeastern Massachusetts. Emergency crews responded to as many as forty homes, with over eighty individual fires. At one point, as many as eighteen fires were burning at once, and Andover officials struck a maximum ten-alarm response.

First responders from as far away as Boston and Manchester, New Hampshire (thirty-five miles away) rushed to shut down the gas lines and prevent further explosions. Local schools and community centers were converted into emergency shelters. By the end of the night, one person was killed, twenty people were injured, and over thirty thousand residents were forced to evacuate their homes. On the following day, Massachusetts governor Charlie Baker declared a state of emergency and appointed state officials to oversee the management of the disaster.[1]

Calamities like the Merrimack Valley gas crisis present opportunities for the church to be the hands and feet of Jesus by providing people's physical and spiritual needs. Even as the Free Christian Church in Andover was dealing with its own issues from the gas crisis, it supported the community by using its benevolence fund to offer financial support to local families. The church also mobilized its membership to volunteer with local agencies and ministries that were assisting people affected by the gas disaster.

Though the acute crisis came under control within a few days, the reverberations lingered for months. The business community bore the burden longer than anyone. Gas-dependent businesses and workplaces, such as laundromats and restaurants, remained unable to open. Lost revenue and low morale mounted. Discouragement set in, especially during the winter months. The gas company promised to cover business losses incurred as a result of the crisis, but business owners had to jump through the hoops of demonstrating lost commissions and wages to employees, which cost valuable time and energy. While residents returned to their homes, business owners and employees were losing their livelihoods.

Heidi Janson owns a bridal shop in Andover, Massachusetts. She is also the founder and CEO of the nonprofit Brides Across America, which provides free wedding dresses to military brides. She was physically and emotionally exhausted from trying to keep her small business running. Imagine a cold chill running down a bride's back as she tries on a shimmering white wedding dress—not from anxiety about her upcoming wedding, but because the bridal shop literally has no heat in the middle of a New England winter. Like other local small business owners, Janson needed encouragement and support.

The pastoral staff at the Free Christian Church was aware of the needs in the business community, but they weren't sure how to address

---

1. Stanglin and James, "Nearly 40 homes," para. 1–10.

them. Churches usually minister to individuals and families, not businesses and organizations. What is the church's role and responsibility in ministering to its local business community? Should the church consider workplaces and businesses a part of its parish? If so, how should it engage this sector of the public square? Should pastors try to evangelize entire companies? Should churches use their benevolence funds to help a small business make payroll? The church's business is to proclaim the gospel of Jesus Christ, but does the gospel have anything to offer the business community? And how can the church benefit from a relationship with the business community?

The Chasm between the Church and the Business Community

Like the church's relationship with other parts of the parish that we will explore throughout this book, there is a vast chasm between the church and business community. People tend to view the church as a place for sacred work and the business office or factory floor as a place for secular work, with little room for overlap between them. This unfortunate sacred/secular divide has even contributed to the misguided notion that there is a legal separation between church and business.

Why is this? Perhaps the business community is skeptical about associating with religious institutions because of the barrage of church scandals over the past few decades. Or maybe the church is reluctant to form a relationship with the business community that has been beleaguered by stories of fraud and unethical financial practices. It is also possible that the church and business community simply do not believe they have anything in common—after all, there is a widespread misconception that the sole mission of business is to make money and the mission of the church is to make people more religious.

Regardless of the reasons, there is a disconnect between the church and business community. Even Christian business owners tend to think of these as completely separate arenas. They worship in the sanctuary on Sunday and work in the office Monday through Friday. But when Sunday worship and Monday work are compartmentalized like this, churches and businesses miss out on important opportunities to facilitate human flourishing together.

The business community could benefit from a meaningful dialogue with the church. The Bible contains an immense collection of business principles that apply to everyone from entry-level employees to top executives. The gospel offers a redemptive solution for a wide range of workplace problems. For instance, in a business atmosphere that is often dominated by cutthroat competition and a compulsion for profits at any cost, employers can learn valuable lessons about fair wages and workplace productivity from the apostle Paul's teaching in 1 Corinthians 9:7–10:

> Who serves as a soldier at his own expense? Who plants a vineyard and does not eat of its grapes? Who tends a flock and does not drink of the milk? Do I say this merely from a human point of view? Doesn't the Law say the same thing? For it is written in the Law of Moses: "Do not muzzle an ox while it is treading out the grain." Is it about oxen that God is concerned? Surely, he says this for us, doesn't he? Yes, this was written for us, because when the plowman plows and the thresher threshes, they ought to do so in the hope of sharing in the harvest.

When workers have the hope of sharing in the harvest by earning fair wages, receiving good benefits, and participating in profit sharing programs, they are more likely to be loyal and productive employees. Likewise, employees develop a deeper appreciation for the products they make when they are able to consume a portion of them. Vermont's Ben & Jerry's ice cream corporation is famous for its policy of giving every employee two pints of ice cream for every eight-hour shift. While this fringe benefit of free ice cream may not make their employees healthier, it definitely makes them happier. When generosity triumphs over greed, everyone in the company is blessed.

A company vice president could also employ the apostle Paul's words in Ephesians 4:25 as a motto for establishing a company culture of honesty and integrity: "Therefore each of you must put off falsehood and speak truthfully to his neighbor, for we are all members of one body." Shareholders and investors have a high degree of confidence in companies where transparency and trust govern the chain of relationships between executives, management, employees, and consumers.

Just a few verses later, Paul presents some communication principles that could transform toxic workplace atmospheres into environments of mutual support and encouragement. Sadly, too many people have worked for bad bosses who berate them in front of their peers and badmouth them behind their backs. Similarly, many employees would rather complain about their supervisors and gossip about their coworkers than confront the real relational problems that plague workplaces. Some employees even steal from their employer and pursue personal gain at the expense of the company. In Ephesians 4:28–29, Paul presents a relational theology that addresses all of these common workplace problems:

> He who has been stealing must steal no longer, but must work, doing something useful with his own hands, that he may have something to share with those in need. Do not let any unwholesome talk come out of your mouths, but only what is helpful for building others up according to their needs, that it may benefit those who listen . . . Get rid of all bitterness, rage and anger, brawling and slander, along with every form of malice. Be kind and compassionate to one another, forgiving each other, just as in Christ God forgave you.

Imagine a workplace where these principles are actually practiced—where kindness, compassion, and forbearance replace malice, slander, and bitterness—where coworkers use their tongues to build one another up rather than tear each other down—where employers and employees view their work as a means to bless others rather than just benefit themselves—where people at every level of a company extend mercy and forgiveness to each other in the same way Christ does through the gospel—where the priority of business is human flourishing and the common good, not amassing personal wealth.

In all of these biblical passages, it is important to remember that Paul is speaking to the church, but the principles can just as easily be applied to any business. The Bible offers guidance for virtually every business and workplace problem: from understanding the purpose of work, basic business ethics, dealing with discouragement from vocational burnout, anxiety about automation and unemployment, stress about volatile markets, to finding a proper balance between work and rest.

Timothy Keller and Katherine Leary Alsdorf, in *Every Good Endeavor: Connecting Your Work to God's Work*, offer a stark contrast between businesses that are molded by brut pragmatism versus those that are shaped by the gospel. They point out the unfortunate fact that sin influences every business culture because every individual worker is a sinner. When sin is unrestrained in a business culture, it results in poor service, polluted rivers, unjust compensation, entitlement attitudes, dehumanizing bureaucracy, and power grabs. But they also offer a compelling counter-narrative by applying the gospel to business:

> The gospel centered business would have a discernable vision for serving the customer in some unique way, a lack of adversarial relationships and exploitation, an extremely strong emphasis on excellence and product quality, and an ethical environment that goes "all the way down" to the bottom of the organizational chart and to the realities of everyday behavior, even when the high ethics mean a loss of margin. In the business animated by the gospel worldview, profit is simply one of the many important bottom lines.[2]

If business leaders want to create successful and sustainable companies that truly promote the common good, they would be wise to build their businesses on the rock of God's Word and the gospel of Jesus Christ rather than the shifting sands of utilitarian efficiency.

Just as the church can make valuable contributions to the business community, the opposite is also true. The church can learn a great deal from the business community. Unfortunately, many pastors and church leaders either passively neglect or actively ignore good business practices that could improve their church's organizational and financial health. Many churches are gospel-centric and spiritually minded, but they suffer from lackadaisical leadership structures, inadequate communication systems, haphazard meeting methods, deficient financial policies, and poor administrative practices.

The church is not a business; nor should it be managed like a business. But it can benefit from good business habits. For instance, a local church could hire an astute businesswoman, either Christian or non-Christian, to assess its administrative practices or improve its fiscal policies. The pastoral staff could visit a corporate boardroom to observe how to run an efficient meeting. The church leadership board could read a book from the business world to help them address a particular organizational weakness.

If the church really believes that all truth is God's truth, it will welcome wisdom from all sources, including the business sector. When I was a student preparing for pastoral ministry, one of the most insightful leadership books I read was James M. Kouzes and Barry Z. Posner's *Credibility: How Leaders Gain and Lose It, Why People Demand It*. It is neither a Christian book nor does it quote any verses from the Bible. It is written by business academics for business leaders, but it emphasizes the biblical ethic of credibility as essential for good leadership. In this regard, what

---

2. Keller and Leary Alsdorf, *Every Good Endeavor*, 167.

is true for the business leader is also true for the church leader. Whether a person is a CEO of a multinational corporation, or a pastor of a small-town church, Kouzes and Posner help leaders understand the importance of earning credibility:

> Credibility, like reputation, is something that is earned over time. It does not come automatically with the job or title. It begins early in our lives and careers. People tend to assume initially that someone has risen to a certain status in life, acquired degrees, or achieved significant goals is deserving of their confidence. But complete trust is granted (or not) only after people have had the chance to get to know more about the person.[3]

By elucidating the difference between assumed and earned credibility, these business authors saved me from making a multitude of unnecessary mistakes in the early years of my ministry. Pastors, like business leaders, must understand that credibility is not conferred through academic achievements or hierarchical titles, but it is attained by maintaining integrity, building healthy relationships, and providing faithful service over a long period of time.

In addition to gleaning organizational and leadership practices, there is an even more compelling reason for the church to engage the business community: the church benefits when the local economy prospers. As the people of Israel were about to endure seventy years of exile in Babylon, God spoke to them through the prophet Jeremiah 29:4–7:

> This is what the LORD Almighty, the God of Israel, says to all those I carried into exile from Jerusalem to Babylon: Build houses and settle down; plant gardens and eat what they produce. Marry and have sons and daughters; find wives for your sons and give your daughters in marriage, so that they too may have sons and daughters. Increase in number there; do not decrease. Also, seek the peace and prosperity of the city to which I have carried you into exile. Pray to the LORD for it, because if it prospers, you too will prosper.

Rather than insulating themselves from the pagan culture of Babylon, God directed his people to make the best of a bad situation by building houses, planting gardens, and settling in for the long haul by marrying, starting families, and increasing the population. And as far as it depended on them, they were to pursue the political peace and

---

3. Kouzes and Posner, *Credibility*, 25.

economic prosperity of the city because they too would be beneficiaries of a flourishing environment.

As God directed the Israelites in Babylon, the modern church can seek the peace and prosperity of its own local economy and business community. Instead of isolating itself over differences in values or worldview, the church can pursue relationships with business leaders, pray for companies that provide employment and a broad tax base, and build partnerships with businesses to bless the community. When local businesses flourish, the whole region profits from new economic development and population growth. As new people move into the community to fulfill jobs, the church will gain new opportunities for outreach, evangelism, and discipleship. When the church blesses its business community, it too will be blessed.

The Pastor as Bridge-Builder between the Church and Business Community

Now that we have surveyed the chasm between the church and business community and have explored some ways that both entities may benefit from a relationship with one other, let's consider how the pastor can serve as a catalyst for "new parish" ministry by becoming a bridge-builder between these important sectors of the public square. Some church members, who are captive to a compartmentalized culture, may protest their pastor pursuing relationships with "secular" business leaders. They may insist that their pastors spend all of their time doing the "sacred" work of shepherding, prayer, preaching, soul care, and proclaiming the gospel of Jesus Christ. While these practices constitute the core of pastoral work, they should not be limited to the church membership. If pastors are going to have any influence beyond the walls of the church sanctuary, they must cast a vision for new parish ministry to their own congregation.

As pastors seek to build bridges between the church and business community, they would be wise to begin by establishing a robust business and workplace theology in their churches. Many faithful church attenders have never heard a single sermon about business or work, let alone participated in a discipleship program that addresses these important matters. They have listened to hundreds of sermons on issues such as "Growing in Your Relationship with Christ" or "Five Steps to a Better Prayer Life" but have never heard their pastor address issues such as vocational calling, business ethics, or how the gospel redeems work in a broken world. Likewise, many Sunday school classes study subjects like the Lord's Prayer and the Apostles' Creed, but the content is hardly ever applied to real situations people face at work. How does "thy kingdom come, thy will be done" relate to a gas station clerk who lacks motivation to get up and go to work on Monday morning? How does "suffered under Pontius Pilate" pertain to the company manager who just got fired for blowing the whistle on a CEO's unethical financial practices?

So, how can pastors tackle these topics through the church's teaching ministry? First, they can initiate a sermon series with a vocational emphasis. They might consider preaching an expository series through a whole book of the Bible and highlight the vocational motifs imbedded in the text. The four Gospels contain a treasure trove of vocational themes, along with the books of Genesis, Proverbs, and Ecclesiastes.

Similarly, pastors may preach an expository/topical series titled "Overcoming Obstacles in the Workplace" from the book of Nehemiah or "God's Providence in a Workplace Romance" from the book of Ruth. In series like these, pastors can draw attention to how God works through human work, whether it is rebuilding a city wall (Neh 4), winnowing barley on a threshing floor (Ruth 3), or operating a vineyard (Prov 31:16). Pastors could also preach through portions of biblical books to help their congregants understand theological themes like being created for work (Gen 1–2), the burden of work (Gen 3), the dignity of work (1 Thess 4), the dangers of laziness (Prov 19:15), and the importance of rest from work (Deut 5:14–15).

Moreover, pastors may develop and deliver a topical sermon series on business and work like the one I presented during my church's year-long faith and work initiative. I titled the series "The 6 E's of Exceptional Employees": Ethics (Phil 1:27; 1 Thess 4:11–12), Excellence (1 Cor 10:31; Prov 22:29), Endurance (1 Cor 4:12–13; Prov 14:23), Encouragement (1 Thess 5:11–22; Eph 4:29–32), Evangelism (Matt 28:16–20; 2 Timothy 4:1–2), and Entrepreneurism (Prov 11:10; Rom 12:6–8).

Second, pastors can promote a theology of work by teaching on these topics. This could be done in a variety of ways, such as creating a weekly Bible study series or a one-time seminar on the theology of work. Any of the theological content from the previously mentioned sermon series could be used in these formats. Or the pastor might consider organizing a group to read one of the fine books from the modern faith and work movement. (See the *For Further Exploration* section at the end of this chapter.) A book can be assigned and read over a specific duration of time (maybe a month), and then one evening can be designated for the group to gather and discuss the book. My church had great success with this model when large groups read and discussed Ken Barnes's *Redeeming Capitalism* and Tom Nelson's *Work Matters: Connecting Sunday Worship to Monday Work*.

Third, pastors could initiate a faith and work forum at the church and invite a local business leader to talk about their company and the role it plays in the community—or a few business leaders to participate in a panel discussion to explore regional economic matters and employment issues. Forums like this, which showcase the needs and resources in a particular community, could lead to the formation of a unique church and business partnership.

A number of years ago, my church formed a partnership with a local restaurant and catering company. Even though the owners do not attend our church, we have built a strong relationship with them and their business. Among other events, our church uses their elegant ballroom for our annual Christmas banquet and children's pageant. They bless us by donating the use of their space and giving us a discounted price for catering. We bless them with direct business and by promoting their company in our church and community. Many of our church members book their business for wedding receptions, funeral luncheons, and holiday business parties.

Fourth, pastors could initiate a series of faith/work testimonies during the Sunday morning worship services. A faith/work testimony is an anecdote or short story about how a person's faith influences their work. The pastor could solicit volunteers or choose specific parishioners from diverse vocational backgrounds to share a five- to ten-minute story with the rest of the congregation. Every pastor and church can establish their own guidelines. When I led this initiative at my church, I asked individuals to answer one or more of the following questions:

1. What kind of work do you do? How did God call you to this type of work? How did you know that this was what God wanted you to do?
2. How does your faith affect your effort, ethics, and/or evangelism in your workplace?
3. How do you see your work contributing to the kingdom of God?
4. Who are the beneficiaries of your work? How does your work minister to others?

5. What are some of the specific joys and challenges you have experienced as it relates to your faith and work?

During this initiative, our church heard many powerful stories, including a registered nurse whom God specifically called to care for geriatric patients, a dairy farmer who receives joy from providing milk to nourish people's bodies, an airline pilot who shares the gospel with his crew on international flights, a medical administrator who prays for every person on her patient list when she arrives at the office each morning, an auto mechanic who gains satisfaction from putting safe cars on the highway, a businessman whose faith guides him through difficult ethical dilemmas, a high school special educator who shows the love of Jesus to students who suffer from mental disabilities, a parole officer who supervises sex offenders who live in the community, a dental hygienist who shares her conversion story with people while she cleans their teeth, and a large animal veterinarian who offers pastoral counseling to his clients in the agricultural community.

The whole church was inspired by such a wide variety of ways their fellow church members connect their faith to their work. It caused everyone to think deeply about how their faith influences their work. Some people felt convicted about compartmentalizing their faith and work. Others were challenged to implement ideas that they learned from others. And to my surprise, a few even felt compelled to consider a career change. Faith/work testimonies are an excellent way to integrate a theology of work into the life of the church.

Fifth, pastors can bring the workplace to church by organizing commissioning services, which are special ceremonies to pray for people who serve in specific vocational roles. Churches commonly employ commissioning services for people entering "sacred" positions like pastoral ministry, missionary service, or military chaplaincy, but they rarely commission people in "secular" professions like carpentry, coal mining, or cosmetology. But does God favor evangelists over economists? Does he value commentary writing more than custodial work? Does he prefer the monk in the monastery to the mechanic in the automotive shop? If the purpose of all work is to glorify God and facilitate human flourishing, why do churches perpetuate this sacred/secular divide by commissioning so-called "sacred" forms of work but not others? What message does this send to people whom God has gifted and called to work in the healthcare field, the financial district, or a construction site?

David W. Gill, one of the pioneers of the modern faith and work movement, is a champion of commissioning services for people who are called to "secular" work. He states:

> Recognizing and commissioning our parishioners for the work they do during the week is a powerful message that their work matters not just to them but to their brothers and sisters and, above all, to God himself. They are called to serve the Lord in and through their work, to be an ambassador of another way of life and work.[4]

He goes on to observe that it is so easy to slip into an attitude that work doesn't really matter except maybe for the paycheck and the tithes that support God's real work. But this is bad, unbiblical theology. God does care about our work. It is one of the primary ways we love God and our neighbors. It is about so much more than the money.[5]

Commissioning services are a creative way to bless church members who serve in a wide variety of vocations—from politicians in the state house to machinists at the pulp mill. But commissioning services need not be limited to parishioners in the pews; they can be extended to people in the community who rarely darken the doors of the church.

One year, my church planned four commissioning services for vocations that are widely represented in our local community: legislators, farmers, educators, and fire/rescue workers. We wanted to reach out beyond our church by inviting people from our community to participate in the commissioning services. For Educator Sunday, we sent invitations to every employee at our area schools, from the custodial staff to the superintendent and school board members. We even moved this service from the church sanctuary to the elementary school gymnasium to accommodate all of the extra guests who would join our congregation for this service.

We strategically planned every aspect of the service for maximum impact on the educators who did not have a relationship with our church. The service was scheduled for the Sunday before the first week of the new school year. The liturgy and hymns followed educational themes, I preached a sermon from Mark 12:28–34 titled, "Jesus, the Greatest Teacher of All Time." The superintendent, who was a former music teacher, played a piece on classical guitar for the offertory. And we asked

---

4. Gill, "Commissioning," para. 3.
5. Gill, "Commissioning," para. 3.

the longest tenured teacher in the district, who was entering his fiftieth year of teaching agriculture at the local high school (and happened to be a member of our church), to share a testimony about how his faith influenced his teaching career.

The climactic moment of the service came when we asked all of the current and retired school employees to stand; we publicly thanked them for their service to the community and we prayed for God to bless their work. Many educators were moved to tears as they expressed their gratitude to our church for honoring their work.

Pastors can utilize this commissioning model for vocations that are present in their own parishes. The service can be designed to fit the community context and the specific vocation that will be commissioned. It should be gospel-centered but not have such a bold evangelistic agenda as to cause guests to feel manipulated. As parishioners within and outside the church see how their work coincides with God's work, they will gain a clearer understanding of who God is and what he has done to redeem us from the brokenness in our world.

As pastors build bridges by bringing the business community to church, they can also take the church to the business community. Pastors can begin in a small way by visiting their church members in their places of work and business. Of course, some workplaces, like government agencies and state penitentiaries, may be off-limits without proper clearance, but many other workplaces can easily accommodate a pastoral visit.

By doing this, pastors develop a deeper understanding of the types of work that are represented in their churches. Church members often feel honored when their pastor takes a vested interest in their work, and they would be delighted to give their pastor a firsthand glimpse of what they do. Pastors can tour facilities, be introduced to coworkers, or even participate in some aspect of the job. The farmers in my congregation cherish the times they taught me how to bail hay, operate a corn chopper, and make maple syrup.

While pastors are conducting workplace visits, they can ask insightful questions and offer encouragement and appreciation. They may even be able to pray for their parishioner and fellow coworkers in the midst of their daily duties. Sometimes a simple pastoral presence can bring peace to an anxious work environment.

Workplace visits not only help pastors empathize with their parishioners' vocational joys and struggles, but provide opportunities for pastors to meet new people and broaden their own life experience as well.

The workplace and business community are untapped gold mines for sermon illustrations. Who wouldn't be intrigued by sermons with stories from the stockyard to the stock exchange?

Another way pastors can bring the church to the business community is by developing personal relationships with local business owners and members of their chamber of commerce. Many business owners would welcome an invitation from a pastor to learn about their company and its role in the community. Pastors could either drop by the business location or set up a lunch meeting to discuss community issues like economic challenges, employment problems, networking opportunities, resource sharing, and potential partnerships. Even if the relationship doesn't immediately evolve into a formal affiliation, building good rapport is an essential step for any future collaboration. Never underestimate the power of community presence and personal relationships.

Likewise, pastors may even consider becoming a member of their local chamber of commerce, which is a voluntary association of businesses, nonprofit organizations, manufacturing industries, service sectors, banking institutions, legal firms, and medical centers. These chambers work with their municipal government to strengthen and develop the local economy. They usually serve as a central hub for the local businesses and are often responsible for coordinating community events. They provide opportunities for pastors to connect with hundreds of people and show support for the business community.

Pastors can also bring the church to the business community by encouraging their parishioners to consider starting a Bible study at their workplace. While it is outside the purview of most pastors to personally lead Bible studies at individual workplaces, they can equip and encourage their church members to reach out to their fellow coworkers and form such a group. The study could be conducted in a company breakroom, lounge, or even off-site. They could study a book of the Bible, read a devotional book together, or explore biblical themes that are relevant to their job.

One step beyond a workplace Bible study is membership in a Christian vocational association or society. Many vocations have some national organization that brings Christians in particular vocations together for mutual support and encouragement. For instance, the Christian Medical and Dental Association provides educational resources, networking opportunities, and a public voice for Christian healthcare professionals and students. Transport for Christ connects truck drivers to Christian community so that they will never feel alone on the highways and interstates. The Christian Legal Society is a fellowship of Christian attorneys dedicated to serving Jesus Christ through the defense of religious freedom and provision of legal aid to the needy. Cowboys for Christ is an organization of men and women who work in the cattle, horse, and rodeo industries. Their mission is to share the gospel of Jesus Christ with people involved in the rodeo circuit.

Pastors can prod their parishioners to participate in a national association that matches their vocation. These societies provide Christian fellowship and ministry opportunities beyond the local church, and they pool vocational resources together and use them to make an impact beyond their local communities. These groups help their members to view their vocation as kingdom work.

Finally, pastors can take church to the business community by encouraging their church members to use their vocational knowledge, skills, and networks entrepreneurially. Amy Sherman, author of the book *Kingdom Calling: Vocational Stewardship for the Common Good*, observes that many churches already contain some talented individuals who are thinking about leaving their career to birth some entrepreneurial enterprise that provides a creative solution to a thorny social problem. God may be calling a businesswoman to launch a nonprofit agency to provide business coaching and start-up financing to inner-city entrepreneurs. Or perhaps an architect and a real estate developer in the church may collaborate together to address the city's affordable housing crisis.[6]

Sometimes God calls people to extravagant vocational enterprises, but fear and anxiety hold them back. Here is where pastors can offer personal encouragement and inspiration to help such dreams become a reality. As a result of my church's faith and work initiative, a young hospital budget analyst in my congregation approached me about an idea to for our church to start a program that provides microloans to ex-convicts who cannot acquire a conventional loan to start a business. We would work with our local prison ministry to identify potential candidates and then form a team of business owners from our church to mentor the candidate through the process of starting a business. This vision has not yet materialized, but we haven't given up on it. But even if this idea never comes to fruition, I am grateful for people in the church who look for

---

6. Sherman, *Kingdom Calling*, 183.

ways to use their vocational skills to solve spiritual and social problems in the community. This is the epitome of a new parish model for ministry.

Conclusion

At the beginning of this chapter, I mentioned that the Free Christian Church of Andover was praying about how they could respond to the business community that was demoralized by the Merrimack Valley gas crisis. The church was not in a position to provide for the business' financial needs, but it was able to come alongside the business owners and be a source of support and encouragement for them.

In January, following the Christmas rush, the Free Christian Church networked with the Andover Business Center Association and the local chamber of commerce to host a business appreciation night for businesses that were affected by the gas crisis. The church held the event at a local microbrewery, and their worship band played soft jazz for background music throughout the evening. The church catered hor d'oeuvres and bought one glass of beer for all attendees. At the beginning of the event, the pastors welcomed everyone and briefly explained their theology of work. They articulated the fact that God cares about businesses and that the Free Christian Church wants to see their local businesses flourishing for the good of their community. Then they took a few moments and publicly prayed for all of the businesses. The rest of the night was reserved for mingling and improving morale.

Some business leaders in the church also used this as an opportunity for their colleagues to "meet their pastor." Many employers and employees were surprised to learn that a pastor actually cares about people's work and that a church would sponsor such an event. In the weeks that followed, some business owners felt so loved by the church that they started attending worship on Sunday mornings. The event, which the church appropriately titled "Taking Care of Business," was a huge success!

This compelling story illustrates how one church embraced a new parish model of ministry by engaging its local business community during a time of crisis. The pastors took the initiative to be present in the public square and mobilize their church to reach beyond its own walls. Pastors and churches need not wait for a disaster to prompt them to engage their local business community. There are business owners and workplace leaders in every city and town who need the gospel of Jesus Christ for the salvation of their souls and the betterment of their businesses. Perhaps pastors can help their church members see that the business community is part of their parish. And as pastors lead their churches to return to the parish, may they take care of business by taking care of business.

For Further Exploration

1. Kenneth Barnes. *Redeeming Capitalism*. Grand Rapids: Eerdmans, 2018.
2. Steve Garber. *Visions of Vocation: Common Grace for the Common Good*. Downers Grove, IL: InterVarsity, 2014.
3. David Gill. *Workplace Discipleship 101: A Primer*. Peabody, MA: Hendrickson, 2020.
4. Tim Keller and Katherine Leary Alsdorf. *Every Good Endeavor: Connecting your Work to God's Work*. New York: Riverhead, 2012.
5. Tom Nelson. *Work Matters: Connecting Sunday Worship to Monday Work*. Wheaton, IL: Crossway, 2011.
6. Amy Sherman. *Kingdom Calling: Vocational Stewardship for the Common Good*. Downers Grove, IL: InterVarsity, 2011.

Engaging the Business and Workplace Parish

Interview

DAN CARSWELL HAS OWNED and operated Blouin Bros. Oil Company in Enosburg Falls, Vermont since 1997. As a full-service energy business, Blouin Bros. supplies home heating oil, propane, kerosene, diesel and gasoline, and motor oil and hydraulic oil to homes and businesses throughout northwestern Vermont. Carswell is also the chairman of the elder board at the East Franklin Union Church in Franklin, Vermont and serves as the community as president of the board of directors for the Northern Tier Center for Health (NOTCH), a federally funded community-based nonprofit healthcare corporation.

Q. **How did you get into the energy business?**

Well, an opportunity fell into my lap. Since I was already in the heating and plumbing business, it was mentioned to me that Blouin Bros. Oil was for sale. So, I tried to secure the funds to purchase the company. It was meant to be! The Blouins, who started the company in the 1940s, offered me a fair price, and after thirteen months, we had a closing, and the deal was done. I was especially blessed to be cash positive from the day I took over. I've never gone without a paycheck even though I had to borrow money to buy the place. Not many businesses can say that. I was truly blessed! I've been very fortunate; the business has been quite successful. Over the years, the company has grown considerably—some years by more than 10 percent.

Q. Do you view your vocation as a calling from the Lord? Why or why not?

Absolutely, no question! First of all, I was gifted with the aptitude to know what I know. I did not choose my own path; it chose me. That was through opportunity, but also you when you're being called to do a certain thing because it becomes your passion. I don't think that happens by accident. I always had an ability to figure out how things work and solve problems. When I was about thirteen, I wound up helping the plumber who was doing the plumbing in my parent's basement. I knew this was something I could do. I went to junior college, but it wasn't ready for me, and I certainly wasn't ready for it. So, I trained to be a plumber and soon became proficient at maintaining boilers. I wound up working as a boiler technician at a hospital for handicapped children in New Hampshire and I've been in this business ever since, trying to keep people warm and comfortable.

I still feel passionate about my work. Every situation I go into is like solving a puzzle—the diagnostics are challenging, and I have to figure out how to make it work better and more efficiently. As the technology advances and heating systems become better, I have to continue to learn and grow. There are days when I don't like what I do, like today as soon as I leave you, I have to go fix a boiler that has been perplexing me for weeks, but by and large, I still love what I do. I'm blessed in that my giftedness, passion, and opportunities have all converged into my vocational calling.

Q. How does your business serve the community?

We fulfill the needs of homeowners and businesses to deliver the products they need to operate, whether it be chopping hay or heating their homes. We do it on time and offer competitive pricing; we offer twenty-four-hour service and stand behind what we sell. I believe that our business had a good reputation in the community. We've been able to offer special discounts to churches and other nonprofit organizations in the community.

Q. Do you view your business as a ministry? Why or why not?

In its own way, yes, but we're not the pulpit on the corner. However, I've had many instances at work when I've become the counselor and discuss people's difficulties, and that's where the ministry presents itself. Since I'm often in people's homes, they feel comfortable talking to me about their hardships. It usually happens when I am busy, but you have to take the time and give people what they need—whether it is just someone to listen to them vent or give them reassurance. I don't require or request this of my employees, but I often hear about it. I certainly demand that they get their work done, but you have to take time with people—our customers are part of our family.

Q. What are the most significant joys and challenges of being a business owner?

Honestly, I enjoy the independence and autonomy that comes with owning my own business; I don't have to justify my decisions to anyone. That being said, there's no harder boss than yourself. I never truly have a day off because I'm always thinking about what I could or should be doing to make the business more successful; I always bear the burden of responsibility. Even when I'm on vacation, it is difficult to disconnect from the obligations and concerns that come with owning a business. But even in the midst of responsibility, there is great joy in knowing that my business provides a livelihood for my employees and their families. I know all of my employees well—we're really like family.

As far as challenges, like any business owner, I'm always thinking about work, especially sustainability. I'm always concerned about the future. The energy market is volatile—oil prices, legislative issues, and climate change rhetoric are always threatening to put us out of business. I still believe that many people in our country need oil and propane to heat their homes and do their work, particularly in rural states like Vermont. But it is difficult to be vilified day in and day out in the national media. We are simply trying to help our local people get the energy they need to survive, but there are many political agendas driving the energy industry and there is a lot of inaccurate information in the press. There are two sides to every story!

Q. Has your Christian faith and involvement in the church helped you as a business owner? If so, how?

Immensely. My Christian faith guides my business ethics—the difficult decisions that I have to make every day and the way I treat people, whether they are employees, customers, or community members. Also, there are days when, if I did not have forgiveness in my heart, I wouldn't be able to do what I do. When I get ripped off or someone takes advantage of me, I have to remember the forgiveness that Christ has extended to me and then extend that same forgiveness to others. To be a good business owner, I have to keep my heart focused on heaven when evil will exist no more.

Q. How can your pastor help you be a better businessman?

By doing what you're doing right now, because you are making me think about what I do. I think that is one of the most important things a pastor can do—make people examine themselves or at least examine why they do what they do. As a matter of fact, this conversation has forced me to think about some of our policies. Whenever we're finished, I'm immediately going back to the office to review those policies to make sure that they are in alignment with biblical values. You've given me some resources to help me serve other people better!

2

Engaging the Science and Technology Parish

Jon Paul

> *A principal characteristic of technique . . . is its refusal to tolerate moral judgments. It is absolutely independent of them and eliminates them from its domain. Technique never observes the distinction between moral and immoral use. It tends on the contrary, to create a completely independent technical morality.*
>
> —JACQUES ELLUL

I WAS SITTING IN a conference boardroom with the most brilliant person I had ever met, and I was totally intimidated. As part of the Ockenga Fellows Program, our cohort of early career pastors was having a dialogue with Dr. Rosalind Picard, the founder and director of the Affective Computing Research Group at the Massachusetts Institute of Technology (MIT) Media Lab, about her research in Affective Artificial Intelligence (AI). Although I was a science major during my undergraduate studies, I knew I was out of my league as soon as she started her presentation. I confess that, at first, I wasn't particularly interested in Affective AI (I didn't even know what it was), but through the course of the conversation, I became fascinated by her cutting-edge inventions and how they are alleviating various forms of human suffering, such as autism, epilepsy, depression, sleep problems, stress, dementia, and post-traumatic stress disorder.

As a result of our discussion with Dr. Picard, I developed a desire to learn more about modern scientific research and technological development, especially how these complex issues intersect with Christian faith, morality, and ethics. But since I had little background knowledge of Affective AI, I felt inadequate to contribute to this conversation. So, like Mary before Jesus' feet, I just sat there and listened.

As a pastor, my formative education centered around the subjects of theology, preaching, and church leadership. My seminary curriculum didn't cover scientific topics like AI, genetic engineering, or nanotechnology, nor did it prepare me to think about such matters from a theological perspective. Since these themes were rarely, if ever, raised, I had never really reflected on their relationship to pastoral ministry. But during our conversation with Dr. Picard, I realized that the world is inundated by new scientific discoveries and technological advances, and these breakthroughs are relentlessly reshaping society. As I listened, I wondered: "How should Christians react to these technological advancements and the rapid and complex changes they bring to our lives? Do pastors have a role and responsibility to engage the scientific community as part of their wider parish? If so, what should it look like?"

Theologian Leonard Sweet argues that "it is important that theologians and people of faith at least try to understand what is going on. The danger level is high. Genetic engineering, robotics, AI, IT, and nanotechnology come compassless, rudderless, and utterly heartless, and they come into a 'my truth' culture totally unprepared to deal with normative questions."[1] Sweet's admonition is apropos. Many people of faith (including pastors) are either skeptical of the scientific community or intimidated by it. There is a pervasive belief among many Christian communities, especially evangelicals, that science and faith are incompatible, and that most scientists have an anti-Christian agenda.

Indulging the reasons for this perceived incongruity is beyond the scope of this book, but it will suffice to say that, broadly speaking, the Christian community lacks the theological conviction and acumen to thoughtfully engage scientific and technological issues. For instance,

---

1. Sweet, *Rings of Fire*, 141.

how often do pastors address scientific issues in their sermons? When do churches ever host small group conversations about new technologies and the moral questions they raise? How many Christians either blindly accept technological promises as gospel truth or turn a blind eye and pretend they don't exist? How many Christians believe that science undermines biblical truth and is, therefore, harmful to a Christian worldview?[2]

Over the past century, we have lived in a world of unfettered technological development, and the pace continues to accelerate. But is it a good thing? Just because technology creates the ability to do something, does that mean we should do it? What are the unintended consequences of new technologies? The rate of technological advance appears to be outpacing society's ability to evaluate the moral and ethical implications. The late cultural critic Neil Postman, in his *Technopoly: The Surrender of Culture to Technology*, warned: "Information is dangerous when it has no place to go, when there is no theory to which it applies, no pattern in which it fits, when there is no higher purpose that it serves."[3] Is there a place for pastors in the technological community? Is there a place for science in the church? How can pastors return to the scientific and technological parish and address these issues from a theological perspective? But let's first evaluate some of the benefits and drawbacks to science and technology in its current state.

Science and Technology: The Good, the Bad, and the Ugly

Artificial Intelligence can now be used to predict an autistic child's disruptive behavior in a classroom. A wristwatch-sized device, discretely worn by a student, can detect minute variations in skin reactions that indicate a change in mood before even the most astute observer could pick up on any cues that something is wrong. When the child's mood begins to escalate into a behavior that could disrupt the whole class, the device signals a teacher who can then intervene and spare the classroom from incident and interruption. This technology is a triumph for the teacher, student, and the whole class.

---

2. Elaine Howard Ecklund, professor of sociology at Rice University, documents the reasons why so many Christians fear the scientific community and offers suggestions on how to overcome it. See Ecklund, *Why Science and Faith Need Each Other*.

3. Postman, *Technopoly*, 63.

But this same AI technology that aids students in a classroom can also be used to exploit gamblers in casinos. A camera in a slot machine may be programed to detect emotion through facial analysis. When signals identify that the gambler might be ready to cut his losses and leave the game, the automated system can signal a cocktail waitress to bring a warm smile and a free drink to convince him that his luck is about to change. This pleasant encounter compels the gambler to feed more money into a machine that is specifically designed for him to lose.

Likewise, automation in manufacturing may increase the accuracy, precision, and efficiency of a production process, but it may also eliminate jobs and cause unemployment. Every day, automated machines buy and sell shares on the stock market, with little or no human oversight. This form of automation may increase convenience and profitability, but it may also eliminate the moral and ethical dimensions from the human decision-making process. The problem isn't necessarily the technology itself; it is how technology is utilized. God's wisdom is needed to navigate the good, the bad, and the ugly of science and technology.

The Good

In 2020, the COVID-19 pandemic swept the globe and caused various levels of shutdowns, lockdowns, and quarantines. Countries and communities alike scrambled to adapt to the new challenges. Technology-based solutions were implemented across a wide spectrum cultures and sectors of the public square. Schools moved to distance learning; businesses shifted their labor force to remote working; and churches transitioned to online worship. While they were far from perfect, people applied new technologies to maintain everything from government operations to church ministries. These expressions of human ingenuity (and many others) are good because they reflect God's goodness and his cultural mandate for humans to use their creative abilities for the common good of society.

The Bible teaches that human beings are created in the image of God. Genesis 1:26–27 proclaims:

> Then God said, "Let us make mankind in our image, in our likeness, so that they may rule over the fish in the sea and the birds in the sky, over the livestock and all the wild animals, and over all the creatures that move along the ground." So God created

mankind in his own image, in the image of God he created them; male and female he created them.

Creating is one of the ways human beings reflect the image of God. While humans cannot create *ex nihilo*, out of nothing, as God can, they can use their God-given creativity to subdue the earth by developing new techniques to adapt the natural resources God provided. Consider the many good uses of technology in healthcare. Pharmaceuticals, biotechnology, and advances in medical equipment have brought healing and renewed hope to people suffering from horrendous diseases and medical conditions. New messenger RNA (mRNA) technology has allowed the rapid creation of COVID-19 vaccines. Robotic surgeries are making procedures safer and more successful. Medical imaging technologies can detect cancers at earlier stages and dramatically increase survival rates. These good uses of technology help prevent disease, alleviate pain, and generally promote human health and flourishing.

Stewardship is another way that humans reflect the image of God. God is the supreme king, but he gave mankind the ability and authority to care for his creation. Human beings reflect the image of God when they develop technologies that improve ecological conservation and environmental flourishing. For instance, plastics increase human convenience, but their byproducts pollute the earth. What technology can be created to balance convenience and conservation?

As a part of the BioBuilders club at their high school, two teenage girls from my town are researching and experimenting with splicing plastic-degrading enzymes with bacteria. They hope to develop a bacteria-based technology to degrade plastics that end up in the ocean. These students are drawing attention from experts in the field.[4] They are also attracting God's gaze by developing technologies that facilitate stewardship of his good creation.

Technology can not only be used to solves problems, but it can also be used to prevent problems from arising in the first place. Automobiles are now equipped with advanced safety features like forward collision warning, automatic emergency braking, blind spot warning, pedestrian detection, lane assistance, and advanced airbags, just to name a few. But even the most advanced automobile technologies still require human common sense. Consider the 2012 story about a group of students who followed the GPS in their rental car into the ocean because "it told us we

---

4. DiNatlae, "Ridding."

could drive down there."[5] However, technology generally improves safety in everything from homes and healthcare to transportation and tourism.

Beyond individual health and safety, technology can keep family and friends connected across the globe. Human interaction and relationships are fundamental to what it means to be created in the image of God. The doctrine of the Trinity affirms that the one God is eternally distinct in three co-equal persons. God is relational by his very nature. When humans live in harmonious relationship with one another, it reflects the image of God. High-definition video calling now enables relational contact in ways that would otherwise be impossible. During the COVID-19 pandemic, telecommunication features like Facetime and Zoom not only kept physically separated families connected, but they were essential for relational entities like businesses, schools, hospitals, and churches to function remotely.

Whereas telecommunication technologies give people the ability to maintain relationships across great distances, social media platforms like Facebook and Twitter provide opportunities for people to communicate with others broadly and instantaneously. Important announcements and messages can be broadcast to large groups in a matter of seconds. By having a thoughtful social media presence, pastors and churches can connect with their neighbors who otherwise may never step through the doors of the church. Many churches utilized social media communications during the COVID-19 pandemic shutdowns. Even though "livestream" and "virtual" worship services are not as meaningful as live, in-person events, they provided a relatively convenient and effective alternatives amid unfortunate conditions.

Likewise, other media-based technologies can be powerful tools for gospel ministry. The Jesus Film Project is a Christian ministry that seeks to share the message of Jesus through video. One of our church's ministry partners, Erick Schenkel, is the former executive director of the Jesus Film Project. He recently shared that the app version of their film is now available in over 1,700 languages. The Jesus Film Project claims that over 500 million people have indicated they have made decisions to follow Jesus.[6] Regardless of one's opinion of the film, the impact of this media technology is undeniable.

---

5. Fujita, "GPS Tracking Disaster", para 5.
6. See https://www.jesusfilm.org/about/history.html.

Many technological advances and scientific achievements reflect God's goodness and image in human beings. They make valuable contributions to human flourishing and the common good of society. They make the world a better place by increasing safety, alleviating human suffering, enabling relationships, and solving various problems of human life. But before anyone draws a false conclusion that science and technology is always good, we must consider some of their unintended consequences. Except for God himself, every source of light has a dark side.

The Bad

Although God gave human beings the capacity to create technologies to subdue the earth (Gen 1:26–30), the Bible consistently warns against placing inordinate value on created things. All creations, human and divine, must be kept in their proper place in relation to their Creator. In Romans 1:25, the apostle Paul asserts: "They exchanged the truth about God for a lie and worshiped and served created things rather than the Creator—who is forever praised." God alone is the object of worship. When a person's significance or security comes from a created thing rather than the Creator, they are guilty of idolatry. Psalm 20:7 declares: "Some trust in chariots and some in horses, but we trust in the name of the Lord our God." Science, and especially technology, have competed with God for human allegiance since the days of Cain and his descendants, who built the first city and developed the early technologies of tentmaking, livestock domestication, musical instruments, and metal tools (Gen 4:17–22).

One of the adverse effects of technology in modern times is addiction to electronic devices (televisions, computers, video games, iPads, smartphones, etc.). I personally witness the negative impact of technology on children all the time. It is a now common to see a toddler entertaining herself by playing games on a cell phone while sitting in a grocery cart. In the not too recent past, children would ride up and down the aisles and ask questions about the menagerie of products, grab at cereal boxes, and participate in social activity with other shoppers, even if it was just to make a cute comment or funny face. Today, children are hardly even aware of their surroundings because their eyes are glued to a handheld screen.

Similarly, electronic devices have changed a child's experience in the waiting room at the dentist's office. In the past, when big brother was at his six-month cleaning, the waiting room would become a place for little sister to investigate and explore. In addition to people-watching, there were always the magazine rack, an eclectic collection of toys, and, of course, the aquatic life in the obligatory fish tank. By engaging these activities, little sister would learn the important skills of creativity and patience to cope with the uninspiring experience of waiting. Patience is a fruit of the Holy Spirit (Gal 5:22) but our instant access to information and entertainment is causing our children to become increasingly impatient.

In a 2019 report, the World Health Organization suggests that children under the age of one year old should have zero sedentary screen time and children between the ages of one and two should have no more than sixty minutes per day. According to the report, if the guidelines for screen time are followed along with appropriate physical activity, sleep, and nutrition, children will be healthier, less prone to obesity and disease, and will be more likely to have better mental and physical condition later in life.[7] And yet, caregivers are quick to hand devices to children or plop kids in front of screens for long periods of time.

Adults are also susceptible to the dangers of technology. We witness adults in our community growing less patient and more frustrated. Technology offers the false promise that life's questions can be answered immediately, and the difficult problems of our existence can be solved quickly. In a world where Siri and Alexa respond instantly to our questions, it is easy to be lulled into a belief that whatever problems we face, someone must be able to come up with an answer or engineer an adequate solution on the spot. There is a false faith that technology will eventually address all of life's woes. But as Christians, we know that technology can't solve all of our problems. We understand that life must include suffering. Jesus said, "If anyone would come after me, he must deny himself and take up his cross and follow me" (Matt 16:24). And again, Jesus warned his followers "In this world you will have trouble" (John 16:33).

Not only will technology not alleviate all of life's troubles, but there are also instances where technology makes us more vulnerable, due to the unconstrained rate of implementation. This is particularly the case for the older members of our community. Many are forced to adapt to new technologies such as electronic applications for services, online

---

7. "WHO guidelines."

financial transactions, and electronic claims processes. Some people have not learned the skills to adequately navigate such systems. Consequently, they may not receive necessary services, lose money, or become victims of fraud or identity theft.

These addictions, frustrations, and vulnerabilities make it clear that technology is sometimes bad. Technology does not automatically improve human life or lead to progress for society. Furthermore, when the dark side of technology is exploited for evil purposes, the results are downright ugly.

The Ugly

Cyber criminals worm their way into computers where valuable personal and financial information is stored, wiping out bank accounts in an instant, plunging victims into poverty. Fake news can be spread across multiple social media platforms with the malicious intent to perpetuate conspiracy theories and radicalize groups of people towards violence. Explosives can be configured to release deadly pathogens in a bioterrorist attack against innocent civilians. Technology becomes an ugly tool in the wrong hands.

Under the influence of sinful people, technology can lose its good power to reflect the creator God, and instead can be twisted into a temptation to replace God. When technology becomes increasingly disconnected from the Creator, its use drifts more and more from God's good purposes towards whatever warped or evil agenda exists in the minds of the one in whose hands the technology lies.

The biblical story of the Tower of Babel is an infamous example of technological arrogance and ugliness. Even though God gave the world a fresh start after the great flood, Noah's descendants quickly deviated back into lifestyles of decadence and debauchery. In just a few generations, the world once again became consumed by conceit and corruption. Consider Genesis 11:1–4:

> Now the whole world had one language and a common speech. As people moved eastward, they found a plain in Shinar and settled there. They said to each other, "Come, let's make bricks and bake them thoroughly." They used brick instead of stone, and tar for mortar. Then they said, "Come, let us build ourselves a city, with a tower that reaches to the heavens, so that we may

make a name for ourselves; otherwise we will be scattered over the face of the whole earth."

As the human race settled on the plain of Shinar, they launched into a two-phase process of tower building. Since ancient Mesopotamia didn't have stone available, they took it upon themselves to manufacture their own building materials. With incredible human ingenuity, they created kilns to bake bricks and mined bitumen (asphalt) to make mortar. These new technologies gave them the ability to build waterproof structures as sturdy as stone.

With mass production of the proper materials, the people shifted to phase two of their presumptuous project—building a city with a massive tower. The infamous Tower of Babel was not a simple watchtower or defense rampart, it was a monstrous ziggurat (a square or rectangular structure engineered with multiple tiers and staircases and a shrine on the top) designed to make a statement to the watching world. It was a man-made mountain that served the dual purpose of national pride and pagan worship. With its foundation on the earth and pinnacle in the clouds, it would supposedly give humans access to heaven and provide a convenient stairway to heaven so the gods could come down and bless their city and civilization.

The builders of Babel employed the most advanced technologies to that point in human history, but to what end? Genesis 11:4 reveals that the people's motivation for building the Tower of Babel was to make a name for themselves and not be scattered all over the earth. These city planners were hoping to achieve fame and eternal glory. They sought significance and security through their own achievements. They arrogantly believed that they could make their own way to heaven, independent from God. They put their faith in their own ingenuity rather than trusting God to take care of them. They were trying to consolidate their power and protect themselves by urbanizing, rather than scattering over the earth, as God desired. The people were no longer trying to be like God; they were trying to bring God down and manipulate him to be more like them. The entire effort reeked of human hubris.

The people's advancement and use of technology only gave them a false sense of power and control. Technology and human achievement could not genuinely address their anxieties and vulnerabilities. And, of course, when the project at Babel backfired, the people's fears were realized as they ended up scattered.

There is nothing inherently wrong with the technologies of city building, civil engineering, architectural design, manufacturing building materials, or even urbanization, but like all human endeavors, it always comes back to the motivation of the heart. The episode of the Tower of Babel should compel modern people to question their motivation for technological advance. When technology promises progress, independence, self-sufficiency, it might be prudent to pause and ask, "Progress at what expense?" and "Independence from whom?" and "What is the real purpose of pursuing this goal?"

Today, the same ugly power of technology exists. Technology can give people a sense of power and self-reliance that diminishes reliance on God. Unchecked, some people will use this sense of power and control to exploit and harm others. The same technology that guides the shipment of useful goods can be used to track and traffic human beings. Drones fitted with meteorological equipment to monitor weather can be fashioned with weapons to assassinate political opponents. These are just a few of the evil uses of technology.

It would be convenient if all technologies fit neatly into the categories of good, bad, ugly. If it were that simple, the recommendation would be to use technology for good, avoid the bad, and condemn the ugly. The problem, however, is that technology and its implementation fall into categories of moral and ethical ambiguity.

Take for example the medical technology of gene editing. Yes, the technology can offer an amazing promise to prevent and cure inherited diseases that otherwise would be debilitating or life-threatening. But what are the unintended consequences of this technology? Could the manipulation of human genes lead to the creation of a superrace of humans? Is this making us better humans or is it dehumanizing (or both)? Will parents be able to engineer designer babies with enhanced bodies? Is this technology safe? And what are the ethical obligations towards children born with the DNA from three people: an egg from one, sperm from another, and mitochondrial DNA from a third?

What are we to do? On the one hand, it would be unwise (and nearly impossible) to try to reject and avoid technology. On the other hand, we put ourselves in peril if we indiscriminately utilize every available technology. Where can we find a balance? Does the Christian church even have anything to offer to these complex issues? How can a church leader get a seat at the table to speak into these matters? How can pastors have a voice in the midst of this moral and ethical complexity?

The Pastor in the New Technological Parish

The first step for the pastor in the new technological parish is to develop a personal theological position and moral convictions about the use of science and technology. One of the major problems with technology in our world is that it lacks moral conviction. In order to engage the world of science and technology, pastors need to make sure that they have a firm grasp of these issues in their own minds and hearts. The pastor needs to ask, "What is my view of technology? Do I personally have firm convictions about these issues? Is my personal use of technology in line with what I believe?" In such a technologically advanced society, it is easy to uncritically get caught up in technology use without considering the potential consequences of our own actions.

One concept that should guide our personal convictions around technology use is the notion of sabbath. In our "plugged-in" and ever-connected world, it becomes vital to take time to rest from constant communication and information. On my day off, I find it refreshing to stay off my phone and computer as much as possible. Even so, I do not often go the whole day without checking communications. But even a few hours without the barrage of messages helps me to have the space to just be quiet and listen to the Lord and to others around me.

Another guiding theological concept is incarnation. At the heart of the Christian faith is the incarnation of Jesus Christ, who did not work remotely but took on human flesh and came to earth to make his dwelling among people. As John 1:14 says, "The Word became flesh and made his dwelling among us." In his human condition, Jesus walked with people, taught people, and touched people. God could have shouted from heaven, but in his sovereignty and love, he came to us.

In ministry leadership, it is easy to communicate from a distance and to rely solely on remote and electronic communication. Those can be great tools to efficiently communicate with a lot of people. But if we take incarnational ministry seriously, we need to remember to take the time to be with people, face-to-face.

About ten years ago, our church had the opportunity to put this principle into practice. We had made the decision to become a multi-site ministry. Operating as a video site would have reduced effort, costs, and provided for consistency in the teaching. However, when it came time to make the decision, we opted to establish a live-preaching site. We felt that the proximity and authenticity of a fully live and in-person ministry was a better option, rather than just relying on the teacher-on-a-screen experience.

But we also acknowledge that there are some churches that utilize video preaching effectively. It would be too simplistic to say the solution is to avoid technology as much as possible in the life of the church (although I have one colleague who proudly holds that view, refusing even to use a microphone). Taking the first step of developing theological and moral convictions around these issues will guide the use of technology in the pastor's personal life and the life of the church. And it will give pastors wisdom and credibility to engage the technology community beyond the walls of the church, in the new parish.

The second step that a pastor can take to engage the new technological parish is to equip his or her congregation to use technology thoughtfully and wisely. A simple way to do this is by facilitating conversation forums about technological issues. Seth Anderson, one of the contributors to this book, invited a geneticist to his church to talk to students about genetics and the moral and ethical implications of advancements in this field. Introducing students to these topics helps break down the sacred/secular divide relative to issues of faith and science. By attempting to bridge this divide, young people develop a framework for integrating their faith into a wide variety of subjects.

As part of the confirmation program at our church, we host a Q&A session with the confirmands where they are invited to ask any question they want to a panel of "experts" in the church. In addition to pastors and theologians, we include a college mathematics professor on the panel. The students have appreciated his contributions during these events as he brings scientific credibility and insight to questions of faith.

Another way to equip the congregation is to provide resources to parents who want to help their children navigate a technology-saturated world. The pastor does not necessarily have to come up with original content for this type of equipping. There are numerous books and articles written on these subjects which can be used as a starting point for discussion.

Parents also need to be equipped to understand the value of sabbath including technology sabbaths for themselves and their children. One of my colleagues has instituted regular "technology sabbaticals" as part of his discipleship ministry with students. While it has been difficult to convince students to stay away from screens, he said that some of the greatest moments of breakthrough and spiritual growth have happened while they are "unplugged."

To further equip the congregation, churches can also provide opportunities for parishioners to support one another as they engage issues of technology together. Public forums for the church and community have proved effective. Our church has regularly hosted what we call "Our Cultural Moment" events. Each event includes a faith-based perspective on current cultural issues of interest. Typically, a local expert presents a brief lecture and then people discuss the issue in "table-talk" style smaller groups. Some of our topics have included technology, economics, race, and politics. The events have been well attended and received. Opportunities to gather people from the church and community around topics of mutual interest abound.

Pastors do not necessarily need to create new programs or reinvent the proverbial wheel to equip the church. Many towns host forums like this at public libraries and other civic venues. People love to share their opinions around these issues, and it is relatively easy for pastors to join the conversation by attending these events.

However, pastors should exercise caution when participating in these forums. Our local library hosted an informational talk and discussion about climate change with a university professor as the guest presenter. According to the local newspaper, the event "quickly erupted into a series of name-calling and yelling before police were called to help disperse people from the event."[8] I don't know if the presence of a pastor would have made a difference at the meeting, but it goes to show how these conversations are not just about pure science but about deeply held beliefs and values. These are precisely the type of conversations to which a pastor should bring the perspective of faith.

Beyond personal conviction and equipping the church around issues of technology, the third step a pastor can take to engage the new technological parish is to directly connect to members of the science and technology community. How can pastors gain access to this sector of the public square? The best place to start is by leveraging relationships with people in the church who work in science and technology fields. While the pastor doesn't often have a seat at the table in the technology industry, any number of parishioners may be leaders in these fields. Pastors may, therefore, make connections to these fields through these key people. A pastor can ask them about their fields of expertise, visit their workplaces, and affirm their role as people of faith influencing their world.

---

8. *The Eagle-Tribune*, "Climate change."

Broadly speaking, I knew that Steve (my parishioner) worked in the science and technology field, but it wasn't until I actually visited him at his workplace that I learned he is a chemical engineer in the research and development arm of a prominent pharmaceutical company. Steve collaborates with a team of scientists who are developing new treatments for cancer. This visit opened the door for me to seek his guidance on multiple medical treatments and healthcare issues. My personal relationship with Steve has broadened my knowledge of pharmaceuticals and has given me access to experts who can help me make informed decisions about scientific and technological issues. It has also given Steve and his colleagues an opportunity to bounce their moral and ethical questions off a pastor. They can help me become a more knowledgeable pastor and I can help them be more moral scientists.

Perhaps a pastor's presence in a technology company can, at least in a small way, bring faith into these fields. One time I visited Patti, my parishioner who works in large medical device company in our community. After my visit, one of her co-workers asked her, "Why was your pastor here?" Patti told her coworker that her pastor cares about her and the work their company is doing to make medical equipment safer and more efficient. The coworker was so intrigued by the situation that she began to ask Patti questions about God and faith, in a place where these topics seldom come up in conversation. Sometimes a pastor's physical presence can have a positive impact, even in a research laboratory or technological workshop.

Likewise, pastors can engage the science and technology parish by encouraging and edifying specific individuals who work in these fields. My parishioner Jim is a high-tech cyber security expert for a large internet service provider. He doesn't receive a lot of accolades for his work, but he plays a crucial role in preventing ugly uses of technology. He protects vulnerable people from cyberattacks that expose sensitive personal information and threaten their well-being. In my role as his pastor, I have helped him understand the importance of his vocational/technological calling. God has called him to be a warrior in the spiritual battle between good and evil that is waged in cyberspace and on computer screens; his job is to protect the public by thwarting the worst intentions and wicked plans of wrongdoers. Pastors can engage the technological parish by encouraging and edifying people like Jim.

As a pastor who serves in a community where some of the largest employers are science, technology, and educational institutions, I have had the privilege of visiting some high-profile technology companies and building meaningful relationships with the people who work in these places. In some regions that lack these resources, it may be difficult for pastors to engage science and technology leaders on their turf. But pastors can still build relationships and partnerships with the science and technology faculty at their local university, community college, or high school.

My colleague and co-author, Jason McConnell, pastors a church in a rural area. He was invited to speak at a nearby university about the intersection of the natural and supernatural world, a topic that was intended to engage the scientific community at the school. A biology professor saw a poster promoting the event and decided to attend. The content piqued the professor's interest enough for him to ask Jason to meet another time and continue to explore the topic. This initial encounter has led to an ongoing relationship of mutual learning. If Jason had not ventured out of his church study and onto the campus for this event, he would not have made this connection. He would have missed a valuable opportunity to learn from the science community and share the gospel with them.

Developing personal theological positions and moral convictions, equipping the congregation, and directly engaging the community are simple ways to minister in the technological parish. Most of these ministry ideas require little background knowledge and minimal effort. Pastors are busy, but if they want to reach people in the science and technology parish, they must be willing to learn, engage, and build personal relationships with people in this sector of the public square.

Conclusion

In our conversation with Dr. Picard at MIT, one of my colleagues posed a question that has stuck with me. He asked, "When you go to church, what are you looking for from your pastor, particularly in sermons?" I tried to imagine what I could ever preach that would be useful to a such a brilliant scientist. I remember being struck by the simplicity of her answer. It had nothing to do with intellectual acumen or scientific relevance. She just wanted a pastor to point her and others to the love of God through Jesus Christ. Dr. Picard went on to write:

> I once thought I was too smart to believe in God. Now I know I was an arrogant fool who snubbed the greatest Mind in the cosmos—the Author of all science, mathematics, art, and everything else there is to know. Today I walk humbly, having

received the most undeserved grace. I walk with joy, alongside the most amazing Companion anyone could ask for, filled with desire to keep learning and exploring.[9]

My experience with Dr. Picard made me realize that no matter how much I know (or don't know) about science and technology, pastors have a part to play in this parish. Pastors can help scientists think about the opportunities, goals, and liabilities of developing technologies. We have the unique ability to bring the wisdom of God to the good, the bad, and the ugly of new technology. But even better, we bring the God of wisdom with us wherever we go.

For Further Exploration

1. Nicolas Carr. *The Big Switch: Rewiring the World, from Edison to Google.* New York: W. W. Norton, 2009.
2. Francis S. Collins. *The Language of God: A Scientist Presents Evidence for Belief.* New York: Free Press, 2009.
3. Elaine Ecklund. *Why Science and Faith Need Each Other: Eight Share Values that Move Us Beyond Fear.* Grand Rapids: Brazos, 2020.
4. Jacques Ellul. *The Technological Society.* New York: Vintage, 1964. Neil Postman. *Technopoly: The Surrender of Culture to Technology.* New York: Vintage, 1993.
5. Neil Postman. *Technopoly: The Surrender of Culture to Technology.* New York: Vintage, 1993.
6. Leonard Sweet and Mark Chironna. *Rings of Fire: Walking in Faith through a Volcanic Future.* Colorado Springs, CO: NavPress, 2019.

---

9. Picard, "I Got Smart", 72.

Engaging the Science and Technology Parish

Interview

Eryck Bredy is the founder and president of Bredy Network Management Corporation (BNMC), a New England-based company which provides Information Technology support, cloud services, and IT consulting services to a variety of clients. Eryck graduated from Harvard University in 1987 with a bachelor of arts degree in biochemical sciences. Eryck serves as an elder at the Free Christian Church of Andover, Massachusetts.

(The day I interviewed Eryck, my computer crashed, so I had to take notes by hand. The first pen I grabbed didn't work either. I was frustrated but Eryck found the situation ironic and humorous considering our topic. The following are from my handwritten notes.)

Q. **How did you get into the technology field?**

After graduating from Harvard, my focus was financial services. I'm a "numbers guy" so it was a natural fit. I started my own financial services business. Over time, I found that my financial planning clients kept asking for help fixing their computers. So, I decided to start a consulting company and pretty quickly my IT business outgrew my financial services business—I've been doing IT work ever since. It started with just network consulting but later grew into full-service outsourcing of server, desktop, and network management and support.

Q. Has your Christian faith and involvement in the church helped you in your work? If so, how?

It absolutely helps me in my work—it gives me perspective. Without faith, business is non-fulfilling. Yes, it can be fun and exciting in some respects, but when people depend on you to help them with their technology, it creates a constant pressure. People depend so heavily on their technology that we are put in a position where we constantly feel the fear and guilt of letting people down if we can't fix all of their problems immediately. Without faith, I would constantly be chasing perfection, which is impossible. As a Christian, I trust God's success, not my own. God has gifted me to do this work so I do it the best I can to glorify him, and the pressure to be perfect is lifted.

Q. Do you face any unique moral or ethical dilemmas in your particular work?

I occasionally lose clients because some of my competitors are willing to lie to them. I strive to always tell the truth. The hardest part of telling the truth comes when a prospective client asks if our solution is going to meet all their needs, especially in terms of disaster recovery. Because they don't understand all of the technology, it would be easy to paint a rosy picture about what we would be able to do (as some of my competitors do). But instead, we try to educate our clients about recovery point objectives and realistic timelines. We try to paint an accurate picture instead of just making empty promises.

Q. How can a pastor better support people in technology fields? What would be helpful?

Just keep preaching the gospel of Jesus Christ and the humility of the gospel. A big part of the problem in technology is the leading edge/bleeding edge—the desperate push to develop the next great thing. It creates immense pressure to be successful through self-sufficiency. The gospel is about God-sufficiency. Pastors need to remind us that we can never fully be self-reliant. I've seen a lot of people in tech fields who are driven by a "god complex" that ultimately leads them astray. A good example was the dot-com bust and all the carnage that came from people who were puffed up by their own successes. It doesn't matter to me that you don't know my field.

Just keep preaching the gospel. Start with the fear of the Lord, help us understand his grace, and help us to see that all that we do is for his kingdom and his glory. That's what you can do!

3

Engaging the Healthcare Parish

Justin Frank

"At least two kinds of courage are required in aging and sickness. The first is the courage to confront the reality of mortality—the courage to seek out the truth of what is to be feared and what is to be hoped. Such courage is difficult enough. We have many reasons to shrink from it. But even more daunting is the second kind of courage—the courage to act on the truth we find."

—ATUL GAWANDE

On Monday morning, I received a telephone call from a surgical nurse at my local hospital. After verifying my name and birthdate, she said, "I have a memo to schedule you for an emergency procedure." She arranged an appointment for Thursday because some of my symptoms were similar to the cancer that was currently afflicting my father. Shaken, I followed through with my plan to take my children to the coast for the day. Later that evening, while driving home, my phone rang again. It was my sister. Our father had just died.

As a pastor, I've visited countless patients and prayed with anxious families pacing emergency room waiting areas. I've hovered over hospital beds and held the hands of the dying as they breathed their final breath. But with these two phone calls, I found myself on the other side of this familiar situation. I had to reckon with a reality that I've preached about many times: mortality. Death and dying had become personal. As I simultaneously mourned the death of my father and mulled my upcoming medical procedure, I reflected on the fact that mortality in the modern world forces almost everyone into unavoidable encounters with the healthcare system.

This is why medicine and healthcare are universal subjects in American public discourse. How many times each week—each day—do we come across news about some aspect of the healthcare industry? Every time we turn on the radio, scan newspaper headlines, or scroll a newsfeed on our computer, medical stories abound. We overhear doctors discussing the efficacy of patient care and debating the ethical implications of new medical technologies. We listen to politicians pontificating about access to healthcare and the governance structures that provide the best outcomes (or at least the ones that will them get elected). We hear economists strategize about ways to cut healthcare costs and streamline services, and the list goes on and on.

Hospitals and medical clinics are institutional centerpieces of every American community. They are visible shrines that represent one of our nation's deepest values. For instance, my city of Augusta, Maine is the home of Maine General Hospital, a point of pride in the city and a facility constructed at a cost of over 300 million dollars. I have no doubt there are people in my city who don't know where our church building is located, but they know where the hospital is, and how to get there. It is, therefore, not surprising that healthcare jobs are expected to grow faster in the next ten years than the average for any other occupation.[1]

This, of course, was all true before the onset of the COVID-19 global pandemic in March 2020, but now the healthcare rhetoric has exploded exponentially, ranging from rising death tolls to potential cures and preventive measures like vaccines, social distancing regulations, travel restrictions, stay-at-home orders, and wearing face masks in public places. The pandemic has reshaped the world as we know it and has shifted the healthcare conversation to center stage for the foreseeable future.

With all the complexities involved in healthcare, where should pastors begin to engage this sector of the public square? Since most pastors

---

1. According to the US Bureau of Labor Statistics, https://www.bls.gov/ooh/healthcare/home.htm.

are isolated by the disciplines of their own profession (theology, preaching, spiritual caregiving), how can they confidently speak to issues related to anatomy and physiology or pharmacology? Should pastors be expected to understand the minute details of healthcare policy or the moral and economic implications in the health insurance debate?

Even if pastors did begin to speak out about healthcare, who would listen? According to a December 2018 Gallup poll,[2] the top three most trusted professions in America were all in healthcare—nurses, doctors, and pharmacists (in that order). A whopping 84 percent of those questioned rated nurses' honesty and ethical standards as high or very high, and only 2 percent as low or very low. Doctors and pharmacists came in a bit lower in the second and third spots, at 67 percent and 66 percent high or very high, respectively. Clergy? Not the worst (that's Congress) but significantly lower, with 37 percent ranking clergy integrity as high or very high, and 15 percent as low or very low.

With a lack of necessary medical knowledge and credibility, how can pastors meaningfully engage the healthcare community as part of their parish? The answer starts with a recognition that, for all the wonders of modern medicine, there are massive existential questions that medicine cannot address. Modern society values physicians over pastors, but this was not always the case. The fourth-century church father Gregory of Nazianzus points out an older perspective when he compares the work of pastors and physicians: "ours [pastors'] is more laborious, and of more consequence." But why is the pastor's work harder and more consequential? Gregory opines that it is because of "the nature of its subject matter, the power of its science and the object of its exercise."[3]

Gregory of Nazianzus is not the only one who has observed medicine's deficiencies. Dr. Atul Gawande, surgeon, Harvard Medical School professor, and writer, puts it bluntly in his *New York Times* best-selling book, *Being Mortal*: "The problem with medicine and the institutions it has spawned for the care of the sick and the old is not that they have had an incorrect view of what makes life significant. The problem is that they have had almost no view at all."[4]

This, Gawande writes, is a major problem, especially when it comes to the final moments of human existence, when the practice of medicine,

---

2. McCarthy, "America's Most Trusted," para. 1–2.
3. Nazianzus, "Reflections," para 16.
4. Gawande, *Being Mortal*, 128.

so focused on physical healing, can help a patient no more. When people are dying, the most important questions and relationships in life are front and center. The practice of medicine has no answer for these questions, no prescription for handling the relationships. According to Gawande, the healthcare system often ignores the significance of these fundamental realities altogether. Gawande puts it forcefully:

> [T]he way we [medical professionals] deny people this [engagement with the most significant issues of life while in the process of dying] . . . out of obtuseness and neglect, is cause for everlasting shame. Over and over, we in medicine inflict deep gouges at the end of people's lives and then stand oblivious to the harm done.[5]

It is pointless to debate whether doctors or pastors are more important, and the very question implies a false dichotomy of dualistic assumptions. However, these poignant words from an ancient pastor and modern physician reflect the necessity of caring for both body and soul, a conviction that Jesus himself highlighted on multiple occasions (Matt 9:10–14; Mark 2:15–17; Luke 5:29–32). Medicine alone has no answer for the deepest questions of human existence; science cannot heal the soul. But when medicine and faith meet—and when pastors and physicians work together to care for the whole human being—everyone benefits.

There is obviously a huge gap between healing medicine and human meaning. So, how can pastors begin to bridge this gap? How can they engage the healthcare sector? I want to focus on three areas for pastoral engagement—meaning, morality, and the ministry of presence—all of which are rooted in a theology of the imago Dei, the religious belief that all humans are created in the image of God and bear God's likeness in body, mind, and soul.

Engaging the Human Need for Meaning

My son Samuel was born on a bright September afternoon. After my wife endured a painful labor, a peaceful stillness settled over the hospital room and time seemed to stop. The warm glow of autumn sunset seeped through the window shades while my wife and I took turns cradling our baby in our arms, whispering prayers, and gazing into his enquiring eyes that embraced the world outside the womb for the first time. For all three of us, it was a moment filled with indescribable awe and wonder.

---

5. Gawande, *Being Mortal*, 128.

It is a cliché to say that birth is a spiritual experience. But clichés evolve because they capture some aspect of a universal truth. I have conversed with many people who wouldn't consider themselves religious, and yet, they have used similar terms to describe the birth of their children. The process of birth and the marvel of infants themselves, testify to something "more" than a bundle of atoms and molecules in motion—to some greater story yet to be told—to some veiled transcendent reality peeking through.

In modern America, this wonderful, spiritual experience typically takes place in a hospital, with trained medical personnel on hand. Of course, most hospital rooms are filled with the pain and anxiety of death, not the peace and joy of new birth. This is sometimes true even in the maternity ward. The neonatal intensive care unit was not far from the room where our Samuel was born—the unit where his older brother was rushed a few years earlier when he was born purple, limp, and silent, not breathing. Our midwife and the nurses responded quickly, and his brother survived. Not all do. Hospitals are host to the heights and the depths of human emotion, and they are places where many people embark upon a quest for human meaning.

Gawande recounts an encounter with a patient named Jewel Douglass and his attempt to help her make complicated decisions about how to deal with advanced cancer. Such decisions, he concludes, cannot be made outside the larger consideration of meaning. "For human beings," he writes, "life is meaningful because it is a story: A story has a sense of a whole, and its arc is determined by the significant moments . . . A seemingly happy life may be empty. A seemingly difficult life may be devoted to a great cause. We have purposes larger than ourselves."[6]

Medical professionals are often trained, Gawande writes, to value "safety and survival," and to ignore larger questions of meaning. But, he argues, this is a profound mistake that misunderstands the centrality of these questions to human life. This is true not only when facing death, but also when enduring suffering.

Patients and their family members are not the only ones in the hospital who are searching for meaning. I have spoken to many medical professionals who tell stories about the toll caregiving takes on them and the constant question of meaning their work raises. Dr. Francis Collins is the director of the National Institute of Health. In his *New York Times*

---

6. Gawande, *Being Mortal*, 239.

best-selling book *The Language of God*, he writes about how interacting with real patients, many enduring chronic pain and grim diagnoses, shook his understanding of the world.[7] When he started medical school, Collins was an outspoken atheist. Rather quickly, however, his experiences treating patients began to change him.

What stood out to Collins most about his patients who were sick and dying was the "spiritual aspect of what many of them were going through."[8] He saw the powerful sense of meaning in the midst of hardship that faith gave to many of his patients. One day, his reflections on all of this came to a head as he spoke with a patient:

> My most awkward moment came when an older woman, suffering daily from severe untreatable angina, asked me what I believed. It was a fair question; we had discussed many other important issues of life and death, and she had shared her own strong Christian beliefs with me. I felt my face flush as I stammered out the words, "I'm not really sure." Her obvious surprise brought into sharp relief a predicament that I had been running away from for nearly all of my twenty-six years: I had never really seriously considered the evidence for and against belief.[9]

Questions of ultimate meaning represent one area where pastors can help patients and healthcare professionals. American society has largely sidelined theology for disciplines deemed more practical and scientifically verifiable, but the shift toward the practical and scientific has avoided the existential questions of human life—questions which theology directly addresses. "Far from being impractical," theologian Kevin Vanhoozer argues, "the pastor-theologian is (or ought to be) a holy jack-of-all-existential-trades."[10]

If pastors are going to help people discover meaning in human existence, they must be engaged in ongoing biblical and theological reflection. Theologians deal with the reality of God and his relationship to his creation. Christian theologians, in particular, find ultimate meaning in the person and work of Jesus Christ as revealed in the Old and New Testament and church history. As the apostle Paul wrote in his glorious description of the "cosmic Christ" in Colossians 1:16, "all things were

---

7. Collins, *Language of God*, 19.
8. Collins, *Language of God*, 19.
9. Collins, *Language of God*, 20.
10. Vanhoozer and Strachan, *Pastor as Public Theologian*, 104.

created by him and for him." In Colossians 2:3, we are taught that in Christ "are hidden all the treasure of wisdom and knowledge." It is the pastor's privilege to shepherd people into a deeper understanding of Christ and his sovereignty over everything in the world, whether material or immaterial.

This often takes the form of helping people understand how the truth of the gospel relates to the realities of sickness and suffering and death. Why does God allow these things to happen? How are we to bear the weight of them?

Recently, a member of my congregation asked for healing prayer in the manner modeled in James 5. I agreed to pray for him the following Sunday, and at the end of the service, I announced that I would be praying and anointing with oil, inviting any who wanted to join us to come forward. A large crowd came, and several others stepped forward to also ask for anointing and prayer.

The very next day, that church member went into the hospital in extreme pain, and he was diagnosed with stage IV cancer. Medically, there was little more to be done. Two days after public prayer for healing, we sent out a message asking the church for continued prayer as he prepared to transition to hospice. When I spoke with him, he said "Pastor, I'm just sorry for you that you have to explain this to everyone." Why, just one day after such a powerful time of prayer, was he doomed to such a swift death sentence? How could this be God's plan? How would his family, doctors, and nurses find meaning in a series of events like this?

When questions like these come from the parish (inside or outside the church), pastors must be prepared to answer them. Such inquiries require emotional sensitivity and theological competence. Pastors must have more than clichés and sentimentality. The pastor's native language is theology, and people need pastor-theologians to address life's most difficult questions and quandaries. Pastors, if properly prepared, are in a position to speak meaning to apparently meaningless situations. The Bible, indeed, addresses the purpose of life, the inevitability of death, the reason for relationships, the goal of work, the origin of evil, the objective of suffering, and many other crucial questions about ultimate meaning. Pastors must contextualize these abstract principles to people's daily lives.

Engaging Moral Questions of Life and Death

After I finished preaching one Sunday morning, I was notified that the husband of one of our church members collapsed while getting out of bed that morning. The ambulance rushed him to the hospital and the doctors determined that he had suffered a massive cerebral aneurysm. By the time I arrived, he was on life support. The wife was shell-shocked as she waited outside his room in the critical care unit. After waking up beside her husband every day for the last thirty years, she wondered if he would ever wake up again.

I was sitting beside her when the doctor delivered the devastating news. Her husband was functionally brain dead and there was nothing more they could do for him. His body was kept alive by a breathing machine. After the doctor explained the severity of the situation, he carefully broached the possibility of removing life support. The wife was her husband's power of attorney, but he had no advanced directives. In her bewildered state, she not only had to wrestle with her emotions but also her moral responsibilities.

The doctor left us to talk with each other. We discussed two questions. Would her children, who lived out of state, be able to make it in time to see him before he died? And would she be morally culpable for ending her husband's life if she authorized the removal of his breathing tube?

The doctor presented the facts clearly and compassionately, but he offered no moral direction. Her beloved husband was brain dead, but his body was still functioning due to life support—which if removed, would cause him to die. She looked to me for guidance. She asked, "What is the right thing to do?"

A few years later, a friend and his wife disclosed to me their long and painful struggle with infertility. They had recently decided to begin fertility treatment and pursue in vitro fertilization. They are conscientious people; they always consider their ethical conduct and the implications of their actions. As he shared the story, he told me how shocked they were by the medical community's apparent disregard of moral reflection in the IVF process. Having determined the goal of helping them get pregnant, the medical professionals involved offered one treatment after another, each as the logical next step toward their goal. But every treatment option had serious side effects and raised significant ethical questions. They read extensively about the ethics of fertility treatments, but it was difficult to keep up with the technological developments. And their doctors didn't encourage any ethical reflection.

My friend told me about the moment that crystalized their concern. Having arrived at the clinic for an appointment, he and his wife were handed a sheet of paper to fill out before being brought in to see the doctor. The sense they got from the office manager was that this was a formality, just a signature or two before heading into the doctor's office. But when my friend read the form, he realized it required them to make decisions regarding what would be done with the unused embryos created in the IVF process.

These embryos would be created from his sperm and his wife's egg, and just like every other embryo at the moment of conception they would each be fundamentally unique—each with its own unique DNA sequence. They believed this made the embryo an actual human being, not just a potential one. Given time, these embryos could and would develop into fully functioning daughters or sons.

What was the moral status of these embryos? What were the medical and moral implications of how they handled them? What was the right thing to do? And how could they decide any of this in the moment they were given in that waiting room?

Medical ethics are practical ethics, often with weighty consequences. People are making decisions (often life-and-death decisions) regarding their bodies and the bodies of their loved ones. Doctors, nurses, social workers, and medical administrators contemplate these questions as well. And often people don't start to think about ethics until they are personally confronted with the situation in our own life. At that point, how do they to decide what to do?

Science alone cannot tell us whether something is morally right or wrong, even though it is commonly invoked as if it can. Educator and cultural critic Neil Postman has argued that the use of science as moral authority developed in the aftermath of the Enlightenment's rejection of God's revelation as the source of authority in society. With God removed, people have been "searching for an alternative source of moral authority ever since."[11] In our increasingly technological society, science itself has achieved a high pedestal of moral authority. Postman called the appeal to science as an unimpeachable moral authority "Scientism." Scientism, he wrote, is "the desperate hope, and wish, and

---

11. Postman, *Technopoly*, 160.

ultimately the illusory belief that some standardized set of procedures called 'science' can provide us with an unimpeachable source of moral authority." He gave a practical example:

> Science can tell us when a heart begins to beat, or movement begins, or what are the statistics on the survival of neonates of different gestational ages outside the womb. But science has no more authority than you or I do to establish such criteria as the "true" definition of "life" or of human state or personhood.[12]

Again, we are back to questions of meaning. What is a human person? What is a human person worth? What are human rights and who has them? And whose rights have priority when they come into conflict? The answers to these questions are found in varying conceptions of the meaning of life. They are also all questions that science cannot answer.

While some view science as moral authority, one wonders if anyone is actually pausing to consider ethical ramifications of modern medical technologies. Biotechnical companies are constantly exploring new frontiers that promise stunning benefits for humanity, but they also raise new moral questions. In the words of Jeff Goldblum's character in the film *Jurassic Park*, some scientists seem "so preoccupied with whether or not they could that they didn't stop to think if they should." The drive for innovation and profit fuels a competitive push forward, but it leaves little time or space to reflect on moral implications or unintended consequences.

Moral questions are usually emotional and weighty. Many doctors and medical professionals agonize over the morality of certain aspects of their work. Patients and their families are confronted by medical crises and the moral questions that immediately follow. They are forced to make difficult decisions without time to think through all of the moral ramifications.

Consider again the two situations at the beginning of this section: the woman considering the morality of removing her husband from life support and the couple contemplating their moral obligation to the embryos created from the union of their own biological life. As Christians, we believe that God is the author of life and the ultimate moral authority in the universe. If this is true, who can bridge the gap between biblical revelation and the ethics of modern medical practices? Once again, pastors are uniquely poised to engage this sector of the public square, especially in conjunction with scientists, physicians, and other healthcare professionals.

---

12. Postman, *Technopoly*, 160.

Pastors do not need to be masters of every technical issue confronting medicine and healthcare, but we should, at the very least, be attentive to developments that affect people in our congregations. Moreover, pastors need at least a working understanding of the issues for them to be a moral voice in the public square.

When I served a congregation in Gloucester, Massachusetts that was made up of a number of newly married couples and young families, I was surprised by how often ethical questions regarding fertility came up in conversation. So, I began reading about the complexities of fertilization and encouraging couples during pre-marital counseling to consider all of the issues and talk about them.

When I was called to my current church in Maine, many people in my congregation were starting to face end of life issues (after all, Maine has the oldest population in America). To help our church community reckon with the realities of meaning and morality in death and dying, we coordinated a presentation of the PBS Frontline documentary *Being Mortal*, based on Atul Gawande's book. Following the film, we hosted a panel discussion made up of a medical social worker, a doctor, a lawyer, and a pastor (me), to answer questions from the audience. The event was immensely helpful to the church members who attended, but unfortunately we missed an opportunity to engage the broader community. When we duplicate this event in the future, we will promote it with the whole parish.

There are other opportunities for pastors to engage public dialogues involving medicine and morality in the broader parish. For instance, pastors may testify before the state legislature on medical issues. In recent years, many states have weighed the moral implications of issues like healthcare accessibility, the legalization of marijuana, and physician-assisted suicide. As states continue to grapple with the morality of medical legislation, will pastors be there to provide a prophetic voice? Pastors might also consider serving as a member of a healthcare ethics committee or a provider/patient advisory board at a local medical center. Groups like these often welcome a pastor's presence and perspective around their table.

But if pastors have a desire to engage the healthcare sector, yet they are struggling with how to gain access, they should start by asking healthcare professionals in their congregations to assist them. These parishioners work in the public square daily and have the knowledge and relational capital to help pastors find entryways into these networks.

However it may happen, there is a great need for pastors to weigh in on the moral questions of life and death.

Engaging the Human Need for a Ministry of Presence

Andrew Bomback knows doctors. He is the son of an accomplished doctor, he is married to a doctor, and as a doctor himself, he teaches medical students at the Colombia University College of Physicians and Surgeons. His short book *Doctor* paints a portrait of doctors as real people amid a rapidly shifting landscape in the healthcare industry. He has witnessed firsthand how medical care has changed from a personalized practice into the big business it has become today.

One of the most obvious changes is in the doctor/patient relationship, which is no longer determined by the wholistic needs of the patient, but by the time constraints imposed by corporate executives and new technologies. He gives an example from his own practice—when he sits down with a new patient, he explains why he is going to look at his computer while they talk. "I type all my notes," he tells them. "With his fingers ready to go above the keyboard, he explains, "That means sometimes I have to look at my screen, but I'm always listening to you."[13]

This is not the instruction Bomback received in medical school, where he was encouraged to maintain eye contact while speaking with patients. It is also not what his old-school father does. Confronted with a technology (the computer) that would change his interactions with patients, he resisted. At the time of the writing of the book, his father had just turned seventy. He had been practicing medicine for over forty years and was still working for a private practice. That practice, perhaps as a concession to his father's sterling reputation, hired a scribe to take notes on his patient interactions so he didn't have to use a computer and type his notes himself during his patient interviews.

The pressures of modern medicine have changed the human dynamic in its practice. Years ago, primary care physicians would come to the hospital when someone was sick. The physician, who had a personal relationship with the patient, would be able to offer a valuable perspective. But in today's fast-paced environment, inpatients are generally cared for by hospitalists who only know the patient through what they can read on a chart.

13. Bomback, *Doctor*, 58.

The depersonalization of the healthcare industry has created an opportunity for pastors and churches to fulfill the human need for the ministry of presence. The ancient Christian practice of caring for the sick can be traced back to Jesus' example and teaching. Jesus taught that at the final judgment, one of the marks of those who are truly saved will be that in their lives they visited the sick (Matt 25:36). Furthermore, Jesus indicated that in such visits they had not just done a kind deed for a particular sick man or woman. Rather, "Inasmuch as you did it to one of the least of these my brethren, you did it to me" (Matt 25:40). That Jesus places such immense personal value on visiting the sick speaks volumes about the importance of Christians being personally involved in the ministry of presence today.

People need care beyond their bodies, though they don't always know how to ask for it. One nurse wrote, "Most people tend to isolate themselves as they struggle." She mentioned one mother whose "son has a chronic illness which requires a hospital admission for weeks at a time through the year." The mother told the nurse how people visited all the time at first, but then the visits dropped off and she wasn't able to attend church for a while, and her pastor hadn't checked in and she didn't want to bother him. "It's really lonely," the mother said, "but we're doing okay."

The nurse wrote that she would love to see the church caring for families over the long haul. She is convinced that this kind of ongoing care for the sick can be a profound public witness to families and the medical professionals caring for them. She wrote that this "entails pastors and parishioners being present to form trust and relationship so when things get really hard; they are the ones who are there to pray with families and speak truth into their lives."

Hospital visitation is a core part of the pastor's work, but pastors are not the only ones who can or should do it. As Kevin Vanhoozer writes, "If pastors themselves cannot visit . . . then they should at least train elders who can."[14] Church members can be trained to conduct meaningful visitation with the sick and dying, whether it happens in the hospital, nursing facility, or a person's home.

Pastors should also be aware of opportunities to embody God's love to doctors, nurses, and other hospital staff who work in the medical parish. Healthcare professionals are exposed to the types of traumatic and stress-inducing situations that can negatively affect their own mental and

---

14. Vanhoozer and Strachan, *Pastor as Public Theologian*, 155.

physical heath. According to a 2018 report by the American Psychiatry Association, suicide rates for doctors are "more than double that of the general population."[15]

In addition to the normal stress of the work, habitual losses influence physicians' own sense of meaning and purpose in life. Many healthcare workers gain a sense of meaning by giving of themselves, but these same professionals lose their patients, and a sense of failure diminishes their confidence and joy. Pastors can address these needs through an intentional ministry of presence. The purpose of this pastoral presence, Vanhoozer writes, "is to communicate the gospel by embodying Christ, God's love for the world . . . Only when pastors come to see the context of a person's life, at particular times and places, can they minister the word in the particular ways that direct people in the way of Jesus Christ."[16]

This ministry of presence in the medical parish begins by showing interest in the lives and work of healthcare professionals. When asked, "How can pastors better serve doctors who are in their church?," one doctor answered, "Periodically ask healthcare professionals how they are doing; emotionally, physically, spiritually." A nurse wrote that when she was new in her profession she had a hard time seeing it as being service to God. "I remember thinking my service didn't count because I was receiving a paycheck for it," she wrote. Pastors could have a huge impact by simply inquiring about their vocation and then connecting it to faith. This is especially true if the pastor is engaged in a regular visitation program and has established relationships with the medical staff.

The ministry of presence can be enhanced when it is combined with the ministry of prayer. A nurse suggested that when pastors pray with patients, they can also pray for the nurses and doctors. She wrote, "I overheard a pastor praying for me once and it was very powerful." Another wrote, "When pastors are willing to directly engage the nursing staff, it has great value." One of my pastoral colleagues, while visiting a member of his congregation in the hospital, asked the attending doctor if he would like prayer as well. When the pastor prayed, the doctor was deeply moved and even began to cry. Afterward he repeatedly thanked the pastor for the prayer.

The ministry of presence can also be strengthened when pastors combine their efforts with hospital chaplains who are already hired by the

---

15. Farmer, "When Doctors," para. 11.
16. Vanhoozer and Strachan, *Pastor as Public Theologian*, 156.

hospital to care for the spiritual and emotional needs of the sick. When I first moved to Augusta, I served on a board with the head chaplain at our local hospital. He invited me to visit him so he could give me a tour of the hospital. He not only helped me find my way around, but he introduced me to the other chaplains on staff. That chaplain has since moved on to another position, but he encouraged me to build relationships with the chaplains—a custom I have continued regularly.

This practice has led to further ministry opportunities. For a while, one of the chaplains was ordained by the Unitarian Universalist church in town. But whenever a patient mentioned any connection to a Baptist church, she would quickly refer them to me. She once told me that I was her "favorite Baptist." Because she trusted me, her referrals made it possible for me to serve people in the hospital who didn't have relationships with a pastor or church. Pastors and chaplains are natural partners for offering the ministry of presence in a new parish perspective.

Conclusion

When my doctor ordered the medical procedures that would screen me for signs of the cancer that was killing my father, he told me that maybe my father would save my life. At the time, he meant that the knowledge of my father's cancer could uncover a predisposition to a similar cancer. It turned out that he was right; the procedures revealed early stage growths that could easily be removed before they developed into full-on cancer. This may well have saved my life—or at least saved me from a battle with cancer.

However, it wasn't my father who saved me. It was the doctors and nurses who have dedicated their lives to diagnosing and treating illness, and whose knowledge and skill made the difference. In the same way, the doctors, nurses, and social workers tended to my father and my family throughout his long decline. I am profoundly grateful for all of them. It was both painful and beautiful to watch my two sisters, who are nurses, care for my father in his last days. As I intimately observed their compassion and competence, I gained a new perspective on how they and their colleagues care for people who would suffer tremendous pain without them.

At the same time, in my father's last days, visits from pastors and friends gave us strength and comfort. When my dad asked for people to come and sing hymns around his bed, the pastors from his church arranged a worship service in his room. People brought instruments, lyric sheets, and even elements for communion. It was a time we will never forget. When my father died, his pastor returned to visit with us and plan the funeral service.

And after my surgery, while I was lying in the same painful position that mirrored my father's, I received a call from my doctor. Good news—the results of my biopsy were negative! But I also received a phone call from a friend, a skilled pastor, who was able to help me process my grief, fear, and deepened sense of my own mortality. As he pointed me to Jesus' love and power and prayed for me, I was able to cry for the first time throughout the whole ordeal. His work was as healing as any surgeon's.

One of the notable aspects of the ministry of Jesus Christ is that he spent so much of his time with the sick and suffering, touching and teaching them, and healing their diseases. The work of healthcare professionals is Christlike work. But the same Jesus who healed the physical bodies of so many also said: "What does it profit a man, to gain the whole world and lose his soul?" Human life is more than mere biology. Meaning, morality, and the ministry of presence is found at the intersection of biology and theology. And this is why pastors must engage the parish of medicine and healthcare.

For Further Exploration

1. Andrew Bomback. *Doctor*. London: Bloomsbury Academic, 2018.
2. Mark W. Foreman. *Christianity and Bioethics: Confronting Clinical Issues*. Eugene, OR: Wipf and Stock, 2011.
3. Atul Gawande. *Being Mortal: Medicine and What Matters in the End*. New York: Metropolitan, 2014.
4. Elisabeth Rosenthal. *An American Sickness: How Healthcare Became Big Business and How You Can Take It Back*. New York: Penguin, 2018.
5. Kevin J. Vanhoozer and Owen Strachan. *The Pastor As Public Theologian: Reclaiming a Lost Vision*. Grand Rapids: Baker Academic, 2015.

Engaging the Healthcare Parish
Interview

JOANNA BUSHFIELD HAS BEEN a nurse for over twenty-five years. She earned her RN from John Abbot College in Montreal, Quebec, and holds a bachelor of science in nursing (BSN) from the University of Ottawa. She was a nurse at the Royal Victoria Hospital (Quebec), Massachusetts General Hospital, and the Beverly Hospital in Beverly, Massachusetts. She is currently a registered nurse in the neonatal care unit and a lactation consultant at the Boston Medical Center.

Q. **What do you wish pastors knew or understood about working in healthcare?**

I wish pastors understood what nurses "do" and the scope of our practice. I suppose this is true of any profession, that we can feel very misunderstood (pastors only work on Sundays, right?). Within the healthcare community each profession does understand the role of the other. When pastors walk into a hospital not knowing the difference between a nurse, nurse's aide, doctor, and occupational therapist, it shows a level of ignorance that diminishes their credibility with the healthcare community.

Q. **How can pastors better serve patients who are in their church?**

I think it really depends on the person and the situation. As a family on the "patient" end, we benefited from encouraging notes (which we'll treasure always) and practical help with childcare, well-timed meals, and gift cards. I guess my experience is a bit unique because through all of these we have been the pastor's family [Joanna's husband is a pastor on the North Shore of Massachusetts.] But I think that it's helpful if pastors are ensuring this practical care is happening (meals ministry, point person, etc.).

Visits with the sick are tough. As a nurse for many years in maternity, I think it's completely inappropriate for anyone who is not in the immediate family to be there. New families need to focus on bonding, breastfeeding, and getting all the rest and teaching they can take in during their very short hospital stay. I have seen enough eye rolls and tears when pastors arrive to believe that the mamas agree even if they don't think they'll feel that way. I think a phone call or text or bouquet of flowers from the pastor is a lovely gesture with plans to stop by the house for a *brief* meet/greet/blessing with the new baby after a week or two.

Of course, this is different if it is a family that has experienced past or present pregnancy losses or undergone extensive IVF when there could be immediate spiritual needs that might be right on level with the physical needs of the family. If the infant is in the NICU, it is beautiful if the hospital allows the pastor to come and pray over the family and baby (those always bring me to tears—even when the baby is completely "healthy"). In this case, sitting with the family (especially if it's a very sick baby when the family has nothing to "do") in the waiting room or taking Dad for a cup of coffee can be a huge support.

As for patients in the hospital for other reasons, it's so individualized. I think pastors (anyone!) should ask the question "Should I visit?" before "When should I visit?" If someone is in the hospital they are obviously in need of specialized care and if that care requires all their available energy (therapy, testing, teaching, etc.) then it's not appropriate to visit. For the most part, pastoral visits should be kept short and include a time of prayer and shared Scripture. Those things make such a difference. And please, do pray for the nurses as you pray—that they would have energy and wisdom as they care for the patient, thank God for the skill and compassion they have shown, and ask for a blessing over them in their lives and practice (I overheard a pastor praying for me once and it was very powerful). I know most pastors know these things (but trust me, there are a few who don't!). And when you leave, going out of your way to thank the nurse for her care of your parishioner is appreciated. For the most part, nurses really do care about their patients and it's nice to have that acknowledged.

Q. If you had the chance to directly address pastors, is there anything you would love to say to them about healthcare and the medical profession?

We are told in church that we are "sent" into our workplaces. Even as a nurse providing hands-on care of the sick, it was very hard to see my work as missional early on. Especially as a young nurse, I think I would have found it so helpful to be recognized (not publicly at all but just in interactions with my pastor) as having the privilege to serve God so directly with my vocation. I remember thinking my service didn't count because I was receiving a paycheck for it. Having a pastor ask a simple question like, "How does your love for the Lord impact your daily practice?" or "How does Scripture speak to you in your nursing?" or "How do you think the Lord sees you as a nurse?"—what we should be asking regardless of our vocation, but those questions or acknowledgment might have been helpful to me early on.

As a nurse (and now I speak of current work at Boston Medical Center as well), I see the most amazing things . . . birth, hope, recovery, good news all mixed together with addiction, abuse, death, loss, violence, homelessness, poor outcomes, such brokenness that sometimes I am numb as I come home. There has only been once in twenty-three years when I felt like I could bring this to a small group to pray for me. I just don't think many people understand the heaviness that a nurse might see/experience even in one shift alone. I have never felt that anyone outside of the hospital really could appreciate that.

In all of the above, I am reminded of the calling pastors have to help the church be the church—encouraging the body to be visiting the sick and to be asking these questions and praying for each other. It really doesn't need to be the pastor—but the pastor can set an example while the church is learning.

4

Engaging the Political Parish

Matthew Wigton

"Culture is the root of politics, and religion is the root of culture."
—RICHARD JOHN NEUHAUS

EASTER SUNDAY IS THE holiest day of the Christian year because it celebrates the glorious resurrection of Jesus Christ. However, one Easter Sunday stands out in the life of my church for a very different reason. Our worship service included a congregational prayer time that resembled an open mic night at a neighborhood bar. The service spun out of control when one church member stood up and prayed for Israel, and then another member immediately countered by offering a passionate prayer for Palestine. The dueling prayers exploded into a political jousting match over the complicated matter of Middle East peace—all amid the ironic rays of sunlight shining on a crowded sanctuary of pastel-clad visitors on Easter morning.

This incident not only provided the impetus for terminating the open mic prayer time, but it showcased the inescapable reality that pastors cannot avoid politics within the life of the church. Responding to political issues is a regular part of a pastor's role, sometimes even on Easter Sunday.

This reality mirrors the fact that we are citizens of the kingdom of God and American society, simultaneously. As such, we all play a part in the political drama. The words of the Declaration of Independence, "We hold these Truths to be self-evident, that all Men are created equal, that they are endowed by their Creator with certain unalienable Rights, that among these are Life, Liberty and the pursuit of Happiness" echo through the centuries and demand that we all participate in politics at some level. To refuse to engage in the system by saying "I am not political" is still a political choice.[1] Our actions (or inactions) impact others, whether it is electing a president who may send our children to war or voting for a local school levy.

The onset of the COVID-19 global pandemic underscored the critical need for wise pastoral political engagement. This global health crisis agitated the political divisions that already lurked beneath the surface. People were isolated, scared, and confused about what and whom to believe. Pastors are actually in a great position to calm fears and facilitate civility in times of crisis. And if they act wisely, they can offer hope to fractured political systems and healing to hurting communities.

The term "politics" is often used narrowly to refer only to elected officials or "professional politicians," but the political sphere actually encompasses a much wider range of activity, from the relatively benign gesture of registering a pet, to establishing educational standards, to executive orders from the White House. At all these levels, our unique system requires balancing power between the majority and minority voices in our democracy. Who should have the power in any number of daily decisions in our lives, all of which are political in nature?

As with any public figure, but uniquely as the leader of a politically diverse congregation, this puts the pastor in a particularly delicate position. Given the enormity and magnitude of issues, how much energy should pastors dedicate to political matters? Should the pastor engage, ignore, or flee from the political systems? Furthermore, what is the pastors' role in balancing power within their churches? And in doing so, to what extent should pastors reveal their own political positions and exercise their influence within their congregations? How can pastors navigate the political minefields in their congregations and communities? At some point, every pastor will develop a posture toward politics, but the question is: Which one?

---

1. Keller, "How Do Christians," para. 1.

A View from the Dump and the Human Condition

It is not lost on me that the Hebrew word for hell, "Gehenna," can be translated as "dump." In the picturesque seaside town that surrounds my congregation, the location of the town dump (or the transfer station) is one of the most hotly debated political issues. Much of the contention centers on the very existence of the dump. All town residents are required to cart their own trash to the dump, which requires everyone to own at least a car, or more ideally, a truck, and to have the physical strength to regularly haul trash. Additionally, they are required to pay for a dump sticker and buy special government-mandated blue bags that are often of inferior quality (and require double bagging), a policy that increases costs and environmental waste.

All these requirements provoke abuse, which, in turn, has necessitated a full-time security guard to confront the perpetrators, making the dump feel more like a small-time prison. Moreover, our town's demographics are disproportionately shaped by baby boomers, so the facility hours are problematic for working families. From my personal perspective, the facility is unjust, immoral, and a humongous waste of money in comparison to the more common practice of curbside trash pickup.

However, many people in my congregation and community love going to the dump. For many, socializing at the dump's Swap Shop (a hoarder's paradise) is the highlight of their day. To complicate matters further, members of my congregation work at the dump, so what am I to do? As a resident, I have some very strong feelings about our town dump, but as a pastor, should I use the pulpit to promote its removal? I am confident that, if I pushed my pastoral weight around, I could lead a successful campaign to trash the transfer station.

This is, of course, an example of a petty First-World political problem, but it is a problem, nonetheless. If we can't resolve the town dump conflict, how will we ever solve the far more serious and complicated issues of racism, immigration, affordable housing, student debt, national debt, cybersecurity, sex trafficking, healthcare, war, and abortion? Each of these political matters have moral and spiritual components because they involve human beings, who are created in the image of God.

Every political issue is related to a human problem. And from a theological perspective, all human problems can be traced back to the fall of humanity in the garden of Eden (Gen 3). The sinful human condition can only be solved through the atoning work of Jesus Christ

(Col 1:20–23). Since the gospel is the ultimate answer to every human problem, the church is called be a part of the reconciliation process by working with its political representatives—to pursue acute solutions and promote the common good together. Thus, the gospel provides the primary motivation and framework for political engagement.

Returning to the Parish

Central to our "return to the parish" perspective on pastoral engagement in the public square is a re-evaluation of the basic reasons for political engagement. Why get involved in politics? On one side of the spectrum is pure altruism: God's care for the world and declaration of its goodness may compel us to care for it as faithful stewards (Gen 1–2). This stewardship mandate is often only applied to creation care, but it also provides a primary reason to engage the governmental systems that oversee our towns, cities, and nation.

Many people get involved in politics out of genuine "altruistic" motives. They seek to leverage power for the good of society, from advocating for a specific issue to helping marginalized people groups. For example, as result of large-scale political advocacy, laws were passed to protect and empower people with disabilities. There are many good people who have dedicated their lives to using political power to promote social justice and societal flourishing. These faithful public servants are more likely to be lightning rods for public criticism than recipients of praise for their hard work of passing laws to improve life. The word "politician" carries a negative connotation in American culture, but there are many civic leaders who genuinely labor for their constituents and pursue the common good. As pastors return to the parish, these political leaders can become excellent partners for facilitating human flourishing.

On the opposite side of political altruism is the pursuit of power for self-interest. For some, politics is about achieving or maintaining power for a particular person, party, special interest, tribe, or state. This is true at all levels, whether someone is trying to win the majority in Congress or funding the local school budget. This is why labor unions and lobbyists spend millions of dollars on elections: to control legislative agendas for their respective constituents.

But, as justified as these motives may be in themselves, what does Jesus say about power? Jesus turned the pursuit of power on its head in the gospel. Instead of seeking the power that was rightfully his as God incarnate, Jesus voluntarily gave up his power (and his life) to accomplish the work of redemption. Jesus' followers are therefore called to model this sacrificial life. The Gospel narratives depict the Jews' misguided political expectations; they wanted a political Messiah who would liberate them from Roman oppression. Especially on Palm Sunday, many of them pressured Jesus to take up power, but Jesus resisted power and chose the path of the cross. Thus, we should be cautious about the pursuit of power as one's key motivation for political involvement.

So, if political involvement is not about the pursuit of power for the sake of self-interest, why should pastors get involved with politics? Engagement in the political sphere is necessary because it is explicitly related to the lives of people, both within the congregation and the community. If we take the greatest commandment seriously, loving our neighbor means being involved and caring for those in our actual neighborhood. The Christian pastor has the opportunity to model a different approach to political engagement than that which is often showcased in our culture. The pastor's concern is ultimately centered around the flourishing of the common good and the genuine welfare of his or her parish. In this, the pastor models power without self-interest. The call to faithful stewardship applies to all, but pastors practice this responsibility in a unique way based upon their position within the community.

As an aside, this raises the question, is the role of a pastor different from that of a layperson when it comes to interacting with the political public square? In some ways, the answer is "not much," but on the other hand, the pastor is called, in unique ways, to be the servant leader of his or her congregation and to model good practice. A pastor is already a public figure and leader in the community. Over time, a pastor will be asked political questions and thrust into political situations. A concrete example of this is that I regularly lead the prayer at town events and provide counsel for leaders and have been called on to help during times of crisis. This is in part because of my position as a pastor, as I have worked hard to cultivate relationships within my town.

So, if pastors decide to engage, how should they approach this complicated, scary, and explosive world of politics? There are no easy answers, and the uniqueness of each parish will impact the way one responds. Nevertheless, three different postures stand out: the partisan pastor, the passive pastor, and the present pastor.

The Partisan Pastor

The tragic events of September 11, 2001 took place during the first month of my freshman year at college. I was working as an intern at a consulting firm, where I remember sitting in the office as we watched the towers fall on live television. It was a horrific moment with global and long-term ramifications. As the day wore on, offices starting closing, airplane trips were canceled; people donated blood, called loved ones, expressed fear, and shared rightful concern. Later that evening, feeling confusion and even a bit of panic, I wandered into a local church. The sanctuary was packed. As soon I sat down the minister started preaching on what policy the US should pursue in response to the attacks.

At a critical time like this, the pastor may have had some really good points regarding US foreign policy, but, in my estimation, he missed an important opportunity to minister to those present who were confused, angry, and afraid. As the embers of the fallen towers remained hot, his congregation needed to be in lament, "weeping with those who weep." The sorrow of that day demanded pastoral leadership that was pointed to the hope and mercy of God, not conjecturing about future policy moves. Not only will I always remember the events of that day, but I will also never forget the pastoral mistake made that night. This pastor was more concerned about making political points than ministering to the needs of a shell-shocked congregation.

This pastor represents what I call the partisan pastor, one deeply involved in and known for political engagement and views. This kind of public engagement is both laudable and compromising in terms of the pastor's role in the congregation. On the one hand, the partisan pastor presents a powerful point of view that may have great merit from a political perspective. Most often, the partisan pastor has strong convictions in the tenets of a particular political party or cause. These convictions drive their ministry and are regularly enunciated in public settings. Consequently, the partisan pastor tends to be widely known in connection with his or her distinct political positions and loyalties.

Examples of the virtues of partisanship are numerous, leading to positive and redemptive change in the world. At the turn of the twentieth century many clergy in America were part of the temperance movement, preaching against the evils of alcohol. This movement had major political power, sending a number of representatives to Congress and mounting credible third-party presidential candidates for several decades.[2] Their most noteworthy success was the passage of the Eighteenth Amendment, banning the sale of alcohol.[3] One does not have to support Prohibition to appreciate the concern for the abuse and damage that can be done through alcohol. More recently, the work of the Ten Point Coalition led to significant reforms and attention on the violence plaguing Boston in the 1990s. This was a collaborative effort of several Boston pastors.

And in 2012, Massachusetts's voters narrowly defeated a ballot initiative, known as "Question 2," to legalize physician-assisted suicide. This outcome was widely attributed to the work of Roman Catholic clergy. The Boston Archdiocese coordinated a statewide campaign against the question. Partisan pastors have a history of getting goals accomplished and influencing government leaders. The risks and rewards should probably be evaluated on a case-by-case basis.

The incentive for these kind of bold political initiatives by pastors can be found in the strong prophetic voices in the Old Testament. Much can be said of the political boldness of prophets like Samuel, Isaiah, or Malachi. What about Esther in the courts of King Xerxes? Likewise, there are the bold and wise examples of Nehemiah and Ezra, who practiced political shrewdness that contributed to the flourishing of their communities. But perhaps there is no greater example of speaking truth to power than Moses and his confrontation with Pharaoh. And we could go on; throughout the Old and New Testament, we find example after example of God's people actively confronting and engaging in the political spheres of their day.

But prophetic preaching (not to mention partisanship) has its hazards. Regrettably, left unchecked, this point of view risks the danger of being driven by talking points and the corrupting influence of power, even if done unconsciously. How many times have we seen Scripture being prooftexted as a basis for supporting one's personal perspective? Even if well-intended, blind political engagement most often leads to a limiting perspective, which, in turn, has the potential of being disunifying within both the congregation and the community around it.

---

2. Roger Babson of Gloucester, Massachusetts (my neighboring town) was the 1940 nominee and the founder of Babson College. He was also one of the first to predict the 1929 Wall Street Crash. The party still existed in 2020, but with little national relevance.

3. Repealed by the Twenty-First Amendment in 1933.

The danger of pure partisanship is a natural byproduct of our day. Unfortunately, we see it everywhere. In our present culture, we are quick to demonize those with whom we disagree. This is based on our works-based sense of self-righteousness. If our view is "the righteous view" then it easy to demonize those who don't share this same sense of "our righteousness." In other words, our political views and actions can become akin to works-based righteousness. A gospel-based position seeks to apply the mercy and grace of Jesus toward our views and the views of others. A partisan pastor is tempted to demonize those who don't share the same views. Such a response is echoing the zeitgeist of our culture and may encourage the growth of a congregation of self-righteous partisans.

The reality is that a pastor is no different from anyone else. Everyone has a political point of view—deeply held values and beliefs that have been shaped by their upbringing, education, and life experiences. The problem comes when we as pastors, especially, fail to acknowledge the existence of our own partisan proclivities and do not think critically outside of our self-affirming echo chambers. The examples are numerous: The partisan pastor might preach a sermon against abortion without any sensitivity to the myriad of reasons why women choose to pursue abortions. A pastor may make a snide remark about persons who have concerns about immigration laws without sensitivity to the many struggling laborers in Appalachia who feel they have had all their jobs outsourced to foreign workers.[4] Likewise, a partisan pastor could make a sarcastic joke about "Trump voters," without considering why he received 46 percent of the 2020 popular vote. These illustrations demonstrate that real life issues are often more complicated than the way they are presented in politics.

Jesus offers us an example at this point. On the one hand, Jesus was bold and culturally engaged. He was straightforward with the religious and political leaders of his day, confronting their hypocrisy and promising future judgment. However, he was able to be bold and prophetic while careful to avoid the partisan traps put out by the Pharisees and Sadducees, and avoid endorsing the movement of the Hebrew zealots. Jesus' followers and his enemies were united in the fact that they represented diverse bipartisan coalitions! From Simon the Zealot and Zacchaeus the tax collector to the Samaritan woman at the well, Jesus' political connections were all over the map. He interacted with the Roman political

---

4. *Hillbilly Elegy*, by J. D. Vance, provides a fantastic look at hardships faced by those living in the Rust Belt.

leaders with honesty and respect, but their power struggle was not his main objective.

We need to learn from Jesus' example. There are many cases where preaching will intersect with deep and thorny matters of the political world. These connections need to be made carefully with the realization that, not only are they coming from our own partisan perspective; they are also coming from limited knowledge of any one of a number of issues. For example, pastors are not usually trained as economists or as experts on climate change. In relating biblical truths that address economic issues or environmental issues, the pastor has the opportunity to model for his or her congregation ways in which information should be processed wisely but with humility. In doing so, the pastor has an opportunity to be forthright about a point of view, while also modeling how to address diversity of opinions.

The approach of the partisan pastor, then, is our first posture for political engagement. Positively, the approach is effective for producing societal change and motivating people towards action. Negatively, it also risks exploiting people for political gain, marginalizing those with opposing views, and diminishing credibility.

The Passive Pastor

On the opposite side of the spectrum from the partisan pastor lies the politically passive pastor. This pastor avoids politics, and, in doing so, tends to be countercultural in his or her approach to society, some may even say escapist. In this, the focus of the passive pastor tends to be inward on his or her congregation rather than to engage outwardly into the community. As a result, the partisan pastor would be reticent to weigh in on political matters of the day.

There are, of course, many admirable reasons to adopt the position of political withdrawal. As we have already illustrated, politics can be messy. It invariably involves multiple perspectives and this, in turn, involves conflict. The passive pastor avoids conflict as all costs, and some might suggest, for good reason. If unity in the church is a central concern throughout the New Testament, maintaining it can be viewed as essential: "Keep politics out of the congregation" should be the battle cry, for the sake of a congregation! A case can be made for this, given the reality that there is a plurality of political views, even within the congregation.

A pastoral colleague of mine lived in a small town that was divided on the question of whether or not the community should build a new school building. Those in favor of a new building claimed that they advocated for the children, and they accused the other constituency of opposing children and teachers. A third group argued that it was a fiscally irresponsible decision to build a new school and that the district should regionalize like everyone else around their area. Another group was concerned about the environmental impact of building a school near a wetland and brought a lawsuit against the town.

My colleague had representatives from all camps in his congregation and the ensuing debate spilled over into church functions. The worship service and fellowship hour became divided, with the various camps sitting together and refusing to talk to those in other camps. Seeking to keep the peace, my friend did not take a position on the issue. Consequently, each side assumed that the pastor opposed their position and became very angry with him for not taking a public position. What was he to do? This demonstrates the detriment of assuming a posture of political passivity.

There are certainly examples in Scripture that, at least on the surface, seem to support this passive posture. The book of Proverbs is full of admonitions regarding the call to be quick to listen and slow to speak. From the beginning of the Old Testament, God called his people to be set apart and holy as God is holy. Is this holiness not best pursued apart from the corrupt kingdoms and cultures of the world? Israel repeatedly got themselves into trouble by syncretizing their society with foreign nations (and foreign gods). From this perspective, the church would seem to be better off withdrawing from the worldly concerns of the state. Nations do rise and fall, so one could argue that engaging in "secular" politics is at best a waste of time and at worst a first step toward idolatry.

Likewise, the early pages of the New Testament demonstrate political clashes between the kingdom of God and the kingdom of Man. Although Jesus, Paul, and other early Christian leaders demonstrated knowledge of the geopolitics of their day, they were not concerned with directly engaging them. In many ways, it was their lack of response to the politics of their day that may have been their strongest political statement. Is there a more powerful political picture in the New Testament than the Suffering Savior hanging beneath a sign of political propaganda, unwittingly declaring to the world that this Jesus is the King of Jews? What strange irony: the passive suffering of the Servant changed the world.

The history of the church is also full of examples of passive approaches to the politics of the day. Monasticism is a classic example of seeming political passivity: Starting as an attempt to preserve the Christian faith by withdrawing from the widespread corruption and of the church and the empire, the monastic movement and its political withdrawal was seemingly successful in preserving many components of the Christian faith. By escaping to cloistered communities in obscure locations these communities were able to for a time escape some of the political pressures of their day.

As one offshoot of the Anabaptist tradition, the Amish are an example of a people group who have successfully created a way of life that has withdrawn from the daily grind of contemporary culture and political pressures. One does not have to fully agree with the Amish approach to respect the concept and attractiveness of their lifestyle.

The challenge, of course, of maintaining Christian fidelity within a state of withdrawal from the culture is always difficult based upon the reality that total withdrawal from the world and its systems is never fully possible. Monasticism is a classic example of this. Many of the ancient monasteries were eventually intertwined with the politics of the parish based upon their finances and property. As poor European peasants encountered the eventual wealth and power of the monasteries (from outside their walls), it was only a matter of time before there was to be a political clash. Likewise, the political powers sought to use these far-flung outposts to secure their reign and control their subjects.

On the other side of the spectrum, the Amish, although maybe more successful in their ability to be disengaged, as a group has forfeited its ability to impact society. It has become a quaint side attraction—a curiosity and historical footnote—rather than a force to impact society. The Amish are literally a slow-moving buggy, as it were, on a fast-moving cultural freeway. Therefore, complete disengagement is almost impossible, but ironically, to the extent it is, it has its own unfortunate consequences.

Significant current examples of the failure of this passive approach facing the church today can be found in the checkered history of the church and clergy with regards to issues involving civil rights, the rise of nationalism, immigration, climate change, and the welfare of working mothers. Recent protests in relation to police brutality and the Black Lives Matter movement have furthered the discussion about the relationship between the church and racism. Failure to stand for righteousness and justice, using the excuse of "not wanting to get involved in politics," can at times be a cowardly cop-out and an unwitting support of evil.[5] Has the failure of many pastors and churches to address racism made them complicit in evil? Has their silence and seclusion actually propagated the problem?

Likewise, the recent evolution of the #MeToo movement has brought to light the way that many pastors adopted a passive posture toward sexual abuse within the church. This approach failed to fully acknowledge a significant evil that has affected the lives of many victims, and in some cases, emboldened patterns of criminal conduct. Such inactions hinder and harm the credibility and global witness of the Christian church.

These examples suggest that, ironically, adopting a passive posture toward politics may mitigate divisions in the short run, but it can also inadvertently lead to greater division down the road. By ignoring political issues in our community, pastors may be complicit in injustice and political corruption, which, in turn end up becoming the source of great social conflict and unrest. To care about the first part of the Great Commandment that is the hallmark of the passive position—"to Love the Lord your God with all your heart, soul and mind and strength"—and ignore the second—"to love your neighbor as yourself"—is impossible. The gospel message suggests that these two commandments are joined at the hip, and if one is ignored, the other is ignored, resulting in the mandate of the church being compromised.

The scope of passive pastoral political involvement, then, runs a continuum from escapism to limited engagement. As with the partisan pastor, there are pros and cons to the posture of the passive pastor. But is there a better way? This leads us now to a third posture for pastoral political engagement.

The Present Pastor

The partisan and passive pastor are postures on the edges. We now move to the center and look at the present pastor. "New parish" ministry encourages pastors to engage the public square with wisdom and winsomeness, with dignity and respect. It helps pastors to be present without getting co-opted or polluted. Somewhat symbolically, in my case, I serve an old historic church physically in the very center of my town of Rockport,

---

5. For a more detailed treatment of this topic, see McCaulley, *Reading While Black*.

Massachusetts, an ancient seacoast town that has become a vacation destination. What an opportunity for me and my congregation to engage in the civic life of our little town and the larger region surrounding it!

Former Massachusetts congressman, *Cheer's* actor, and Speaker of the US House of Representatives Tip O'Neill famously said "all politics is local." What he knew was that the national scene is always a reflection of what's going on in all the different urban, suburban, and rural communities throughout the nation. A few national leaders and issues consume much of people's time in political discussions. The truth is that for most pastors, their political focus is more profitable if aimed at the immediate concerns of their church's community, or as it used to be called, "the parish."

A pastor's long-term presence and involvement in the local parish has the potential to have greater impact than when focused on a larger national scale. As the name implies, the key to being a present pastor is showing up in one's town. The present pastor will show up in the community and look for ways to love and serve the community rather than promoting a political agenda.

Much of the political discussion in our culture takes place in artificial environments such as social media or cable news. They are limited by nature of the absence of human presence. Building real relationships with people in the community and working at collaborating on civic projects, however, is a more authentic approach. This is consistent with the incarnational nature of the Christian faith. Taking on flesh, Jesus spent most of his time working with a few people in the region around Galilee. In this way, Jesus accomplished a global mission through a local focus. Similarly, God is glorified, and seeds of the gospel are planted and nurtured, when local churches and pastors are faithfully present in their local communities, loving, stewarding, creating, and adding to the good of the parish.

Part of the reticence of many to engage in the local community is that it takes effort and puts one in a greater place of vulnerability. It is much easier to stay within the safe walls of one's home, church, or church culture. It is also easier to stay within the safe walls of one's preconceived political framework. Positive, redemptive work that helps the flourishing of a city or town takes time, hard work, and patience, and is very practically the act of loving one's neighbor. Figuring out local involvement begins by listening and seeking out the needs of a local community. A pastor could bless a town by starting a neighborhood forum on the science, theology, and politics behind climate change, but such an effort could also be redundant if similar resources were offered nearby. Effective local involvement requires missionally assessing and knowing one's community while undergirded by prayer and wise counsel from seasoned community and church leaders.

Pastors can model good civic engagement for their congregation. There are many ways to love a community politically without running for office or speaking out at a rally. Every town in America has numerous volunteer positions and boards, which need level-headed individuals who will help guide governments in ways that promote human flourishing. What if every member in our churches pledged to find one position of need within their community and took an active role—not out of a political agenda but to genuinely help their town thrive? If pastors take the lead in positive civic engagement, it will carry over into the lifestyles of their congregations. The purpose of this involvement is not explicitly evangelism but to "love our neighbors." These long-term relationships, grounded in respect and credibility, will build bridges for all sorts of ministry and outreach.

In personal relationships, being present is more than being in the same room with someone. Relational presence is a dynamic exchange that takes place through listening, observing, and spending meaningful time together. Likewise, pastoral presence in the parish is refined through a dynamic relational dance that involves listening, observing, and spending meaningful time in the community. Like a fine wine, this dynamic only gets richer with time. In order to assess the needs of a particular parish and places for possible political involvement, a pastor needs to research and understand his particular parish. The following are examples of questions that can help with such an assessment.

Here are key questions that every pastor should be able to answer about their community and church: What are the demographics of the area reached by your church? What are the key historical moments in the shaping of your town/city? What type of government runs your community (city council, board of selectmen, town manager, mayor, town meeting, etc.)? Who are the key political leaders in your community? What are the critical political issues in your region? What is the general political makeup of your congregation? How might this be used as a blessing for your community and what blind spots might this present for your congregation? Do you have friends with differing political perspectives?

As a fledgling pastor, I signed up for what was advertised as a community board that met monthly for usually about fifteen minutes.

It turned out that this board, the "Housing Authority," was a much bigger responsibility and was a five-year term. The board is the governing agency that oversees state and federally subsidized housing for seniors, families, and persons with special needs. I was given an extraordinary education into the myriad of amazing people and challenging circumstances intertwined in public housing. This experience has direct connection with the circumstances of several in my congregation and I now have a working relationship with the leaders of senior and housing services in my community. Through my time on the board, we were able to make some significant improvements to the operations of this organization, which will impact hundreds of residents for years to come. The experience did not directly lead to more people dunked on "Baptism Sunday," but bespoke a pastor involved and caring for the parish. I have a much deeper relationship with my town because of my time on this board.

The song "The Room Where It Happens" (from the hit musical *Hamilton*) describes the proverbial smoked-filled room where the decisions were made and power held, in the days of Alexander Hamilton. The song rightly highlights that in any political context there are the overt powermakers, but they are usually supported by deeper more long-term persons or alliances. An astute political observer is keen to identify the "kings" and "kingmakers." The "kings" are those in official positions and the "kingmakers" are those who hold the real power in a community or region.

Early in my pastorate, it became apparent that the town's Rotary Club was the room where it happens. Many of the town leaders are part of this group, which has had a key role in saving school programs, funding important service projects, and creating community events. This nonsectarian and nonpolitical global organization was founded to promote "service above self." It shares many objectives with the church and is one of the largest humanitarian charities in the world. The expressed purpose of the organization is to bring together people of different backgrounds—what a great place for a local pastor!

Because of my long-term involvement in this group, I am regularly asked questions about religion and have strong relationships with many community, political, educational, and business leaders. I had the opportunity to lead the funeral for a town leader who was not religious but appreciated our relationship. We had a mutual commitment to the flourishing of our town. Our relationship began in the Rotary Club. The point is not to encourage every pastor to join a Rotary Club, but rather to consider different ways of getting involved in organizations that are positively impacting the parish's political sphere. Each community has places like the rotary club where there are opportunities to engage presently in a meaningful way.

There are countless other examples of pastors winsomely engaging the political sphere. I have known several who have served as chaplains for local police, fire departments, or hospitals. Some pastors make a habit of meeting with their elected representatives simply to have a relationship and encourage them. Often the only time a politician meets a pastor is when they are angry about an issue or seeking to push an agenda. It's a wonderful picture of the gospel when the church, led by the pastor, says to a town and its civic leaders "how can we serve you?" as opposed to "here's how we would like you to serve us." This model is grounded in the way that Jesus engaged his local community:

> Jesus called them together and said, "You know that the rulers of the Gentiles lord it over them, and their high officials exercise authority over them. Not so with you. Instead, whoever wants to become great among you must be your servant, and whoever wants to be first must be your slave—just as the Son of Man did not come to be served, but to serve, and to give his life as a ransom for many." (Matt 20:25–28)

Further, there are times when a pastor may find the need to speak or act in relation to a particular local issue. When these times of prophetic witness occur, speaking with those with whom a relationship exists will potentially be more fruitful. Opportunities for local political involvement will vary greatly based on the location of every pastor. The few examples given above could be complemented with many more stories of pastors faithfully and creatively engaging the political sphere across the country. This critical engagement begins when we look outside the doors of our church and observe the governing forces and issues affecting our neighborhoods. As we pray for discernment and ask for advice about ways to engage, opportunities will abound.

Perhaps the COVID-19 pandemic has offered us the most vivid example of creative engagement for the present pastor. The pandemic has created chaos and misery. The endgame remains uncertain. Nonetheless, there are signs of hope and ways that the pandemic is refining our culture and priorities. People have been forced to spend more if not all of their time in their parish. I have seen congregants with strong opposing political views helping one another by providing masks, preparing meals, and offering calls of support. My family has spent more time with our neighbors than ever before. Suddenly, global expansion has stopped, and large cities are seeing massive exodus as people flee to smaller communities.[6] Pastors cannot afford to miss the opportunity to presently engage in this time of crises, creatively being in and loving their respective communities.

What better time, then, to be present in our communities? Given the current political climate where there is so much disagreement and disunity tearing our communities apart, what better opportunity for pastors to engage in their communities in ways that really matter? Whether fully realized or appreciated, our communities need pastors and the message they represent more than ever. This is not a time for partisanship that ultimately divides, nor is it a time for passivity and escapism that eludes our responsibility. We have an opportunity to guide our congregations into respectful but meaningful engagement in the political spheres of our communities.

For Further Exploration

1. Saint Augustine. *The City of God*. Peabody, MA: Hendrickson, 2009.
2. David Brooks. *The Second Mountain*. New York: Random House, 2019.
3. Richard Mouw. *Uncommon Decency*. Downers Grove, IL: InterVarsity, 2010.
4. H. Richard Niebuhr. *Christ and Culture*. New York: Harper and Row, 1951.
5. Scott Sauls. *Jesus Outside the Lines*. Carol Stream, IL: Tyndale House, 2015.

---

6. See https://www.nytimes.com/2020/08/30/nyregion/nyc-suburbs-housing-demand.html.

Engaging the Political Parish
Interview

REPRESENTATIVE LARRY WOLPERT (R-OH) was elected to the Ohio House of Representatives in 2000 and served until 2008. Prior to being appointed as the Joint Committee on Agency Rule Review's executive director, Wolpert served as a commissioner on the Ohio Elections Commission. He served on Hilliard City Council from 1993 to 2000. Director Wolpert had a twenty-year career with the Grange Insurance Companies before entering public service.

Q. **Why have you chosen to devote much of your life to public office and government service?**

I believe it is a calling and experienced verification of this. My church and pastor were very supportive of encouraging candidates to run for office. I felt a calling from the Holy Spirit to run and knew in my heart it was something I should do. I started in Hilliard (Ohio) City Council in 1993 and served in the Ohio House of Representatives from 2000 to 2008 and was considered a candidate for US Congress. I served on the Ohio Elections Commission and now am the executive director of the Joint Committee on Agency Review for the state of Ohio.

Q. **How do you think pastors can contribute to the good of the common square?**

Don't be a wimp. Be strong. Pastors are allowed to have an opinion. Part of the reason that we have so many problems in our country is that pastors have neglected preaching the Bible. Speak the truth of God's word. The fabric of the country has changed because many pastors have failed to correctly guide communities. When we lose our moral fiber we have to turn to civil laws. We have lost our moral fiber. I blame the pastors for much of the problems. Pastors have the potential to lead us back to a respect of the Bible and love for God.

Q. In your experience, how have you seen pastors play a positive role in the political sphere?

I was running for the House of Representatives, and I stopped off at the county party office and someone I had never seen came up and prayed over me. I have never forgotten that experience. When I was in the House of Representatives there was a nondenominational pastor who has a weekly Bible study for members of the legislature.

Q. In your experience, how have you seen pastors play a negative role in the political sphere?

Some don't take the Bible that seriously and pastors who don't hold to orthodox Christianity attack Christian politicians. Eighty percent of the state budget is focused on education, medication, and incarceration largely tied to how society operates and the family structure or lack or structure. Pastors need to address these societal problems that cannot be changed by legislation. An example of this was my experience with the Interfaith Horizon dorm in the Marion Correctional Institute. This ministry was focused on prisoners experiencing transformation through the gospel. The Spirit of God, not humanist principles, changes behavior.

Q. How would you advise a pastor who wanted to engage in politics within their community?

I would say get to know your elected officials; take them out to coffee. Pray for them. Be careful of how you articulate politics from the pulpit. Be supportive of biblically based legislation. I put forth over fifty bills in Ohio. The most important piece of legislation was "the snowflake baby bill," which protects the adoptive parents of an embryo. I was inspired by the listening to Dr. Dobson talk about this issue.

Q. What do you wish pastors knew about public servants?

Public servants are no different than anyone else. Don't put people on pedestals.

Q. How can pastors best encourage and pray for government officials?

Pray for guidance, to be patient, and to be a good leader. My church was heavily involved in Ohio Right to Life and pro-family organizations.

Q. How do you think the COVID-19 pandemic will change politics?

Whoever the current incumbents currently are, they are going to be thrown out. The country is radically changing. The Republican Party will be become a regional party and be significantly changed. The Democratic Party is becoming much more liberal, and significant demographic change is taking place. What is wrong is now right and what is right is now wrong.

Q. Is there anything else you would like to say to pastors?

We live in a democracy that is managed by politics. Take care of your flock and your community. The only way we can turn the country around is by turning people back to God through the work of the Holy Spirit.

5

Engaging the Education Parish

Chris Dunaway

> "The function of education is to teach one to think intensively and to think critically. Intelligence plus character—that is the goal of true education."
>
> —MARTIN LUTHER KING JR.

"I BECAME A TEACHER so I could teach, not to manage kids' bad manners and behaviors. Their parents should be doing that," said Suzanne, a long-time second-grade teacher. Her calm voice betrayed her exasperation as she expressed the sentiment shared by tens of thousands of teachers across the American educational landscape.

Suzanne went on to elaborate about other challenges today's teachers face. Only 20 percent of students in her school district come from traditional two-parent homes. Most students live in single-parent homes or with their grandparents or other relatives. Many students have experienced significant trauma—with at least one parent serving a prison sentence or detoxing in a drug rehabilitation center. In the past five years, two separate students witnessed their mother being murdered. How can students be expected to learn anything at school with that on their mind?

Suzanne doesn't teach in a gang-ridden urban community or an economically depressed rural school. She is an educator in a suburban New Hampshire town that is picturesque enough to appear on a postcard. The median household income is over $60,000 per household, which ranks it in the middle 50 percent of towns in the state. But sadly, Suzanne's story is not unique. It illustrates the myriad of challenges schools face almost everywhere. Students struggle to learn the social/emotional skills to interact well with other students, let alone stay focused in the classroom. Some are constantly cycling through the revolving doors of the foster care system while others live in homes that face food insecurity. And approximately 20 percent of students ages twelve to eighteen report being victims of bullying or cyberbullying.[1]

To combat these problems, it is now commonplace for elementary school classes to begin their day with a "mindfulness moment." Middle schools set aside time for meditation. High school student government leaders receive formal training in conflict resolution—all on top of the traditional subjects like the "three Rs"—reading, (w)riting, and 'rithmetic.

In addition to problems with students, school districts face an array of administrative and bureaucratic challenges, especially ensuring adequate resources to educate their students. Public pre-K–12 schools are funded by a combination of federal, state, and local sources, but there never seems to be enough money to meet all of the needs. Even schools in close proximity to one another can experience gross disparities in funding. In 2016, *The Atlantic* magazine published an article that described how one school district in Connecticut spent $6,000 more per pupil per year than another district fewer than thirty miles away.[2]

These are just some of the many problems that permeate America's educational institutions. Somewhere along the way, the education system has assumed the overwhelming responsibility of resolving society's most daunting challenges: hunger, obesity, poverty, substance abuse, parental abandonment, family dysfunction, and mental illness. It's no wonder so many teachers like Suzanne feel frazzled and frustrated on a daily basis. They are not only required to deliver academic instruction, but they now play the role of parent, therapist, and legal advocate before they even reach the classroom. This is beyond any teacher's pay grade and is enough to drive even the best educators to emotional exhaustion and

---

1. Wang, "Indicator 10"
2. Semuels, "Good School", para. 1.

vocational reevaluation. With so many persistent social problems plaguing our schools, one may wonder about the possibility of churches and schools working together to seek solutions for the common good of the community. As fellow community leaders, could pastors and principals form relationships and learn from each other's expertise? Could churches and schools form partnerships that would be mutually beneficial? What if churches viewed schools as part of their parish and schools considered churches as part of their community? Is the perceived separation of church and school too wide, or is there enough common ground for these institutions to help human beings develop their fullest potential and foster a flourishing society together? Perhaps this is a good starting point for the conversation: the purpose of education.

The Purpose of Education

In the public debates about school problems, people rarely step back to consider the crucial underlying question: What is the purpose of education? While every individual and educational institution would answer this question according to their own ideals, there has been a surprisingly high level of consensus about the purpose of education in America from its inception to today. Even in a pluralistic culture with many competing worldviews, the purpose of education is generally distilled into two primary components: helping people achieve their highest human potential and building a flourishing society.

The Puritans in colonial America believed that education (especially literacy) was essential for understanding the Bible, which is a precursor to human beings discerning God's will and establishing a well-ordered society. Education was so crucial to their vision of "a city on a hill" that they passed laws to ensure that all of their citizens would learn how to read and write. The Old Deluder Satan Act of 1647, which required towns to start grammar schools, was intended to prevent Satan, the "Old Deluder," from deceiving the illiterate and keeping them uninformed about God's ways. Even though the Puritans pursued education for primarily religious purposes, their laws promoted human flourishing on an individual and societal level, and thus became the early foundation of the American public school system.[3]

---

3. See Kamrath, *Miracle of America*.

Many of America's founding fathers, including Benjamin Franklin, John Adams, and Thomas Jefferson, touted education as the means to develop human potential and create a thriving democratic society. This is why, after the American Revolution, they continued to push for a public education system in the new nation. In 1785, Jefferson proposed such a system for the Commonwealth of Virginia. According to Jefferson:

> The ultimate result of the whole scheme of education would be the teaching all the children of the state reading, writing, and common arithmetic: turning out several annually of superior genius, well taught in Greek, Latin, geography, and the higher branches of arithmetic: turning out . . . others annually, of still superior parts, who, to those branches of learning, shall have added such of the sciences as their genius shall have led them to.[4]

Jefferson's plan included progression through three successive stages of education: primary, intermediate, and university, according to students' academic abilities. In his August 13, 1786 letter to George Wythe, he remarked that "the most important bill in our whole code, is that for the diffusion of knowledge among the people."[5] He believed that "no other sure foundation can be devised for the preservation of freedom and happiness" and that failing to provide public education would "leave the people in ignorance."[6]

As America matured, other leaders carried the mantle of education development and reform. When Horace Mann was appointed to the newly formed Massachusetts Board of Education in 1837, he used the knowledge he gained as a teacher, librarian, and legislator to strengthen the public education system. His personal experience with education elevating him from poverty compelled him to strive toward this end for all American citizens. He labored to actualize his creed, "A human being is not attaining his full heights until he is educated."

Likewise, the American philosopher and education reformer John Dewey, acknowledged this dual purpose of education from the latter half of the nineteenth century through the first half of the twentieth century. His educational philosophy did not revolve around the procurement of a predetermined set of skills, but rather the realization of a person's full potential and the ability to use those skills for the greater good. He noted

---

4. Jefferson, "Notes," 268–69.
5. Jefferson, "Letter to George Whythe."
6. Jefferson, "Letter to George Whythe."

that "to prepare him [the student] for the future life means to give him command of himself; it means so to train him that he will have the full and ready use of all his capacities."[7]

In addition to helping students achieve their full potential, Dewey recognized that education is an essential instrument for creating a flourishing society. He wrote:

> The purpose of education has always been to everyone, in essence, the same—to give the young the things they need in order to develop in an orderly, sequential way into members of society ... It was the purpose of the education of youth in the golden age of Athens. It is the purpose of education today, whether this education goes on in a one-room school in the mountains of Tennessee or in the most advanced, progressive school in a radical community ... Any education is, in its forms and methods, an outgrowth of the needs of the society in which it exists.[8]

Even with the rapid cultural shifts brought on by industrialization and globalization in the twentieth century, the consensus around the purpose of education remained largely intact. In 1957, the Association for Supervision and Curriculum Development's (ASCD) Committee on Platform of Beliefs affirmed: "The main purpose of the American school is to provide for the fullest possible development of each learner for living morally, creatively, and productively in a democratic society."[9]

Perhaps Arthur W. Foshay, who served as president of the ASCD and John Dewey Society, best summarized the twentieth-century perspective on the purpose of education, when he wrote:

> The one continuing purpose of education, since ancient times, has been to bring people to as full a realization as possible of what it is to be a human being. Other statements of educational purpose have also been widely accepted: to develop the intellect, to serve social needs, to contribute to the economy, to create an effective work force, to prepare students for a job or career, to promote a particular social or political system. These purposes offered are undesirably limited in scope, and in some instances they conflict with the broad purpose I have indicated; they imply a distorted human existence. The broader humanistic

---

7. Dewey, "My Pedagogic Creed," para. 6.
8. Dewey, "Individual Psychology," para. 1
9. ASCD Committee on Platform of Beliefs, "What Is the Purpose of Education?," para. 3.

purpose includes all of them, and goes beyond them, for it seeks to encompass all the dimensions of human experience.[10]

As with other sectors of the public square, the dawn of the twenty-first century inaugurated many changes to education. Laptop computers replaced textbooks; SMART boards supplanted chalkboards; and the apple on the teacher's desk was usurped by Apple products. Technological advances and increased globalization have created new educational terms like internet research, remote teaching, and multilingual learning, just to name a few.

While global competition and other factors have shifted American education toward greater emphasis on specialized job skills and STEM- (Science, Technology, Engineering, Mathematics) based disciplines, the liberal arts and humanities are still in high regard. Even though educators must constantly adapt old pedagogies and develop new curricula to meet ever-changing cultural needs, the consensus on the purpose of education has remained largely unaltered. Consider the current mission statement of Harvard University, America's oldest and perhaps most prestigious educational institution:

> The mission of Harvard College is to educate the citizens and citizen-leaders for our society. We do this through our commitment to the transformative power of a liberal arts and sciences education.
>
> Beginning in the classroom with exposure to new ideas, new ways of understanding, and new ways of knowing, students embark on a journey of intellectual transformation. Through a diverse living environment, where students live with people who are studying different topics, who come from different walks of life and have evolving identities, intellectual transformation is deepened and conditions for social transformation are created. From this we hope that students will begin to fashion their lives by gaining a sense of what they want to do with their gifts and talents, assessing their values and interests, and learning how they can best serve the world.[11]

Even though institutions like Harvard have long departed from their Puritan roots, they still implicitly affirm the biblical values of human life, the uniqueness of the human mind, and that human beings are created for relationships, citizenship, and service within a community.

10. Foshay, "Curriculum Matrix."
11. See https://college.harvard.edu/about/mission-vision-history.

They recognize that all human beings are endowed with certain gifts and talents and possess the capacity to learn, grow, and develop those abilities—and that education plays a key role in helping people reach their full human potential and fostering a flourishing society.

For the past four hundred years of American history, the education community has maintained this vision and upheld these values. And from the humblest elementary schools to the highest ranked Ivy League universities, educational institutions still share this common mission. And from all indications, it appears that this will continue well into the twenty-first century.

As we continue to ponder the purpose of education, it is interesting to observe that the Christian community may be counted among this historic consensus. Although many Christians may contend that the glory of God is the ultimate purpose of education and faith components like biblical knowledge and spiritual formation are essential for good education, they would largely agree with their "secular" counterparts that the primary aims of education are to achieve human potential and societal flourishing. Compare Harvard's mission statement with the vision and mission statement of Estabrook Christian School, a Christian elementary/middle school in Plainfield, New Hampshire:

> Mission: For every learner to excel in faith, learning, and service, blending biblical truth and academic achievement to honor God and bless others.
>
> Vision: To enable learners to develop a life of faith in God, and to use their knowledge, skills, and understandings to serve God and humanity.[12]

Even though there may be a wide gap between the worldviews presented at Christian and "secular" institutions, they share a common humanitarian mission. Apart from the obvious differences in faith language, the mission statements of Harvard and Estabrook bear a remarkable resemblance.

For Christians, these twin purposes of education should not come as a surprise—they are rooted in a theology that proclaims that human beings are created in the image of God. When God breathed life into the dust of the ground, he created humans in his own likeness. He not only endowed them with brains and the ability to think, but he gave them

---

12. http://estabrookchristianschool.com/about/mission-history/.

the capacity to feel, make moral decisions, and communicate with other human beings. Human beings bear the image of God physically, intellectually, emotionally, socially, and spiritually. In essence, all of these dimensions together are what make human beings human. And none of them are static; they all bear the ability to learn and grow and develop over a life span, which presupposes the need for education.

The New Testament asserts that even Jesus Christ, the perfect human being, "grew in wisdom and stature, and in favor with God and men" (Luke 2:52). This single verse highlights the holistic education he received throughout adolescence and into adulthood. "Wisdom" indicates intellectual/emotional advancement. "Stature" reflects physical development. "Favor with God" signifies spiritual growth. And "favor with men" points to social progress. Even though he was God in human flesh, Jesus still needed education to help him achieve his maximum human potential and contribute to a flourishing society.

Like other Jewish children of his time, Jesus learned the fundamental language arts of reading, writing, speaking, and storytelling. He would have studied the Torah with a local rabbi and learned life skills from his parents, most notably woodworking trades, since his father was a carpenter (Matt 13:55). Throughout Jesus' ministry, he not only displayed a mastery of the Scriptures and spiritual truth, but he also exhibited a basic knowledge of geography (Luke 10:13–16), arithmetic (Matt 18:21–22), economics (Matt 22:15–22), agriculture (Mark 4), meteorology (Matt 8:23–27), and culinary art (John 21:9–14). He used all of this knowledge he learned to teach others. If Jesus took the time to learn these subjects and skills, how much more does the rest of the human race need to be educated to realize their full potential and build a better society? Therefore, the Christian church and education community widely agree on the humanitarian purpose of education. But does this consensus create enough common ground for pastors and churches to partner with the education sector to work toward achieving these goals together?

The Pillars of Education

Interestingly, the church and education communities also share a common vision of the pillars that support the purposes of education. If education is going to help human beings reach their potential and facilitate societal flourishing, it will, at the very least, include the educational pillars of truth, wisdom, and service.

The pursuit of truth has been a central pillar of education at least since ancient times. In the fourth and fifth centuries BC, Socrates formulated his famous "Socratic method," an inductive and dialectical pattern of argumentation that distills knowledge and pursues truth by asking a series of questions. He used this epistemological method to test initial hypotheses and uncover presumptions and assumptions. This approach to pursuing truth was later expanded by his pupil Plato and eventually became the foundation of the modern scientific method and a key component of American legal education.[13]

The pursuit of truth is still a primary pillar of education today. On March 20, 2019, Lawrence Bacow, president of Harvard University, delivered a speech titled "The Pursuit of Truth and the Mission of the University." In his speech he declared:

> Great universities stand for truth, and the pursuit of truth demands perpetual effort. Truth has to be discovered, revealed through argument and experiment, tested on the anvil of opposing explanations and ideas. This is precisely the function of a great university, where scholars in every field and discipline debate and marshal evidence in support of their theories, as they strive to understand and explain our world.
>
> This search for truth has always required courage, both in the sciences, where those who seek to shift paradigms have often initially met with ridicule, banishment, and worse, and in the social sciences, arts, and humanities, where scholars have often had to defend their ideas from political attacks on all sides.[14]

Truth is a pillar of education because it is indispensable for human and societal flourishing. It enables people to view the world as it really is, without prejudice or bias; to understanding oneself and their relationship to the world and other people in it. Truth is essential for authentic communication to occur and makes genuine interaction between people possible. Imagine what it would be like to live in a society where no one told the truth. How could a person discern what is accurate and what is a falsehood? On what basis could a person make important decisions

---

13. See Garret, "Becoming Lawyers," para. 8–10.

14. https://www.harvard.edu/president/speech/2019/pursuit-truth-and-mission-university.

if there was no expectation of the truth? Without truth, life would be chaotic, and society would descend into anarchy.

This is why teachers instruct students in the truths about everything from history and grammar to music and mathematics. If people didn't know the truths of geography, they would be literally lost. If they didn't understand the truths of language, they would not be able to communicate. Thus truth, in all educational subject areas, is crucial for human and societal flourishing.

The church concurs with truth as a pillar of education because truth is a foundational doctrine of the Christian faith. The Bible affirms truth as an essential aspect of God's character. For example, Jesus said, "I am the way, and the truth, and the life (John 14:6), and he called the Holy Spirit "the Spirit of truth" (John 14:17; 15:26; 16:13). A more indirect affirmation that God is truth is Hebrews 6:18, which says that "it is impossible for God to lie."

The Bible uses various forms of the word "truth" 238 times. The term is often employed as an admonition to speak the truth. The apostle Paul provided a good example of this as he instructed the Ephesians about how to live their Christian faith: "Therefore each of you must put off falsehood and speak truthfully to his neighbor, for we are all members of one body." (Eph 4:25). His teaching about truthfulness emphasizes its benefits to individuals (neighbors) and the whole community (members of one body).

Thus, the church and the education community stand on common ground when they consider the pursuit of truth as a pillar of education. But truth on its own is insufficient in achieving human potential and human flourishing. Truth must be applied correctly, which requires wisdom, the second pillar of education.

Wisdom is the ability to use one's knowledge and experience to make good decisions and judgments. In short, it is the prudent application of truth. In education, a basic knowledge of core subjects like reading, writing, and arithmetic are foundational for functioning in the world, but one still needs to decipher which body of knowledge (truths) should be applied in a given situation. For instance, what good is a knowledge of chemical compounds if one is trying to compose a symphony? Or what good is a knowledge of music theory if one is trying to build a garage? Likewise, without wisdom, the truths of mathematics can be used for diabolical purposes, such as developing weapons of mass destruction that prevent human and societal flourishing.

In the introduction to his book *Education and the Pursuit of Wisdom: The Aims of Education Revisited*, Janis Talivaldis Ozolins argues for wisdom being one of the intrinsic aims of education:

> It is not intended to discuss the aims of education further, rather, to simply propose that wisdom is an overall important aim of education since it is involved in the acquisition of knowledge, with the cultivation of virtue and character, and hence, with human well-being. Wise individuals are universally recognized as flourishing human beings because they know how to live well, and this is at least in part because they are able to see the interconnectedness of knowledge and experience they have acquired and reflected upon. They live in harmony with themselves and everyone else around them.[15]

He goes on to make the point that wisdom has never been easy to attain, which is why it has always been an important educational pursuit. Throughout the rest of his book, he explores the historical and philosophical reasons for wisdom being a central pillar of education, and he defends wisdom against the postmodern threats that seek to reduce education to utilitarian and economic functions. Wisdom is essential for "the formation of human persons so they develop the virtues and values that they need to not only live successful lives, but also to be responsible members of their communities, working for the common good, and acting to transform them into just societies."[16]

As with truth, the church agrees with the pursuit of wisdom as a pillar of education. The Bible is filled with references about the value of wisdom and contains a collection of five books known as wisdom literature (Job, Psalms, Proverbs, Ecclesiastes, and the Song of Solomon). The book of Proverbs, in particular, is dedicated to attaining wisdom in all areas of life. It begins this way:

> The proverbs of Solomon son of David, king of Israel:
> for attaining wisdom and discipline;
>   for understanding words of insight;
> for acquiring a disciplined and prudent life,
>   doing what is right and just and fair;
> for giving prudence to the simple,
>   knowledge and discretion to the young—

---

15. Ozolins, *Education and the Pursuit of Wisdom*, 4.
16. Ozolins, *Education and the Pursuit of Wisdom*, 4.

> let the wise listen and add to their learning,
>> and let the discerning get guidance—
> for understanding proverbs and parables,
>> the sayings and riddles of the wise. (Prov 1:1–6)

In addition to the biblical admonition toward attaining wisdom, the Christian church has a long and rich history of pursuing wisdom in education. There is the catechetical tradition in the early church—the Augustinian and Benedictine traditions in the early Middle Ages—Thomas Aquinas and the school of Scholasticism in the late Middle Ages—Martin Luther and the neo-catechetical tradition during the Protestant Reformation—and the Sunday school movement that has dominated the church's educational mission since the late eighteenth century. Teaching and attaining wisdom is a central concern in each of these traditions.

Once again, we find the Christian church and education communities standing on common ground. One wonders if this common ground could create opportunities for both communities to listen and learn from one another. Could the church's long tradition of teaching principles of wisdom virtue such as insight, discipline, prudence, righteousness, justice, fairness, knowledge, discretion, guidance, and understanding—all words used in these first six verses of Proverbs—benefit public and private schools today? Can churches and schools help each other achieve their mutual goals of wisdom in education together?

But even the pillars of truth and wisdom in education are not ends in themselves. They are insufficient for achieving human potential and societal flourishing until they are combined with service, which is the third pillar of education.

Christians readily agree that education must prepare people to serve Christ and the common good of humanity. This is inherent in Jesus' mission of coming to earth. In Mark 10:43–45, while teaching about true human greatness, he asserted:

> Not so with you. Instead, whoever wants to become great among you must be your servant, and whoever wants to be first must be slave of all. For even the Son of Man did not come to be served, but to serve, and to give his life as a ransom for many.

A little while later, when one of the teachers of the law asked Jesus which is the greatest of all of the commandments, Jesus responded: "Love the Lord your God with all your heart and with all your soul and with all your mind and with all your strength.' The second is this: 'Love your neighbor as yourself." There is no commandment greater than these" (Mark 12:30–31). Service is central to Jesus' personal mission and vision of a flourishing society.

Good Christian education doesn't merely pursue biblical/theological content (truth) and virtuous living (wisdom); it actively promotes loving service to other human beings. The apostle Paul reiterates this principle in Philippians 2:3–4, when he instructs: "Do nothing from selfish ambition or vain conceit, but in humility, consider others more significant than yourselves. Let each of you look not only to his own interests, but also to the interests of others."

Educators outside the church walls agree that education ought to prepare students for lives in service of the common good, as was already exhibited by Harvard University's mission statement. Furthermore, Benjamin Franklin, reflecting on the aims of education, wrote that schools are to, "Supply the succeeding Age with Men qualified to serve the Publick [sic] with Honour to themselves, and to their Country."[17]

Modern educators continue to carry the mantle of service as a pillar of education. Doran Morford, a high school teacher and counselor for more than thirty years, asked students at a high school commencement, "As you graduate, everyone is asking you, 'What will you make of yourself?' I want to ask you, 'What will you give of yourself?'"[18]

Valerie Strauss, an education reporter for *The Washington Post*, echoed this sentiment when she wrote, "Education should prepare young people for life, work and citizenship."[19] Dennis Littky, a former middle and high school principal and National Principal of the Year runner-up, asserted that educators should strive to help make students care and want to give back to their community, have integrity and self-respect, and have moral courage.[20]

Since the Christian church and American education system maintain vast agreement on the purpose and pillars of education, one may wonder why churches and educational institutions seldom work together to achieve their common goals of helping human beings reach their highest potential and fostering societal flourishing through the pursuit of

---

17. Franklin, "Proposals," para. 10.
18. Morford, "Commencement Speech."
19. Strauss, "What's the purpose," para 4.
20. Littky and Grabelle, *Big Picture*, 1.

truth, wisdom, and service. Unfortunately, ignorance and fear on both sides have contributed to an unnecessary separation of church and school.

The Separation of Church and School

Since the US Supreme Court ruled school-sponsored prayer unconstitutional in the landmark 1962 *Engel v. Vitale* case, many have asked: What does the separation of church and state mean for America's public schools? Throughout the decades, proponents have hailed the decision, with its renewed emphasis on the establishment clause of the US Constitution, as a victory for democracy. Opponents complain that the court kicked God out of school and hold this case in contempt for many of America's moral woes, from drug addiction to the onslaught of school shootings. But at the very least, ongoing misunderstandings and overreactions to the separation of church and state have led to a culture war that has only deepened the divide between churches and schools and has impeded progress toward human potential and a flourishing society.

Many educators have either been misinformed or misinterpret the laws about religious expression in schools. While it is true that schools cannot endorse a particular religious view or sanction prayer or Bible reading, students have the freedom to express their religious views in class, read the Bible and pray in their free time, and organize religious clubs. Although some people have challenged the traditions of reciting the Pledge of Allegiance with the words "under God" and decorating Christmas trees, the courts have deemed the Pledge a patriotic rather than a religious exercise as the reference to God is civil in nature, and Christmas trees as having widespread secular connotations.[21] Unfortunately, some educators have restricted students' constitutional rights to religious expression due to inadvertent ignorance or intentional anti-religious bias, which has caused some Christians to view the education system with skepticism.

Furthermore, there has been considerable confusion over the role of teachers and religion in public schools. On one hand, the law appropriately restricts teachers from proselytizing and promoting their own religious views with their students. On the other hand, teachers have the freedom to discuss religion and religious texts as they pertain to curriculum and culture. It would be almost impossible to have an honest

---

21. Heinrich, "Ask the Expert," para. 4–5.

dialogue about history, literature, philosophy, music, or world civilizations apart from their religious contexts. But individual teachers who either exploit or avoid these issues altogether have contributed to the fear and skepticism on both sides. Likewise, many Christians have overreacted and demonized the public education system for policies they deem threatening to their faith and worldview. Six decades later, some Christians still blame almost every societal ill on the removal of school prayer. In the wake of the tragic 2012 Sandy Hook Elementary School shooting, some Christians heralded that the reason why so many terrible things were happening in public schools is because "God is not allowed in school." Insensitive sentiments and catty comments like these have eroded Christian credibility in the public square.

Curriculum controversies over issues such as evolution, human sexuality, and an array of social and political issues have caused many Christians to abandon the public education system altogether. In the 1980s, with the encouragement of evangelical Christian leaders like Focus on the Family founder James Dobson, many Christians removed their children from these "secular" influences by joining the emerging homeschool movement. Christian homeschooling networks took a largely antagonistic outlook toward public school administrators and were unwilling to cooperate with public schools they viewed as evil. The ensuing legal battles over the legitimacy of homeschooling fanned the flames of animosity on both sides, exacerbating the rift between churches and schools well into the twenty-first century.[22]

It is a shame that these issues have contributed to a complete separation of church and school in many communities all across the country. Fear and skepticism have led to an institutional isolation that has impaired vision for churches and schools to work together to achieve their common goals. This is precisely where a new parish perspective could calm fears, rebuild trust, and create new opportunities to foster human potential and flourishing communities together.

Practicing a New Parish Perspective in Education

A new parish perspective challenges churches to view every citizen in the community as part of their parish, not just church members. It also challenges pastors to directly engage various sectors of the public square,

---

22. See Stevens, *Kingdom of Children*.

like the local public education system. But with such high walls separating churches and schools in many communities, how can pastors begin to scale these ramparts?

As with engaging other sectors of the public square, new parish pastors would be wise to begin by casting a vision for the church to view their local schools as part of their parish. If they can't convince their congregations that engaging the education system is a worthwhile cause, their personal efforts will at best fall flat, and at worst create conflict.

Perhaps it would be best to start by initiating conversations with church members who already work in the public school system. They will not only have ideas about how the church can engage the school system, but they will have insight on how the pastor can equip the congregation for such an endeavor. Their dual affiliation will add credibility to the conversation from a church and school perspective.

Pastors may also promote a new parish perspective through ministries that already exist in the life of the church. The pastor could pray for the local school community during the corporate prayer time in the public worship service. When my church hosted a commissioning service for our local education community, we prayed for the specific needs of everyone connected to our schools—for the students to study well and see God's fingerprints in history, chemistry, French, geometry, and civics—for parents to encourage and assist their children in their educational endeavors—for teachers and school staff to model the grace, wisdom, and love of Christ to all students.

After the service ended, several teachers and parents told me how meaningful that prayer was to them. "I feel so alone in the school," one teacher remarked. "It helps give me courage when I know my church is behind me as I teach." Prayer is a powerful tool for pastors to prepare their congregations to engage the local education system.

Pastors can also use sermons to teach their congregants about the importance of education, demonstrate a commitment to the education system, and inspire their whole church to serve local schools. It is not coincidental that the pillars of education (truth, wisdom, and service) are prominent themes in spiritual formation. We seek to know the Truth—Christ himself—who imparts wisdom and empowers people to serve their neighbors in love.

Of course, serving local schools should not be limited within the walls of a sanctuary. New parish ministry is about going beyond the church's boundary markers and engaging the public square on its own turf. And if the church is ever going to follow this path, the pastor must get out of the church office and lead by example. In today's society, pastors may not be able to start boarding schools or serve as superintendents as Rev. Cutler in the old parish model, but pastors can build meaningful relationships with education leaders and explore potential partnerships that pursue human development and societal flourishing together. How can pastors do this in the education parish?

Pastoral engagement can start by setting up a simple meeting with the local teacher, principal, or superintendent. Pastors may be surprised by how receptive educators are when they are approached with thoughtful questions and an open mind. Imagine pastors introducing themselves to the local middle school principal (perhaps even offering to buy her lunch) and asking her a series of questions like:

1. What are the greatest strengths of this school system?
2. What are its greatest challenges?
3. What are your greatest challenges in your current role?
4. What is one thing you wish parents in your school knew about your work?
5. What makes you most optimistic about your particular school?
6. Do any resources already exist to help struggling students? Can we partner with them?
7. What one need, if it were met, would make the greatest positive difference in your school? How can our church help meet this need?

When pastors form personal relationships with educational leaders and humbly ask how they can help, it builds trust and credibility while reducing ignorance and skepticism on both sides. And it invariably leads to conversations about how the respective institutions can support one another.

Educators often feel skeptical about pastors and churches who come in with a preset agenda. One principal, expressing gratitude for effective church participation in her school, remarked, "The churches did not come in and say, 'We're here to do this for you.' Instead, they said, 'We're here to serve.'"[23] When another principal was asked about how pastors could learn the needs of local schools, his response was simple: "Ask!"

---

23. Emmanuel Gospel Center Boston, "Boston Education Collaborative."

Pastors can model new parish ministry by getting involved in their local schools. It can begin with relatively easy endeavors such as attending Parent Teacher Association (PTA) or school board meetings. Simple gestures like these enable pastors to meet a broader range of education officials and become more familiar with happenings throughout the school system. When pastors are unassumingly present for such meetings, it communicates care and concern for the school, which ultimately diminishes defensiveness and increases credibility.

Pastors may also consider a higher-level commitment by volunteering to help with a school program, coaching a youth sport, starting a clergy/school advisory committee, or even joining the school board. Jason McConnell, one of the contributors to this book, served on his local school board for six years. Even though it required a lot of time, it put him into contact with hundreds of educators and increased his credibility throughout the community, which ultimately led to many direct ministry opportunities such as weddings, funerals, counseling sessions, and numerous gospel conversations.

When pastors are willing to lead the way, church members may catch a vision for new parish ministry. This was the case with Virginia Brown, a mother of three from an affluent North Carolina suburb. In 2009, when her youngest child began grade school, she began volunteering at a local elementary school in a low-income neighborhood—a different school than the one her son attended. "Why volunteer in a different school?" she wrote. "Because they need me more."[24]

Virginia describes the difference between the school where she volunteered and her son's school: "When I signed the volunteer log today there were six signatures on the page. Four of them were mine. At lunchtime I drove to have lunch with my son, and when I signed the visitor's log at his school there were 50 other names before mine on the sheet, just for this morning."[25] As Virginia came to know the students, teachers, and administrative staff at this school, she learned their heartbreaking stories and challenges, and yet she observed, "The majority of these kids are really, really trying. They have a great desire to learn to read and are proud of their improvement. Their faces light up when they achieve something

---

24. Brown, "Things equal," para. 1.
25. Brown, "Things equal," para. 3.

new... I wish I could show you one child's face who realizes for the first time that he can read."[26]

Eventually, Virginia began recruiting members from her church to volunteer at the school with her. The group quickly swelled to fifteen to twenty women volunteering one day a week. One teacher who noticed the volunteers' selfless and faithful service asked the women why they would give their time in such a way. The volunteers gently shared how Jesus' sacrifice for them prompted their own sacrifice for others. This teacher and her husband began worshiping at Virginia's church.

Likewise, the city where I serve, Portsmouth, New Hampshire, is known as one of the more affluent cities in our state, yet our church learned that nearly a quarter of students in our local schools receive free or reduced lunches. This paved the way for our church to partner with our local chapter of End 68 Hours of Hunger, a national program which packs backpacks full of healthy food to send home over the weekend with students who live in food-insecure homes.

As I conversed with other pastors and educators, I heard numerous stories about church/school partnerships, all of which emerged when a pastor asked an educator how they could serve the school. One church hosts a teacher appreciation luncheon for teachers. Another collects back-to-school supplies for an elementary school in need. A third makes end-of-year gift bags for school staff, and still another organizes a gift card drive to give teachers a night out at a nice restaurant or a movie theater, as an expression of appreciation.

During the COVID-19 pandemic some churches heard how parents who were not able to work from home struggled to find a way for their children to learn remotely, since local schools were closed. In response, these churches opened their doors to local schoolchildren, providing internet access and healthy snacks so the students could continue to learn while their parents went to work. Each of these programs arose simply because someone asked, "How can I help?"

The Boston Higher Education Resource Center (HERC) provides a memorable example of an effective church-school partnership.[27] Struck by the fact that Boston hosts some of the top colleges and universities in the nation, while its public school students (especially minority students) struggle academically, a group of individuals partnered with

---

26. Brown, "Gift," para. 3.
27. https://www.bostonherc.org.

Congregation Lion of Judah (Congregación León de Judá) to begin an organization to serve underrepresented urban high school students and their families. HERC works through out-of-school academic enrichment, career advising, and academic support and retention services to help students graduate from high school and college.

In many ways HERC operates on its own, yet it receives financial, administrative, and operational support from Congregation Lion of Judah. Through HERC, Congregation Lion of Judah is able to serve students in nine Boston public high schools, and 90 percent of students involved with HERC become the first-generation college students among their families. The program is so effective that the Boston Public Schools district itself provides philanthropic support to HERC.

Perhaps the most robust example of a church/school partnership we've encountered is the Boston Education Collaborative, a joint venture between the Emmanuel Gospel Center and the Boston Public School system. Among other things, this collaborative facilitates a wide variety of church and school partnerships throughout the greater Boston area. The collaborative grew out of the US Department of Education's Partnership for Family Involvement in Education initiative in 1999, which encouraged churches to play a more direct role in public education. In 2012, Joshua DuBois, former special assistant to President Barack Obama and executive director of the White House Office of Faith-based and Neighborhood Partnerships, said, "Every child deserves an education that will enable them to succeed in a global economy. Faith and community groups are critical partners in this all-hands-on-deck moment."[28]

Recognizing that churches and other faith institutions are committed to helping children reach their full potential and have a long history of partnering with schools, the Boston Public Schools, under the direction of former superintendent Dr. Carol Johnson, created a community liaison position in 2010 to foster more school and faith-based partnerships in the BPS. She said, "Our students and families are depending on all of us—schools, businesses, colleges/universities, secular non-profit and community-based organizations, and your faith-based institutions—to work together for their success."[29]

Today the Boston Education Collaborative coordinates dozens of creative partnerships between churches and schools. Partnerships

---

28. http://www.churchschoolpartners.org/about/.
29. http://www.churchschoolpartners.org/about/.

include reading buddies, after-school programs, targeted academic support, mentoring, parent engagement, donations, college readiness, school clean-up projects, and recruiting volunteers for school events.

The Blackstone School Partnership is a partnership between Blackstone Innovation School and St. Stephen's Episcopal Church, both located in Boston's South End. St. Stephen's hosts the B-READY Afterschool Program, which serves 220 students every school day with academic and enrichment programs; sixty of the youth participants are Blackstone students.

One of St. Stephen's other key contributions to the school was the transformation of a dusty, poorly lit storage space with out-of-date books and encyclopedias into a state-of-the-art library. After more than a decade without a functional library, the Blackstone now has one of the best libraries in any BPS elementary school. The library has a collection of more than ten thousand relevant books and an online catalog that allows teachers to use the library for lesson planning. Rev. Tim Crellin, vicar of St. Stephen's, said, "St. Stephen's believes that we should love our neighbors as ourselves. And the Blackstone School is our church neighbor. We want to participate in the process of making the Blackstone an excellent neighborhood school."[30]

Not every pastor or principal will have the capacity to coordinate such a robust network of church and school partnerships, but when pastors are committed to new parish ministry in their local school system, it may inspire other church members or school officials to embark upon such an ambitious endeavor. But even if it doesn't, one partnership between one local church and one neighborhood school can go a long way toward helping people (especially children) reach their highest human potential and facilitating a flourishing society. When ignorance is replaced by understanding and skepticism is overcome by mutual trust and respect, the possibilities for church and school partnerships are endless.

Conclusion

Churches used to be at the center of community life, but this is no longer the case. Instead of bemoaning the fact that churches have been pushed to the margins of American society, pastors and churches can minister

30. http://www.churchschoolpartners.org/partnerships/the-blackstone-innovation-school-partnership/.

to their parish by serving public schools, which are at the center of community life in most small towns and large city neighborhoods.

Just as Jesus sacrificially laid aside his own claims to power in order to serve us, we likewise serve our parish—our "place"—not by asserting or grasping for power, but by sacrificially serving our communities. We give our lives for our parishes, even in their imperfections, as Christ gave his life for us in the face of our own sin (Rom 5:8). If churches are called to "seek the welfare of the city" (Jer 29:7), and if schools are in so many ways at the center of community life, we neglect a tremendous opportunity when we neglect our schools.

No one expects pastors or churches to fix every problem in the American education system, but a new parish perspective can initiate relationships and partnerships that strengthen both institutions. Imagine if Suzanne had a Virginia in her classroom. A volunteer—even only one hour per week—who could provide reinforcement in a bleak classroom and encouragement to a frazzled teacher. Suzanne doesn't need someone with a graduate degree; she needs someone who is willing to be a redemptive presence in a public school; someone who is committed to the pursuit of truth, wisdom, and service; someone who has a vision for developing human potential and fostering a flourishing society. As N. T. Wright notes, "Christians are not just to be a sign and foretaste of the ultimate salvation: they are to be a part of the means by which God makes this happen in both the present and the future."[31] This is what new parish ministry is all about.

For Further Exploration

1. Betsy DeVos. *Hostages No More: The Fight for Education Freedom and the Future of the American Child*. New York: Hachette, 2022.

2. James W. Frasier. *Between Church and State: Religion and Public Education in a Multicultural America*. 2nd ed. Baltimore: Johns Hopkins University Press, 2016.

3. Zena Hinz. *Lost in Thought: The Hidden Pleasures of Intellectual Life*. Princeton: Princeton University Press, 2020.

---

31. Wright, *Surprised by Hope*, 200.

4. Todd C. Ream, Jerry Pattengale, and Christopher J. Devers, eds. *Public Intellectuals and the Common Good: Christian Thinking for Human Flourishing*. Downers Grove, IL: InterVarsity, 2021.

5. Mitchell Stevens. *Kingdom of Children: Culture and Controversy in the Homeschooling Movement*. Princeton: Princeton University Press, 2003.

6. Tara Westover. *Educated: A Memoir*. New York: Random House, 2018.

Engaging the Education Parish
Interview

MIKE DABOUL, ASSOCIATE PRINCIPAL at Winnacunnet High School, Hampton, New Hampshire, is featured in this interview.

Q. What is the goal of education, as you see it?

We want students to be better when they leave here than they were when they arrived.

Q. What do you mean by "better"?

It's different for every person. It really depends on their goals. If they want to excel academically, then we want them to do that. If they want to earn a good living, we want to help them learn the skills to earn a good living.

That doesn't have to be a white-collar job. One of my students who graduated several years ago got a job as a marine welder. He's making six figures in his early twenties, doing great for himself. We see that as a success. We didn't teach him how to dive or how to weld in high school, but we gave him the skills to figure out his life. He came in as a freshman with no direction, and he left and made a living for himself. We love stories like that!

Not everybody is supposed to be a stockbroker or lawyer or manager. Society needs all types of people, and it's our goal to train students to fill all those needs that society has.

Q. What are some of your most significant challenges?

Where do I start? In a way, it really comes down to student ownership. For the most part, you get out of school what you put into it. If you want to learn, you'll learn. If you don't want to learn, we can't force you to learn. So, trying to help students see the value of education—trying to help them want to learn—is tough.

Then there are all the extracurricular challenges. Some students have so much going on at home, or they don't have a home, that they can't focus here. If students don't have food at home, they can't focus. It's hard to learn on an empty stomach. So, we feed them breakfast and lunch, but there's no guarantee that they'll have dinner at night, and no guarantee of food over the weekend. Those cases, where the student has trouble going on that's not their fault—those are the really hard ones.

Q. In your years of education, both as a teacher and now as an administrator, what are some of the most significant changes you have seen?

Schools are now in charge of everything. We don't just teach the core subjects anymore. We also teach morality, time management, and self-discipline. Parents expect us to teach the things that they, the parents, once taught their kids. For instance, just last week a student's mother called me and asked me to disable her daughter's school-issued laptop at night. I asked her why she wanted me to do that, and she responded, "My daughter stays up way too late at night on her laptop, wasting time, and she's not getting enough sleep." I responded that she is the parent, so she could make her daughter shut down the computer at night. She responded, "I know I could do it, but can you just do it for me?"

It used to be that when we had a discipline issue with a student, we would call the student's mom or dad, and their parents would take care of it. Now it's not uncommon to hear from the parent, "What do you want me to do about it?" It's like they expect us to discipline their children. It puts us in a hard spot, because parents are refusing, and we know if we don't do those things, students will suffer in the long run, so we do what we can. But it adds a lot to our plate that wasn't on it before.

Q. Do you have any advice for a church leader who wants to serve a local school?

First, I would say find out what's already there. And you can't do that without having a conversation. Call the principal or a guidance counselor and see if there are already programs in place that you can help with. There's no sense in duplicating efforts, and I don't have the time to start a bunch of new things, especially when there are programs in place that are already working. Start by asking!

Q. What if there aren't programs in place already?

It really depends on the school and how they work. Each one works differently. You have to start by asking. But for me, I would have a harder time trusting a church who parachuted in and said, "We're here to help." I'd wonder what their motives are. What's their agenda? But if one of our students asks a teacher to sponsor a new club for Christian students, or when several PTA parents lobby to host a study group at a local church, I'm much more open to that. They're already here. We know them. We trust them. We don't question their agenda. It works best when the person starting a program already has a relationship with the school, like a student, parent, or teacher.

Q. Do you have examples of local churches who have a presence in your school?

Honestly, not many. One local church hosts an appreciation luncheon for our teachers every year. The teachers generally enjoy that. That started because one of our teachers is a member at that church, so she had her feet in both pools. Those are the connections that are easiest—we don't have to do the hard work of building trust.

Q. Are there concerns about violating church/state boundaries?

People are usually more worried about that than they should be. If you want to help, come help! We've got needs, and if you want to help address those, you're welcome. Obviously, don't come with a secret agenda. If we ask you to help deliver meals to hungry students, don't try to slip in religious pamphlets. Don't try a bait and switch. You'll lose my trust really fast, and then you've hurt all the other groups who want to help, too, because I'm going to have a harder time trusting them. But if you really want to help, we welcome that!

6

Engaging the Arts Parish

Seth Anderson

"The arts are a cup that will carry the water of life to the thirsty."
—MAKOTO FUJIMURA

My fourteen-year-old daughter came home from church one Sunday visibly upset. She told us that someone had questioned her desire to pursue a career as a professional ballet dancer. Even though the question was genuine, it was tinged with a disparaging tone—"How can a Christian pursue such a thing?" This disconcerting confrontation raised a myriad of moral questions in my daughter's mind: "Is dancing spiritually compromising? Is it immodest, vain, or sensual? Will the environment of professional dance erode my integrity? Will the rigid requirements ruin my faith?"

Concerns like these arose because our daughter had just been accepted into a summer ballet intensive in New York City. She was the first dancer in her local studio to ever be accepted into such a prestigious program. And she received a full tuition scholarship, which we saw as an affirmation of her skill and gifting, as well as a blessing from God. Her instructor was thrilled and posted her excitement on social media. Even though many family members and friends congratulated our daughter, some within the church community met this news with questions, skepticism, and seeming disapproval.

My daughter's unpleasant encounter is not entirely unique. Unfortunately, she was the victim of the suspicion that currently exists between the church and the art world—an apprehension that has waxed and waned since the dawn of the Protestant Reformation and continues to linger in the twenty-first century. Every generation has to navigate the abyss between faith and the arts. Parents have to discern what art is appropriate for their families' consumption and participation. Pastors have to address concerns about art in the life of the church. And artists, who often exist on the fringes of society, have to decide what to do with the church.

A Threat in Perspective

Throughout the centuries, the Christian church was the art gallery and music hall of Western civilization. The church was not only the chief motivation for generative creativity, but it was often the very venue where art was produced. In the sixteenth century, Michelangelo painted his phenomenal frescos on the ceiling of the Sistine Chapel. Sir Christopher Wren was an anatomist, astronomer, and mathematician, but he became England's most notable architect when he rebuilt fifty-two churches in London after the Great Fire of 1666, including his masterpiece, St. Paul's Cathedral. Johann Sebastian Bach composed his cantatas and concertos at St. Thomas Church in Leipzig, where he served as choirmaster from 1723 until his death in 1750. Communities of faith were captivated by truth, beauty, and goodness. And these virtues were expressed through the arts in and through their places of worship.

Yet, in recent generations, the once strong relationship between the church and the arts community has fractured and faded; both groups have forged separate paths, heading in divergent directions. There are exceptions, though. Even in the late twentieth century, Aretha Franklin's gospel caravan started on the stage of the New Bethel Baptist Church in Detroit long before she was coronated as the "Queen of Soul." But exceptions like Franklin have become increasingly rare. It is now difficult for artists to simultaneously maintain credibility in the church and the wider art world. As values, motivations, and worldviews have grown apart, suspicions have arisen and the chasm between these two worlds has broadened, making them seemingly insurmountable. This gulf has left behind a vast wasteland of kitschy "Christian art" and sacrilegious "secular art." While there are many reasons for the rift between the church and the arts, three, in particular, are worth mentioning.

A Crisis of Truth

The church has long taught that the source of truth is found in God, his word, and his creation, stating that truth is to be viewed as objective. So, Scripture declares, "I the Lord speak the truth; I declare what is right" (Isa 45:19). Further, those who have grown up in the church have heard Jesus say, "I am the way, the truth, and the life" (John 14:6). Some in the church have spoken of this truth as "true truth" or Truth with a capital "T," to distinguish the objective from the subjective, the absolute from the relative. The origin of this Truth is not from ourselves; it's outside of ourselves.

This externally perceived understanding of reality is displayed everywhere in nature. For example, the overwhelming consensus by most people is that the sky is blue and the grass is green. Of course, depending upon the way light may shine in the sky or on the grass, there might be various shades and nuances of how we perceive these objects. God's objective world is complex in many ways. Nevertheless, throughout the ages, there has been a strong confidence in the truth of an objective world.

So, too, for many generations, the art community also reflected this understanding of objective reality. The artist would strive to create an accurate representation of a reality. The closer the artist came to exact representation, the more accomplished the artwork. The goal was to re-create as close to reality as possible the reality of God's creation. For example, multitudes praised Michelangelo's sculpture *David* for his accuracy down to the very tendons and musculature. As author Philip Ryken states, "Art is an incarnation of the truth. It penetrates the surface of things to portray them as they really are."[1]

Art continued in this way for centuries, but challenge and change were on the horizon. M. H. Abrams in his *Mirror and the Lamp*[2] explains that prior to the Romantic period artists would create to reflect truth, as a mirror would reflect its true subjects. But artists also recognized that they were interpreters. Objective truth was questioned more and more, opening the door to the subjective. No longer a mirror, now as a lamp,

1. Ryken, *Art for God's Sake*, 39.
2. Abrams, *Mirror and the Lamp*.

the artist illumines his or her subjective interpretation of what is real and true. Increasingly, the subjective interpretation of the artist has become the central focus of artistic perception within the art world.

Though it was popularized in the Romantic era, we would be shortsighted to think that this was a new concept. Truth, and therefore God himself, has been questioned from the beginning. The very first question in the Bible is, "Did God actually say . . . ?" (Gen 3:1). Here, the diabolical serpent questions God's truth and introduces doubt and subjectivity to humankind. Later on, the Roman governor Pilate hears Jesus, the Son of God declare, "Everyone who is of the truth listens to my voice," to which Pilate responds, "What is truth?" (John 18:37–38). The questioning of objective truth is nothing new, though the church has long resisted it.

Nevertheless, since the church is founded upon objective reality, it has become increasingly threatened by a largely subjective center to art, in form and vision. The arts, in turn, have felt a growing alienation by a worldview of the church that trumpets the objective over the subjective vision of the artist. Both sides have reacted against each other's reality, thus causing an ever-growing rift.

A Crisis of Goodness

While truth has become an active battleground, so has goodness. Goodness refers two things in particular, morality and excellence. In Western Christendom, morality was defined and controlled by the church, and there was a general cultural consensus that God created the universe and established moral boundaries and standards, which if followed would lead to a good life. The art world was measured against these objective standards.

More recently, as the culture embraced growing subjectivism, the art community felt more freedom to push against the limits that the church enforced for so long. What was viewed as "the good" has changed, and the moral universe as we once knew it has been deconstructed. An attitude of "anything goes" seemingly drives the visual arts, theater, cinema, literature, and the like. As a result, the various arts have felt less obliged to simply describe the goodness of life, but "all" of life—the ugly, the grotesque, the benign, the ironic, and the mundane. In fact, the art world has been accused of going out of its way to focus on the dark underbelly of life rather than its lightness. Moreover, the good and the profane are often presented as interchangeable. It's no wonder there has been a growing divide between the church and the arts; it is as if they are focusing on two completely different human experiences.

The crisis of goodness, however, is not only a moral standard; it also refers to an aesthetic standard. Again, in a growing world of subjectivism, the arts have expanded the normal conventions of the various art forms. Whereas once measured against strict standards of aesthetic acceptability, many of the arts have opened themselves up to wide ranges of experimentation of expression. What is the standard for these expressions? No longer do they often rest with more objective criteria, but rather with the subjective judgments of the spectator rather than the artist. "Art is what you want it to be," and every individual observer has the inside track on what the art means.

Consequently, the chasm has increased, not only between the church and the arts, but also between the artist and the observer. If the casual observer is the primary means by which art is to be understood—and therefore appreciated—what makes "good" art is so subjective that it is almost impossible to evaluate. Therefore, the lines between good and bad have become severely blurred.

The Crisis of Beauty

This, of course, leads to the third crisis—the crisis of beauty. The church has, for generations, found the source of ultimate beauty in God himself. So, the psalmist asserts of his desire "to gaze upon the beauty of the Lord . . ." (Ps 27:4). Throughout Scripture, there is something captivating and wonderful about God. All that he has made is touched by his beauty and displays his glory. Beauty is, therefore, understood in the church by its transcendence. To see beauty is to look upward. In his sermon "The Weight of Glory," C. S. Lewis states:

> We do not want merely to see beauty, though, God knows, even that is bounty enough. We want something else which can hardly be put into words—to be united with the beauty we see, to pass into it, to receive it into ourselves, to bathe in it, to become part of it.[3]

In seeing the beauty of this world, we have only to see God, the author of all beauty.

---

3. Lewis, "Weight of Glory," 12–13.

All this, of course, has now changed. No longer is beauty merely the upward gaze. Beauty, if it is even sought after, is sought in places of ruin. Artist and author Makoto Fujimura writes concerning the mid-1990s art atmosphere in New York City, "'beauty' was taboo, not to be spoken of in public. It signified cultural hegemony, imperialist power, the corruption of the past, or the cosmetic sheen of superficial contemporary culture. The art world still resists this word."[4] The idea of the beautiful is minimized at best and ridiculed at worst.

Furthermore, the art community saw many in the church define beauty as idyllic soft lightscapes that refused to face or address the reality of the broken and ugly. They saw right through it as superficial hopefulness that wasn't grounded in the here and now. Perhaps the pendulum swung in the opposite direction. Ryken comments, "Today it sometimes seems as though the art world is struggling to overcome an aesthetic of ugliness."[5] When we lose vision and desire for what is truly beautiful, we begin to embrace the distorted as normal. Superficial beauty has threatened the arts' desire to display reality, and the ugly and even profane has threatened the culture of the religious.

These three crises—of truth, goodness, and beauty—have reached a crescendo and the chasm grows ever wider between the church and the art community. Suspicion has led to separation. Fingers have been pointed, blame has been cast, while fear and mistrust have become regular dancing partners that threaten to clear the floor and end the existence of whatever relationship may be left. And as this culture war continues to rage between them, there are casualties on both sides. Artists have lost their place in the church. And the church has lost its vision for the artist and their art.

So, given this, what is the church to do? Whenever there is a divide, a fracture, or divorce, we need to find common ground. We need a starting point, a reorientation to where it all began and what went wrong. Only then will we be able to move forward together with understanding and grace. The best place to begin is with our own story, the story of humanity.

---

4. Fujimura, *Culture Care*, 25.
5. Ryken, *Art for God's Sake*, 42.

A Theology of Humanity

To mend this rupture between the church and the arts community—between people in the pews and the public square—pastors can act as a liaison by explicating a theology of humanity. By leveraging their credibility with the church and building relationships with artists in their community, the pastor is in a unique position to rebuild the bridge by helping both groups answer questions such as: How does our shared humanity establish common ground? How can artists use their gifts to glorify God and bless other human beings? How can Christians embrace the arts without forsaking their holiness? Should there be aesthetic limits for the sake of our souls? If so, how should they be determined? Why should the church resist its instinct to retreat from the art world by creating its own "safe" and "sanitized" culture of art? How can the church minister to artists inside and outside the church?

Jesus, the master of questions and civil dialogue, bridged divides among the people of his day. He spent a great deal of time in the public square, uniting people with different values and perspectives. Jesus lived and died to redeem all things, including the church and the arts. And in his steps, pastors must be willing to step into their pulpits, and out in the public square to thoughtfully engage in the challenging but rewarding work of a new parish model of ministry. But how? Let us begin with our own shared story of humanity. In order for pastors to engage the arts parish in a thoughtful way, we begin with some theological reflection common to all humanity. What does it mean to be human?

The creative impulse is written into Scripture from the very beginning: "In the beginning, God..." (Gen 1:1). It all begins with God himself. "In the beginning, God created..." He is the creator, the first maker, the first artist. He made color, texture, depth, shape, consistency, size, taste, smell, sound, emotion, movement. It was true, beautiful, and good. The creation is a testimony of our Creator; it declares who he is. "The heavens declare the glory of God, and the sky above proclaims his handiwork" (Ps 19:1). Psalm 8 speaks of the heavens being the work of God's fingers.

Yet for all this glory, there is a crown of his creation—human beings. We are made in the image of God (Gen 1:26–27). We are image bearers of the one who made us, and it was very good (Gen 1:28). The great Creator invites us, his creation, to be co-creators with him. We are given the gift of creativity that is nothing short of mimicking the very activity of the great Creator. Part of being made in his image means we have the desire and ability to create. And not just to create, but to cultivate, preserve, and develop.

A pastor once remarked, "Art is an effort to make something."[6] We exercise our creativity when we take what God has made, and remake it to reflect his glory and beauty. Reflecting on Dorothy Sayers in her *The Mind of the Maker*, we are made and "remade in Christ to be makers with God."[7] Our greatest aim is God himself. We were made to wonder, to glory and deeply enjoy him. It is in this that we find our true identity and greatest purpose—"to glorify and enjoy him forever."[8]

So, the artist is exercising a desire and gift given by God. To create is a living expression of what it means to be human. Because we are made in God's image, a measure of creativity is imprinted in all of us. Yet there is much room to foster and develop this gift. We are called to be skillful in our art. Skillfulness brings glory to God as we practice our craft. The psalmist calls to artists, "Give thanks to the Lord with the lyre; make melody to him with the harp of ten strings! Sing to him a new song; play skillfully on the strings, with loud shouts" (Ps 33:1-2) While some skill can be gained, much of it is given. For example, when the instructions for the tabernacle were given to Moses, God pointed out that he had called Bezalel and "filled him with the Spirit of God, with ability and intelligence, with knowledge and all craftsmanship, to devise artistic designs, to work in gold, silver, and bronze, in cutting stones for setting, and in carving wood, to work in every craft" (Exod 31:1-5; 35:30-36:2).

Is it not significant that the first humans anointed by God's Spirit were artists?[9] Artistry is a blessing and gift from God. It is rooted in his very nature and reminds us that all co-creations find their beginning and ending in God the Creator. Artists are dependent upon God not only for skill, but also for inspiration. Consider a few chapters later in Exodus, "And Moses called Bezalel and Oholiab and every craftsman in whose mind the Lord had put skill, everyone whose heart stirred him up to come to do the work" (Exod 36:2). Any artist can tell you the creativity cannot be forced. There must be a stirring of the heart—a movement, a desire. If our greatest desire is God, then our creativity will reflect him in our creations, just as he is reflected in his creation. His creation was true,

---

6. Piper, "Theology of Art in Five Minutes."
7. Piper, "We Are Makers."
8. *Westminster Shorter Catechism*, Question 1.
9. Sproul, *Truths We Confess*, 463.

beautiful, and good. But then something went terribly wrong in Eden, something that marred the God-given gift of human creativity.

Enter Satan in the form of a serpent as he tempts the first couple. And what a temptation it was! First, he attacked what is true: "Did God actually say . . . ?" (Gen 3:1) by calling into question what God said, and then calling him a liar: "You will not surely die" (Gen 3:4; 2:7). Second, the serpent attacked the very goodness of God, as if God was withholding something good from them—such as the knowledge of good and evil, as well as the goodness of the fruit of the tree. And third, the Great Deceiver even uses beauty as a tool of temptation. Eve saw that the tree was "a delight to the eyes" (Gen 3:6). Satan used God's artistic creation against him, by tempting the creature to usurp the role of Creator. Now the creation says to the Creator, "I decide what is true, what is beautiful, and what is good." By believing the deceiver over their Creator, humankind fell. Sin stained all that was true, beautiful, and good. And now, instead of bearing a perfect image, we all alike bear an image that is distorted and dying.

As a result of the first temptation, we all live in a new reality. Everything in creation and culture was affected, leaving a world filled with anger, injustice, hurt, sadness, pain, despair, sickness, tears, alienation, shame, anxiety, frustration, jealousy, animosity, insecurity—and the list goes on. We have lost our original identity and find ourselves in an identity crisis. Who are we? Why are we here? Where is God? This is the origin of our demise. This is our common story. We are all affected by the fall.

Our brokenness runs deep. We see it in our bodies, in our relationships, in our families, and even on our faces. And we even see it in our art and in the artists who create it. The creativity given to humanity at creation is now used as a means of expressing our fallenness. Much art comes from places of deep pain and darkness. God has given artists the ability to help fallen humanity to both understand and navigate the depth of our brokenness. Art can help us come to terms with what went wrong, to grasp how damaged we are, to see in new ways the real problem that sin has ushered in. Isn't this part of the redemptive story for artists? In revealing the brokenness of humanity in their art forms, they point us toward something better.

Herein lies the challenge both for those that create and those who consume the arts. Through artists and their work, we may devolve into a sense of hopelessness and harm our own souls. In doing so, we unintentionally drag others down with us. We may think that we can handle entering into the abyss of the fall. Or, through the arts, we remind ourselves and each other that we were never created to live in our fallen state, even though we do not possess the ability to be fully unaffected and clear thinking apart from God's presence and hope.

By using art as an expression of brokenness, herein lies a further temptation for both the artist and the Christian: On the one hand, it may be a temptation for artists to descend so far into the fall that their very being is compromised by a darkness that they cannot escape from alone. We observe this all too often by seeing artists tragically end their lives in a moment or season of hopelessness and despair. Living in healthy community could very well help artists to understand their physical, emotional, mental, and spiritual limits and recognize when they're falling into despair. Community also serves to remind them and the community they serve that this is not the end of our story.

This is wonderfully illustrated by John Bunyan in his *The Pilgrim's Progress*. Christian wandered off the path one night and lost his way. He took shelter from the storm but awoke to be captured and thrown into the dungeon of Giant Despair, who tried to convince him to end his life. He sank into a deep despair and entertained the taking of his own life. But it was Hopeful, his traveling companion, also in the dungeon, who pointed him to what was true, and how he had overcome before. Hopeful reminded Christian that he had a key in his pocket that would unlock the dungeon and set them both free.[10] This community in the dungeon that offered clear thinking was the very medicine needed to be able to survive and continue.

The temptation for the Christian church is the opposite, to escape the fallenness around it. Is the church willing to embrace the sorrow and depth of human brokenness? Are we able to patiently sit with people in their pain? Is the church able to extend understanding and grace to artists who expose our fallenness before either jumping to judgment or racing to redemption? Perhaps we need thoughtful pause as we consider our story. For if we don't know how deeply flawed we are, we cannot know the fullness of our need for a rescue.

Now for the good news: Though we are all marred by sin and broken by the fall, God's image has not been removed. We are still very much human and continue to bear the image of our creator—however maligned. Apologist Francis Schaeffer describes us as "glorious ruins" such as that

---

10. Bunyan, *Pilgrim's Progress*, 115.

of a once beautiful European castle—now broken down and overgrown. Even amid the ruin, the remnants of beauty remain. Now it is a broken beauty. As we live in our ruined state, we yearn to be made whole again. We long for Eden. Much of life is spent trying to heal from hurt.

Yet we cannot heal ourselves. We need a savior; one who will come to us, enter in, dwell with us, and bring us out of darkness and into light, out of death and into life. Jesus Christ, the perfect Son of God, brought us a bandage of grace and a balm of peace, to heal a bleeding world, and truth for a confused world. He did not stay hidden in a safe fortress or a sanitized palace, but he descended into our infected places, that we might relearn what is true, retrieve what is good, and reconsider what is beautiful. He came to remake us in God's image, to bring hope, meaning, and purpose back to our lives. He came to bring forgiveness, life, and peace with God and one another.

True beauty is rooted in sacrifice. Artist Makoto Fujimura writes, "Sacrifices are needed to provide beauty in the world."[11] Christ's selfless suffering and sacrifice on the cross of was the most profound act of beauty in history. It was an act of generosity, an act of service. This is redemption at its core, where justice and mercy meet. This beauty, this sacrifice, this Savior, not only changes us, but brings hope to humanity. We often only grasp half of the good news—that Jesus died for our sins, but the other half is that he gave us something of infinite value—his righteousness (2 Cor 5:21). As Christians, we now die to sin and live to righteousness. We have a new identity (Col 3:3-4, 9-10). We are no longer defined by what we have done or haven't done, but by what Christ has done for us. Now we are free to live with a renewed purpose for God and for one another. If you breathe in grace, you will breathe it out.

The same goes for beauty. Again, Fujimura writes, "An encounter with beauty can show us what could be and can make us rightly dissatisfied with the way things are."[12] Beauty gives us a vision for hope, for restoration, for redemption, not only for ourselves but for all humanity. Beauty is available and can be offered to all as we live and share fragments of redemption. Redemption is seen in the normal cycle of life, death, and resurrection. It could be in a simple gesture of a child delighting in a flower and picking it to share with another. When an artist paints of new life, or a dancer displays rebirth, whether they are Christian or not, we all

---

11. Fujimura, *Culture Care*, 56.
12. Fujimura, *Culture Care*, 56.

see redemption. We see what it means to be human, that we are not left in our loss, but begin to regain.

But all of this takes time. We must be committed to the long road of patience. For we are damaged human beings, crippled sometimes severely. To regain trust and rebuild relationship will take time and effort. The writer of Ecclesiastes reminds us that God "has made everything beautiful in its time" (Eccl 3:11). God has made and is remaking beauty in time. We too, as co-creators, can join in that process of remaking beauty for the good of all the world. This is the kingdom of God that has come with Jesus and will one day be restored in its fullness.

Although it may be tempting to conclude the story of humanity at redemption, it is not the end. Redemption is here and at work, but we still live with the pain of the fall. The final chapter of our story is that redemption is leading somewhere. We are headed to a place where there will be no more suffering, pain, tears, and death. Jesus himself says he is making everything new (Rev 21:5). It is there we will experience only true beauty, unaffected by the fall. All things will be renewed to their original perfection. But it will be even greater. To be renewed through our experiences of pain and suffering is better than just being new. With scars still visible, we will know that our pain had a purpose; that death was a necessary entrance into life; that the fall has shown us our need and created a longing for Jesus. On the day of consummation, we will stand in his presence renewed, face-to-face, to worship him for eternity.

This is our story. This is what it means to be human. This is what everyone in the parish has in common. This theology leads us into the public square, not to shout and argue, but to understand and learn more of ourselves and our Creator. It ought to lead us to love and value artists who show us our ruin and redemption, who touch us in our inner being with truths that words cannot express. It ought to foster compassion for artists, fellow humans flawed by sin, yet striving to turn ashes back into beauty. This theology of humanity calls for engagement.

A Thoughtful Engagement with the Arts

How, then, can pastors encourage their congregations to re-engage artists and their world? It begins simply by looking with new eyes, listening with open ears, and a renewed commitment to thoughtful engagement. We often value efficiency and utility, but these are not the friends of thoughtfulness. In order to be thoughtful, we must first look and listen. How can we engage the arts in a thoughtful way, in light of our common human story?

Elissa Yukiko Weichbrodt, an art history professor at Covenant College, is interested the idea of "looking responsibly." She asks, "What does it mean to look faithfully and humbly? Can we recognize truth, can we love our neighbor, can we interrogate our own responses, can we be called to repentance when necessary?"[13]

Looking can lead to thoughtless judgment or to thankful reception. On the one hand, we can look to disparage, judge, or dismantle what is wrong. This is a pharisaical way of looking. It is a looking down upon from a superior position. People in the church may sometimes view art this way, as critical and unreflective consumers.

But we are called to a thoughtful and faithful looking, a looking that acknowledges pain and sin and fractured lives. A looking that admits our brokenness and accepts our story for what it is. A looking that generates lament, empathy, and love. A looking not only to consume, but to contribute to and collaborate with. For example, we have seen art at the center of racial unrest; statues coming down and murals going up. As art communicates longings to a watching world, we must strive to see people instead of politics. Looking reminds us of our creatureliness and points to our Creator and even our Savior. Jesus stopped, looked, and demonstrated empathy, compassion, and invited the needy to be forgiven and be made wholly human.

Looking is always connected to the heart. Art captures a deeper love of God and leads us to greater compassion. We are not just consumers, but those who seek to look faithfully. In the words of Andrew Shaughnessy:

> To study art history, to faithfully view art, often means exposing ourselves to the darkness of history and the human soul. But it also means exposing ourselves to stories that are not our own—stories of men and women made in the image of God. It means finding new tragedies to mourn, more wonders to behold, and learning to love people better by seeing them more clearly. For a Christian, it also means grasping more firmly to hope.[14]

---

13. Shaughnessy, "Expanding the Archive," 54.
14. Shaughnessy, "Expanding the Archive," 55.

For the Christian, there can be a temptation to set up legalistic barriers to protect ourselves from a broken world, to set up rules for what we can and cannot look at, to stamp what is approved and denied, what is Christian and what is non-Christian. God calls us to guard our hearts yet rules often remove responsibility and discourage a thoughtful engagement. For others, the temptation is to move toward license, to live as though there were no boundaries, fostering the attitude of looking at whatever you want. Certainly, there is freedom, but not without wisdom of what will bring honor to God, health to our soul, and love to our neighbor.

We need to ask thoughtful questions. What kind of looking faces the reality of my own brokenness? Is my looking from a heart attitude that desires to honor God and foster a deeper understanding of our story? Where do I see sin, ruin, and pain, and how does it point to my own experience as a sinner and one who is sinned against? What have I seen that I see in my own life, leading me to sorrow and repentance? Where do I see forgiveness and redemption? Where do I see truth, beauty, and goodness? How can my looking expand my view toward my neighbor, and lead to actions of generosity and love? May we look as an opportunity to engage—to crucify selfishness and cultivate love for God and others.

After we learn to look, we are called to listen. Listening requires humility, and the ability to hear from people you may not know or with whom you disagree. Fujimura speaks of artists being border-walkers, who live on the edges and can move in and out of realms of culture with which we may not be familiar. Artists are often held at arm's length and labeled as different and difficult. Yet they have the capacity to teach us about the areas of our communities where we are not connected. They create bridges into territories to which we may never be invited.[15]

A wonderful example of the bridging nature of the arts was seen not long ago in my own community. A young man at our local high school tragically took his own life. A year later, his parents and friends decided to put on a music festival to raise awareness for suicide prevention. My daughter's dance company was invited to perform an original piece that fostered healing and hope. Perhaps like no others, artists have the ability to help us listen to the pain, longings, and hopes of humanity.

Interestingly, my local classical radio station reported a large increase in listeners during the COVID-19 pandemic. Listeners wanted to hear something other than the news. But I believe it's more than that. I

---

15. Fujimura, *Culture Care*, 59.

believe the isolation and loneliness caused people to pursue community connections in new places. The arts not only became a contact point for humanity, but they also brought life and hope in the midst of trial.

When we look and listen, we begin the process of thoughtful engagement. Once we have gained, we are ready to give. Are you weary from engaging in the culture wars and frustrated that you are not reaching your community? Are you worn out from protecting the sacred and protesting the secular? Have you retreated from the public square and bemoaned you have no voice in the culture? The arts provide us a wonderful opportunity to re-engage our congregation and community. So, how can pastors lead this process of thoughtful engagement?

Support the Arts

Pastors can begin by simply supporting and nurturing the arts in their church and community. Joshua Banner says, "A nurturer possesses the initiative necessary to penetrate the outer shell, the crusted topsoil, of a person's life. A nurturer is able to till the soil. A nurturer moves past layers of presumption and self-reliance in order to earn a person's trust so that he will receive love. Each of us will have particular types of artists we are drawn to and who are drawn to us."[16] We invite the young children to come up front once a month to participate in the worship songs with various instruments. This kind of openness communicates that we want artists to discover and utilize their gifts as part of our church community.

As pastor, I have encouraged children to draw during the sermon. We provide notebooks and crayons for younger listeners. In the past, we have posted the artwork on a wall in the church building to which I referred to as the "sermon wall of art." This was a benefit not only for the children, but for all who stopped to look and listen. Hold an arts night at your church. Invite all the artists in the church to come together for an evening of praise as they display their gifts. Pray for artists. Commission artists. Encourage artists in the church to use their gifts in the public square.

Go out and support the arts in your community. Invite people from your congregation to attend a concert, ballet, theater production, or art gallery together. I recently invited several men from our church to a local documentary film about motorcycling. After the film, one of the men who attended nearly jumped out of his seat, and exclaimed, "That's

---

16. Banner, "Practitioner," 130–31.

what I want to do!" Clearly, the film had awakened a deep desire within him to see and experience life differently. One of our elders, who has no children, attends the local classical ballet performances to support our students, as well as others he knows from the community. His presence is deeply meaningful to the students and their parents.

Since a pastor's time is limited, we can take advantage of areas where they are already present, such as school concerts and performances. We can advocate for the arts in schools since they are often the first to get cut when budgets are tight. We can offer space, instruments, and equipment to the community. Our church building and piano is sometimes used for lessons and recitals. Likewise, if the church has the appropriate equipment, it can host film viewings and discussions for the community. Choose films that are rich with themes of creation, fall, redemption, and consummation, and that will generate deep conversation.[17] Supporting the arts is a crucial first step toward building credibility with artists throughout the parish, in the pews and out in the public square.

Collaborate with Artists

Pastors can also find creative ways to collaborate with artists inside and outside the church. As a part of planning weekly worship, pastors regularly interact with church musicians, but what about other types of artists? One of my most memorable collaborations was with my brother-in-law, a visual artist. We partnered together to present a visual sermon. He painted as I preached, and then he explained the painting to the congregation. It was amazing to behold the biblical story brushed onto the canvas. It was especially meaningful for the visual learners in our church.

A few years later, we collaborated again, this time with a larger work capturing the themes from four sermons on the book of Jonah. Excitement in the church grew each week, and a church member even made prints with a description on the back. I have since preached in other places with my brother-in-law's paintings present as visual aids. It is always a compelling collaboration.

There are artists, visual and otherwise, sitting in the pews every Sunday morning. They are waiting for their pastor to invite them to share

---

17. Some suggested possibilities for film discussion: *The Shawshank Redemption, The Count of Monte Cristo, The Matrix, The Lord of the Rings, Bella, Gran Torino, Babette's Feast.*

their gifts with the congregation. They can be incorporated into a worship service, a sanctuary beautification project, an artistic discipleship initiative, a creative evangelistic event, or a Sunday school class that discusses a theology of art and the aesthetic. There is no limit to the ways pastors and artistic parishioners can collaborate for the edification of the church.

There are also ways for pastors to collaborate with artists in the community outside the church. They can ask local artists to participate in a discussion about faith and the arts. They can invite artists to collaborate with the church to host a cantata or concert, a poetry night or a songwriting session, or a visual gallery or theater production. The pastor can either offer space at the church or coordinate an appropriate location in the community. We once invited a community band to play at our ice cream social event. Everyone was blessed by beautiful big band music and bold ice cream sundaes.

Teach the Arts

Pastors can also teach about God's role as an artist. They can preach sermons and teach classes about how to look, listen, smell, taste, and touch what God has created. Jesus taught from fields, spoke of birds and flowers, rocks and animals; he taught from boats and used the wind and waves. When people get to know God as the great artist, their hearts will grow for co-artists. Point out the artistry of his Word. Preach on Psalm 119, an acrostic poem. Speak about the use of narrative, history, wisdom literature, as well as the creative use of language—hyperbole, alliteration, metaphor. The apostle Paul quotes familiar cultural poets (Acts 17:28). Show how Jesus uses parables to effectively communicate important truths. He is the master storyteller. Retell the biblical stories with engagement. Teach about musical instruments in the Bible. Draw attention to dancing in the biblical narrative, particularly Miriam after the Red Sea crossing (Exod 15:20–21) and David as the ark came to Jerusalem (2 Sam 6:16–23). Focus on the beauty of the tabernacle (Exod 26) and the skill and craftsmanship that God gave to those artists (Exod 31:11). Bulletins or screens can be used to feature art relating to the Scripture of the day.

Teaching a theology of art doesn't have to be limited to the church; it can be done in the community. I was once asked to teach an orchestra unit to a local group of students. I invited a composer to come and present some of his music and talk about the process of composition. Many of the students had never met a real composer. If a pastor has a particular artistic talent, he or she might consider teaching a beginners class for the community, such as storytelling, painting, dancing, or learning an instrument.

Participate as an Artist

Pastors can develop their own artistic talents and use them in the church and the public square. I grew up using my artistic gifts in my home church and continue to do so today through music and preaching. When I was about ten years old I joined a children's choir in which I was able to perform at various venues and community events. That was over thirty years ago! But I have stayed connected to the choir and the director who has asked me multiple times to return as an adult to sing at their community concert. The director has also asked me to read Scripture as part of the concert because she knows I am a pastor. Pastors can participate in community theater, choruses, bands, or writing groups. These and many other outlets may lead to natural connections and relationships with other artists in the community.

A Thriving Foretaste of Eternity

When pastors engage the arts parish, they have the unique opportunity to communicate God's artistic heart; his compassionate entering into our brokenness; his desire for redemption through his Son, Jesus Christ; his call to be co-creators with him; his work of restoring truth, beauty, and goodness; his movement of the Holy Spirit in providing skillfulness; and his making of all things new. These realities have already begun and will continue for eternity.

The arts are for all of humanity. Instead of fortifying the false dichotomy of sacred and secular art, may pastors help their parishioners behold art that is broken and beautiful, true to our whole story. For the church to engage in this realm will open new opportunities, build a common unity, and potentially reach those who would never otherwise engage with the church. The arts communicate our story in ways that words cannot. They are able to reach deep within, to show us our Creator, display how far we have fallen, and give us hope for redemption.

Redemption will be complete in heaven. The arts will usher in the consummate worship of the one who alone is true, beautiful, good, and worthy—the great artist himself. There will be a new song before his throne, with these lyrics: "Worthy are you to take the scroll and to open its seals, for you were slain, and by your blood you ransomed people for God from every tribe and language and people and nation, and you have made them a kingdom and priests to our God, and they shall reign on the earth" (Rev 5:9–10). Many things will come to an end, but the arts will continue for eternity as an expression and demonstration of worship to our Creator, Savior, and Redeemer Jesus Christ.

Retreating from the public square into a self-contained, sanitized world may keep Christians safe for a while, but we were never called to be safe. Like Christ, who had the courage to enter into our mess, we are called to return to the parish again and again to engage the arts thoughtfully and creatively for the good of our own souls, communities, and common understanding.

Understanding begins with simple conversations. As a pastor, I pursued the individual in the church who had questioned my daughter about a career as a ballerina—not to scold or correct, but to create an opportunity to learn from one another. I listened to their concerns, and I expressed my own concerns about neglecting a God-given gift and desire to dance. It was a good conversation and hopefully one of more to come.

As a father, I sat down with my daughter. I listened and acknowledged her deflation. We discussed art in general and dance in particular. We talked about how Christ is renewing culture and how he could use her gift to bring life to others. It was, likewise, a good conversation and hopefully one of many to come. At the year-end ballet performance, where our daughter performed the lead role, several community members, including the mayor's wife, remarked that they noticed something different while she danced. They spoke of a radiance that emanated through her presence. They said she "glowed" on stage. Her gift of dance evoked wonder. They asked where her talent came from, and how she could dance with such beautiful grace and poise. They saw God's beauty through the art of dance, and it moved them to wonder and motivated them to ask. It was the Spirit of Jesus in the public square.

May God enable us, through the arts, to engage our parish in new ways, in the pulpit and in the public square. And by his grace, may he renew the whole parish.

For Further Exploration

1. Jerram Barrs. *Echoes of Eden: Reflections on Christianity, Literature, and the Arts.* Wheaton, IL: Crossway, 2013.

2. Michael J. Bauer. *Arts Ministry: Nurturing the Creative Life of God's People.* Grand Rapids: Eerdmans, 2013.

3. Andy Crouch. *Culture Making: Recovering Our Creative Calling.* Downers Grove, IL: InterVarsity, 2013.

4. Francis A. Schaeffer. *Art and the Bible.* Downers Grove, IL: InterVarsity, 2009.

5. W. David O. Taylor. *For the Beauty of the Church: Casting a Vision for the Arts.* Grand Rapids: Baker, 2010.

6. Steve Turner. *Imagine: A Vision for Christians in the Arts.* Downers Grove, IL: InterVarsity, 2016.

Engaging the Arts Parish
Interview

BRYN GILLETTE IS A painter and art teacher defined by his identity as an "ambassador of Jesus Christ, a husband, and a father." He finished seven years as a full-time art, photography, and Bible teacher at Trinity-Pawling School in 2017, and has recently moved with his wife and four children to North Carolina to become the high school art teacher at Charlotte Christian School.

Bryn is particularly excited that his children will now attend the same school that he works at and that their tribe can adventure through life together each day. He is the cofounder of TeamOne:27, a nonprofit dedicated to serving the needs of Haitian orphans and has spent much of his artistic time as an advocate and champion of the needs of Haiti. The unique blend of Bryn's Spirit-filled posture, realistic and abstracted painting style, articulate speaking, and remarkably fast live painting process have made his work highly sought out by church communities, private collectors, and organizations. For more information visit www.bryngillete.com.

> Q. Can you describe your church experiences as an artist?
>
> I love the church. I love what God is doing in his people. From my end, I think it's been helpful as an artist in a church community to see its brokenness, and be gracious, and not take things personally. I think my posture is really important in how I interact with the church. My church was fantastic. I think some of the healthiest things were that they really respected me as an artist and as a believer in the body. They valued the gifts that I was bringing, and they saw their merit. They gave space for me to use them and make

mistakes with them, but it was a safe place to grow and learn. We had a 24/7 prayer ministry, so a lot of my work was birthed from the connection between the pastoral leadership ministry and the worship ministries; as a congregant, as someone who was not on staff, in a very strangely healthy place to bring my work.

So almost fifteen years ago, Dr. Reverend Clive Calver, former president of World Relief, asked me to join him onstage, and I did to paint whatever the Spirit would do—typical for more charismatic churches, but I had never seen that or been a part of that—and for the next twelve years got to do that on a very regular basis, and learn and grow. There were hiccups along the way, but in general it was kind of like a magical, beautiful, Spirit-filled unfolding of me being one part of the body. I think as I left my ego at the door, that's where I think a lot of artists make the mistake—and not be doing it for my name or advantage, but as a service, as one part of the body. As we co-submitted to one another, there was amazing teaching, amazing prayer, and amazing worship, and I got to just bring my gifting into that. That's where it really flourished, and I flourished.

Q. How can a pastor encourage artists within the church?

I think it helps to think about the left and the right brain. Very often church leadership is coming from a linear, left-brain thinking. Neither one is better or worse than the other; they're just different. I think just having that kind of emotional intelligence, that social intelligence, where artists are very often right-brain thinkers. They are creative, intuitive, and holistic; they think from the gut. . . .you can almost see the setting up of gasoline and fire, of where people can misinterpret people's motives, and rub each other the wrong way. I think also that when anyone brings a gift into the body of Christ, there's a real danger that artists can quickly begin to feel used—to serve a utilitarian purpose—even in music arts. It serves the body that way, but it can also very much kind of squelch the creativity within an artist, or their capacity of artistry when it gets streamlined or becomes utilitarian. The answer to that, I think, is letting artists be different, and being okay with that, and having boundaries.

Q. As an artist, what would you want to see from your pastor's engagement with you or with other artists from the community?

The idea of God's kingdom was never to make the whole world an ongoing church service, and have every employee on earth be a full-time minister within the church. It's a subtle undertone, but to truly give your life to Christ would mean to work in full-time ministry and either go into full-time church work or mission work. And thankfully, I think that's being dismantled in this era. But I think a lot of what artists just really need is for a pastor to come alongside them. Ephesians 4 really talks about, that the purpose of the apostles, and the prophets and evangelists, pastors and teachers is to equip and empower everyone, including the artist, to do their work in the kingdom, connected to the body, knowing God's word, deeply in relationship with Jesus Christ, and fed by the Holy Spirit, but doing so out in their spheres of influence.

I think it would be so helpful for the church, and those who lead the church, to see the sphere of the arts as distinct and even separate. What the kingdom of God is going to look like in the sphere of arts is not the same as it's going to be within the church—and that's intended by Christ. The intention is not to make the art world full of Christian art, or art that might even be in the church, but actually full of kingdom-hearted artists, that are, as Makoto Fujimura says in *Culture Care*, becoming the agents of creating healthy culture and beauty and transformation in our cultural estuaries. So I think artists should be given the respect and space, that the pastors really acknowledge their value separate from their utilitarian services to the church, and really doing the work of understanding how they could be equipped and empowered to walk their faith maturely, and do their craft excellently.

Q. How can a pastor best engage both the congregation and the community in the arts?

There are little things like, show up at the galleries, go to the receptions, go to the performances, in the outside world of the congregants and the people associated with the church. It would be wonderful to have those natural bridges. Artists really do have such inroads to wildly different subcultures than those that typically darken the door of a church. It's kind of an easy, natural way for people to connect with culture.

7

Engaging the Multiethnic Parish

Kenneth Liu

> "It really boils down to this: that all life is interrelated. We are all caught in an inescapable network of mutuality, tied into a single garment of destiny. Whatever affects one directly, affects all indirectly."
>
> —Martin Luther King Jr.

Several years ago, a parishioner emailed me and expressed her distress concerning racial injustice and how a particular incident in her neighborhood brought this issue closer to home. As a black woman, she grieved how alone she felt being in a predominantly Asian American congregation, where racial issues concerning black lives were rarely mentioned in the pulpit or discussed as a community.

As I reread her email a few times, I was overcome with sadness and grief for the daily fears and anxieties she has for herself and her children. I also lamented the fact that she felt so alone and had no one to turn to in our community. I was saddened that our community gave very little space to lament together and have substantive conversations about the deep divides in our nation.

The reality is that many churches have not had a great track record in engaging issues related to racial justice and reconciliation. The impulse is to avoid the issue, succumb to defensiveness, or withdraw in helplessness. However, we are in a time in history where ignoring this pressing issue is no longer an option. Rather than remain in a state of helplessness and disengagement, how do we begin to understand these issues, let alone take steps in our journey to minister in our complex and ever-changing world?

Theologian Karl Barth is purported to have said, "A preacher needs a newspaper in one hand and a Bible in the other." In other words, preachers should not only be adept in exegeting the Scriptures but also exegeting the world we inhabit. Not only do we need to be familiar with the narrative of Scripture, but the collective narrative of the parish in which we minister to.

Whether or not there is overt racial strife happening in your community, it is happening somewhere, and it is only a matter of time before people in your church are going to want their pastor to weigh in on these matters. Something or someone is out there discipling and shaping our thinking on race and culture, and you probably don't want Fox News or MSNBC to be the ones who shape your parish.

Depending on your context, talking about themes of race and culture is impossible to avoid. For other contexts, there are many land mines to navigate through when the topic is broached. Our silence on these matters, however, speaks volumes as well. How do we speak pastorally and prophetically in such a time as this, especially in contexts where these issues tend to be avoided? Though we may spend many hours in our study exegeting the text for our sermons on Sunday, are we taking the time to exegete our parish and the context and social location we are presently living in? As pastors seeking to impact the public square, how do we face these complexities with sensitivity, courage, and leadership?

Exegeting the Ever-Changing, Diversifying Parish

My church, the Boston Chinese Evangelical Church, meets in two locations. One of the locations sits on the edge of Chinatown and the South End of Boston. One day after finishing a staff meeting, I decided to walk towards the South End to grab some coffee.

On the way, I spot an elderly Chinese woman walking by with a cart of bottles and cans. To my right, there's a bustling low- to moderate-income apartment complex built in the 1960s where residents are made up of Chinese and other immigrant groups.

After a few blocks, I am surprised to find an abandoned building that used to be a Syrian restaurant. Later, I learned that there was a significant Syrian population in the late 1800s who were primarily Christian. At that time, Boston had the second-largest Syrian population in the US. There was also another wave of Syrian immigrants in the 1960s. Many were urban, educated professionals, and mostly Muslim.[1] As I continued down the street, there is a neighborhood called Villa Victoria, which is a vibrant, historically Puerto Rican neighborhood.

As I approach what I thought was a pastry shop where I could get coffee, I quickly realize it was a little boutique for dog biscuits and other high-end pet supplies. Eventually, I found a café, grabbed my coffee, and headed back to the church. On the way back, it was hard not to notice the large construction cranes constructing the latest high-rise luxury condo.

My short walk to grab coffee became a mini education on the many shifts and changes that have happened in our neighborhood. Our neighborhood is a microcosm of the changes and shifts that are happening in many of our neighborhoods and communities. In fact, many of our assumptions regarding the "inner city" and suburbs are increasingly outdated. Suburbs, once assumed to be racially and financially homogenous, are diversifying at a rapid rate, while urban centers are gentrifying and becoming wealthier and whiter. Urban areas, which used to be the gateway for new immigrants, are being bypassed for the suburbs. For example, recent Chinese immigrants are less likely to start off in Boston's Chinatown, but more likely to settle in surrounding suburbs like Quincy and Malden, which have large concentrations of Chinese.

According to demographer William Frey, there is a migration reversal as a recognizable segment of black people have entered into the middle class. The Great Migration out of the South has shifted out of the North and back to prosperous southern suburbs. Black people are abandoning cities for the suburbs, and black neighborhood segregation continues to decline. Frey states, "Although many blacks still suffer the effects of inequality, along with uneven treatment by the criminal justice system, and segregation is far from gone, the economic and residential environments for blacks have improved well beyond the highly discriminatory, ghettoized life that most experienced for much of the twentieth century."[2]

---

1. "Syrian, Lebanese," *Global Boston*, para. 4.
2. Frey, *Diversity Explosion*.

Our nation is also shifting to a time where no racial group is the majority. By 2040, it has been projected that no one racial or ethnic group will be the majority.[3] At the time of this writing, minorities will be the majority of America's schoolchildren.[4] In addition, the white population as well as its birthrate is in decline. We have reached a momentous shift in the history of our nation's racial demographic makeup.

Not only have our demographics shifted, but so has the role of Christianity in our country. While the West has become increasingly secular, the rest of the world is becoming more religious. The center of Christianity has shifted from the West to the Global South. A century ago, 80 percent of Christians lived in North America and Europe, compared to 40 percent today. In that same time period, Christians grew from less than 10 percent of Africa's population to 20 percent. The Pew Research Center projects that percentage will increase to 40 percent by 2030. In Latin America, where Catholicism has long dominated the religious landscape, the growth of Pentecostalism is estimated to be at three times the rate of Catholic growth.[5]

Christianity has also shifted to the East. In the last one hundred years, Christianity has grown at twice the rate of the population in Asia. But by 2025, demographers predict that Asia is projected to grow to 460 million Christians.[6] Much of the growth is found in China, where both registered and unregistered churches exceed more than 100 million.[7] Already there are more church attenders in China than in the United States.[8] We need to pay attention to these tremendous global shifts, especially as the center of Christianity shifts away from the West.

All this is to say the Global South and East have been coming to the United States, and they are bringing their faith with them. The process of migration typically increases religiosity. Those who don't have faith often become open to faith. Many who immigrate are already Christian or become Christian when they reach the United States. As sociologist Stephen Warner noted, "The new immigrants represent not the

---

3. Yoshinaga, "Babies," para. 8.
4. Yoshinaga, "Babies," para. 7.
5. Granberg-Michaelson, "Think Christianity?" para. 7.
6. Granberg-Michaelson, "Think Christianity?," para. 7.
7. Johnson, "Christianity in Asia," para. 7.
8. Granberg-Michaelson, "Think Christianity?," para. 5.

de-Christianization of American society but the de-Europeanization of American Christianity."[9]

Case in point, I am a child of immigrants. My parents came from Taiwan because of political oppression in the 1970s to study in graduate school in Lawrence, Kansas, where I was born. At the time, my mother was already a Christian. In fact, her great grandfather was the first Christian in the family through the influence of Canadian Presbyterian missionaries in the late 1800s. My father grew up in a nominal Buddhist family, but through the influence of a Taiwanese immigrant church, he also became a Christian. I received a call into ministry and became a Presbyterian minister serving in immigrant and multiethnic contexts.

This shift is seen in many of our cities. Much has been made in some circles that New England is a spiritual wasteland and the least churched region of the United States. While churches overall are in decline, this is primarily among white mainline churches. The Emmanuel Gospel Center in Boston has documented a huge surge of new churches over the past forty years that has been named the "Quiet Revival."[10] It is so named because it's a revival that no one seems to notice due to the fact that most of the churches are immigrant non-English speaking and multiethnic churches.

For some, the change and shifts that are happening in our nation are welcome and exciting. Yet for others, the change is threatening and filled with uncertainty. With increased diversity comes greater misunderstanding and potential for conflict. As a nation, we are also haunted by a history of racial injustice and racial trauma, with wounds that are yet to be healed. It is always challenging to fully understand and comprehend all these complex realities while we are in the midst of them. But how should we think and feel in light of the larger story of Scripture?

Exegeting the Word

In Martin Luther King Jr.'s Christmas sermon on peace, he states:

> It really boils down to this: that all life is interrelated. We are all caught in an inescapable network of mutuality, tied into a single garment of destiny. Whatever affects one directly, affects all indirectly. We are made to live together because of the interrelated structure of reality. Did you ever stop to think that you

---

9. Warner, "Immigrants," para. 3.
10. Daman, "Quiet Revival?"

can't leave for your job in the morning without being dependent on most of the world? You get up in the morning and go to the bathroom and reach over for the sponge, and that's handed to you by a Pacific islander. You reach for a bar of soap, and that's given to you at the hands of a Frenchman. And then you go into the kitchen to drink your coffee for the morning, and that's poured into your cup by a South American. And maybe you want tea: that's poured into your cup by a Chinese. Or maybe you're desirous of having cocoa for breakfast, and that's poured into your cup by a West African. And then you reach over for your toast, and that's given to you at the hands of an English-speaking farmer, not to mention the baker. And before you finish eating breakfast in the morning, you've depended on more than half of the world. This is the way our universe is structured; this is its interrelated quality. We aren't going to have peace on earth until we recognize this basic fact of the interrelated structure of all reality.[11]

King's words ring true in the most fundamental ways we live our lives. The interconnectedness of our world is not an accident, but part of God's design from the very beginning.

Throughout Genesis 1–2, we see God making distinctions, whether it's between night and day, light and darkness, land and sea, animals and humans. God declared all of this good! When God created humans as image-bearers, God created humanity male and female. As image-bearers, we reflect the interdependence of our triune God. By design, we are both different and interdependent.[12] Differences and distinctions were meant to be good, but for all of life to flourish, interdependence is needed. When God put the tree of the knowledge of good and evil in the garden, God made yet another distinction.

"You are free to eat from any tree in the garden; but you must not eat from the tree of the knowledge of good and evil, for when you eat from it you will certainly die" (Gen 2:16). This one command highlights perhaps the most important distinction of all. Although we certainly bear God's image, we are not God. There is a distinction between Creator and creation that must be honored for all of life to work.

However, the distinction between Creator and creation became blurred when humanity believed the lie of the serpent, "For God knows that when you eat from it your eyes will be opened, and you will be like

11. Gilliss, "Martin Luther Kings's," para. 11.
12. Cho, "Why Race."

God..." By eating from the tree of the knowledge of good and evil, not only did humanity attempt to blur the distinction between Creator and creation by wanting to be like God, but it also broke the design of interdependence. Rather than be content as image bearers and co-creators, humanity sought to supplant God. Behind the action is the attitude, "I don't need you." It was humanity declaring, "I can run my life better than you and I can do it without you." It was a declaration of independence from God.

All the divisions we see, whether along racial or cultural lines, can be traced back to Genesis 3. Every impulse to divide and conquer is rooted in the attitude, "I don't need you!" This is where radical individualism and racial superiority find their source. How will people regain their humanity again?

Thankfully God doesn't sit idly by, but from the beginning has been orchestrating our rescue through a promise. When we look at the life of Abram, God instructed him to migrate in Genesis 12:1–2:

> Go from your country, your people and your father's household to the land I will show you. I will make you into a great nation, and I will bless you; I will make your name great, and you will be a blessing. I will bless those who bless you, and whoever curses you I will curse; and all peoples on earth will be blessed through you.

Much of the promise consists of a recovery of what was lost in Eden. The creation mandate in Genesis 1:26–28 consists of a blessing, specifically focused on the seed and the land, and the dominion of them. Fast forward to Abram, and we see that the promise consists of blessing, seed, and land. In addition, the promises contain a multiethnic future where all nations will be blessed through him.

The rest of the Old Testament is a story of the people of God in a continuous search for refuge, rest, and a place to call home. Migration is a central theme where sojourners, refugees, and perpetual foreigners are normative experiences for the people of God. It is a constant state of in-betweens where places that appear to be the final destination are actually just pit stops along the way.

Ultimately, that promise culminates with God migrating from heaven to earth to become a human being just like you and me. Through Jesus' life, God shows us how to be human again. Jesus shows us the life we were meant to live—a life of love and justice. Jesus also dies the death we deserved to die. Through his bodily death and resurrection, Jesus triumphs over sin and death, so that our relationship with God can be made right again. Through the cross, not only are we able to be forgiven, but given the ability to forgive others. Jesus not only restores us to God, but also to each other. The call to love our enemies seems unfathomable unless Jesus did it and gives us the power to do so same.

But living out this new reality wasn't without difficulty. As the Corinthian church was struggling with how to coexist with each other, the apostle Paul used the metaphor of a body to describe who we are to be in Christ:

> Just as a body, though one, has many parts, but all its many parts form one body, so it is with Christ. For we were all baptized by one Spirit so as to form one body—whether Jews or Gentiles, slave or free—and we were all given the one Spirit to drink. Even so the body is not made up of one part but of many. (1 Cor 12:12–14)

Paul makes the case that though we are many parts, we are one body through Christ. We may be different, but we have the same need. And that need can only be met through one person, Jesus Christ. In our baptism, we make a *declaration of dependence*. Jesus brings us you back to God and back to each other to form one body. When Paul mentions Jews or Gentiles, slave or free, he is mentioning the most divided people groups of that day. In our context, who would those people be? Black and white perhaps? Republican and Democrat? Rich and poor? Young and old? These are all identity markers that we use to define ourselves and define others. Some are inherent in us and some are categories we choose for ourselves. Nevertheless, no matter how different we are, there is only one person that powerfully brings us together and unites us. Our baptism in Christ is now our primary identity marker. It doesn't eradicate difference, but it highlights our common need for the only one who can save.

Ultimately, Paul is trying to make the point that it's impossible not to be part of the body if you are a Christian. In life, you can choose friends and lovers, but you can't choose family. People who are different from you are now brothers and sisters whether you like them or not.

This isn't by accident, but by design. If we go against the design and distance yourself from others, you're losing a vital part of what it means to be human. You lose out on the ability to truly see and hear. But it's precisely the differences and diversity within the body that enable us to see God and the gospel from different angles and perspectives. Missiologist Allen Yeh comments: "Nobody has the full picture of God, and though every perspective might be true, each is incomplete in and of itself, and every cultural perspective is needed to fully understand this global God."[13]

As Paul says later in verse 18, this is how God has arranged members of the body. He places people in our lives to show us a different dimension of himself and it's often in ways you'd never expect. Often times it may be uncomfortable! But these are the ways God works in community.

If this is how God arranged the body, then it should change our attitude towards those who are different from us. Let's take a look at vv. 21–26: "The eye cannot say to the hand, 'I don't need you!' And the head cannot say to the feet, 'I don't need you!' On the contrary, those parts of the body that seem to be weaker are indispensable . . ."

If indeed it is true that by design we are created differently, but interdependently, then there needs to be a shift in perspective. Rather than saying, "I don't need you!" we need to shift our thinking to, "I need you more than I realize." Who do we need in our lives? Paul points to the part of the body that "seem to be weaker" and calls them indispensable. Those who at first glance seem like they have nothing to offer, we especially need to listen to because we need their voices more than we realize.

Our parishes are ever-changing and diversifying. We no longer need to travel across borders to experience this. Rather than flee or fight this reality, we are to welcome it. Throughout the Old Testament, Israel was commanded to love the stranger and foreigner among them with the reminder that they too were once strangers and foreigners in Egypt (Deut 10:19). Spiritually, we are all sojourners, aliens, and perpetual foreigners looking and longing for a better world. Hopefully as the body of Christ, we can give the world a glimpse of what it looks like to be a community that values interdependent difference. As we better understand the backstory of our parishes, and what the story of Scripture calls us to be as Christ's body, how do we practically live this out?

From Exegesis to Engagement

Listen

When it comes to engaging our ever-changing and multiethnic world, listening is crucial, especially if you are prone to tune other voices out. If you are part of majority culture, then this is of critical importance. The

---

13. Yeh, *Polycentric Missiology*, 43.

Epistle of James is especially relevant here: "Be quick to listen, slow to speak, slow to become angry . . ."

Listening may seem passive and impractical, but in reality it is both an action and a posture of humility. It's especially important to lean on the voices from the margins. This means going out of your comfort zone to listen and learn from those who are different from you.

Practically speaking, what is on your bookshelf? If you listen to podcasts, who are the people on your playlist? Are they pastors, theologians, and thinkers exclusively from your own theological tribe? Are they only from a Eurocentric and North American point of view? Are they exclusively male? Do you read widely from other perspectives, including persons of color? We are all culturally conditioned and situated persons, so we all approach the text with our own presuppositions, assumptions, and blinders. That is why we need a diversity of perspectives to shed light on the whole gospel.

Bryan Stevenson is a Harvard educated public interest lawyer who established the Equal Justice Initiative (EJI) in Montgomery, Alabama. He grew up in the African Methodist Episcopal tradition, which informed his belief that "each person in our society is more than the worst thing they've ever done." One of the most formative moments in his life was when his grandmother told him, "You can't understand most of the important things from a distance, Bryan. You have to get close."[14] While doing an internship with the Southern Center for Human Rights during law school, Stevenson was tasked to visit an inmate on death row. With no experience working with incarcerated people, he was nervous and did not expect the conversation to last particularly long. It lasted three hours. Little did he know that drawing close would change the trajectory of his life and calling. His life's work at the EJI is to "provide legal representation to people who have been illegally convicted, unfairly sentenced, or abused in state jails and prisons."

Stevenson has dedicated his life to challenging bias against the poor and minorities in the criminal justice system. Stevenson has heard the cries of injustice from our youngest and most vulnerable. Rather than acquiescing to the prevailing attitude of "I don't need you" and seeing people as dispensable enough to be thrown away to die in prison, Stevenson has put his life on the line for the sake of the poor and the oppressed. His life calling began by following his grandmother's advice to get close.

---

14. Stevenson, *Just Mercy*, 14.

In the same way, we cannot fully understand others without first getting "proximate" to others.

What does "getting proximate" to others involve? Gordon Allport is credited with the development of the contact hypothesis. He points out that putting different people together in the same space doesn't change anything unless there's an environment that fosters mutuality, positive interaction, and understanding. He observed that prejudice is a direct result of generalizations and oversimplifications made about an entire group of people based on incomplete or mistaken information. Until you have sustained interactions with people who are different from you and you are in an environment where mutuality is expected and lived into, perceptions and prejudices won't change.

Although diversifying your reading and listening queue is a good start, it is important to seek out flesh and blood relationships that are mutual. As pastors, we are often in the mode of leading. If we want to be led, we usually look to those who have certain platforms or reputations. We like to hear from pastors with the largest churches or those who have planted dozens of churches.

Why not seek out leaders you've never heard of and learn from them? I truly believe when we are in heaven, the heroes of the faith we will hear about will be women and men we've never heard about. They will be women and men who have never shared a conference platform or written a book. They are the people of God serving in obscurity, but not unnoticed by our Lord Jesus Christ. If you are serious about engaging cross-culturally, there are no shortcuts. It will take time to listen and have sustained interactions with others different from you, in order for change to happen. It may mean seeking mentors, coaches, and cohorts who can help you unlearn assumptions and presuppositions you may have and learn from their experiences navigating through dominant culture. Those in the margins have firsthand experience of what it means to be sojourners, exiles, and foreigners in this world. They are living examples that vibrant faith is possible without cultural power, privilege, and position. That is why I think Paul states that those parts of the body that seem weak are indispensable. Paul wants us to see the "weak" differently. We need them more than we think. Our notion of "success" needs to change.

In order to minister effectively in our ever-changing and diversifying world, churches need to be intentional about raising up leaders who are culturally competent. This subject cannot be merely an elective, but a required part of our training. One of the most uncomfortable, yet formative courses I ever took in seminary was "Christianity and the Problem of Racism." The lectures covered many parts of American history I never learned growing up. Just as impactful were our roundtable discussions with my diverse classmates. Stories were told, assumptions challenged, and tears shed. It was an eye-opening experience to hear firsthand the suffering of my black brothers and sisters. Not only did I have to confront my own biases and racism, but I also had to address unhealed wounds in my own life growing up in a predominantly white neighborhood with very few minorities. I owe a great deal to this class for opening my eyes and starting me on a lifelong journey towards justice.

Another practical step is to attend and serve in cross-cultural settings. If you are white, why not attend an ethnic church for a season and sit under the leadership and authority of a person of color? If you are a person of color, why not attend or serve in a context different from yours? If you are already in full-time ministry where it's hard to visit other churches, whenever you have a free Sunday to worship somewhere else, have you considered looking for a church to attend that is different from your own in its makeup and culture? If you have a sabbatical, rather than visit the fastest growing church plant or megachurch in town, why not visit the storefront church with no website? If you can't visit on a Sunday, why not make a cold call and get to know other pastors in your community outside of your tribe?

Most importantly, are you getting to know those in your community, especially those who are the most vulnerable or even invisible? Rather than just hanging out at the local café to get a pulse of your community, are you getting to know those who frequent your local food pantry?

Out of anyone in the world, followers of Jesus should be the ones who see the invisible and dispensable in our society. Who are the people in your community that you need to see with new eyes? Who are voices who have been silenced that you need to listen to?

Learn (and Unlearn)

Not only do we need to listen to the voices of the marginalized in their everyday experiences, we also need to reexamine American history and consider the lens of the marginalized. We often have a very romanticized understanding of the origins of America. For some of us, we might have the perspective that America was founded established on Christian foundations. While there may be merit to this assertion, there are other realities that complicate America's legacy. Much of America's prosperity came through the systematic genocide of Native Americans as well as the forced migration and enslavement of Africans.

Some of us may esteem theological and spiritual giants like Jonathan Edwards and George Whitefield and their role in the Great Awakening. But do we conveniently ignore the fact that both were advocates for slavery and owned slaves themselves? Edwards is known for spending thirteen hours a day in his study theologizing. That was only made possible because of the slaves he owned to assist his wife Sarah.[15] How did Jonathan Edwards, arguably the greatest American theologian, become complicit in such systemic evil? Does this mean all his theological and pastoral contributions ought to be dismissed? Is it possible to hold to his theology but at the same time ask questions relevant to the African American experience?[16] It's not within the scope of this chapter to answer this question, but it should cause us to pause to ask ourselves, "If a spiritual giant like Jonathan Edwards can have egregious blind spots, what about the rest of us?" We need to be self-aware enough to admit that we all are susceptible to blindness, especially in matters related to race.

It's important to keep in perspective that slavery as an institution ended only six generations ago. Jim Crow ended approximately three generations ago, which means those who are in their seventies are the last generation raised under Jim Crow. It's naïve at best or willfully ignorant at worst to assert that African Americans "get over it" because "slavery was a long time ago." The reality is that slavery and "separate but equal" are all rooted in some sort of doctrine or belief. It's rooted in the satanic doctrine of racial superiority, specifically white supremacy. Although slavery is technically abolished, the undergirding ideology still exists and has morphed into different expressions that are not as overt or obvious. The fact that this ideology and doctrine is hidden and subtle doesn't make it any less harmful to people of color. As the old adage goes, "The greatest trick the devil ever pulled was convincing the world he didn't exist." If this is so, then the best way for white supremacy to stay intact yet impactful is to keep it underground.

For example, the wealth gap between white and black people is well-documented. The great migration of black people to Northern cities to

---

15. Meyer, "Jonathan Edwards," para. 14–16.
16. Anyabwile, "Jonathan Edwards."

escape oppression from the South produced another migration known as white flight. Bryan Stevenson once asked, "What if Northern cities and churches had seen this as an opportunity to offer hospitality to refugees?" Instead, the migration was seen as a threat and many white people "escaped" to the suburbs. The government practice of "redlining" designated certain regions as "undesirable" and concentrated the wealth in white neighborhoods. Homeownership then and now is the most significant means of intergenerational wealth-building in the United States. These redlining practices from eight decades ago had long-term consequences in widening the wealth gap that still exist to this day.

Jesse Curtis connects the dots between white flight and the rise of the megachurch movement. He notes: "At the height of the Church Growth Movement's influence, John Perkins blasted the evangelical mainstream for not bothering with breaking down racial barriers, since that would only distract us from 'church growth.' And so, the most segregated, racist institution in America, the evangelical church, racks up the numbers, declaring itself 'successful,' oblivious to the . . . dismemberment of the Body of Christ . . ."[17]

There are other ways in which the ideology of racial superiority permeates our systems and structures. In 1882, Congress passed the Chinese Exclusion Act, which restricted immigration of Chinese laborers and prohibited Chinese naturalization. The Act was in response to the threat of cheap labor from China and marked the birth of "illegal immigration." Later, Congress passed the Immigration Act of 1924, otherwise known as the Johnson-Reed Act, which banned Asians while prioritizing immigrants from northern and western Europe to "preserve the idea of American homogeneity."

My wife's great-great-grandfather came to the America from China at the end of the eighteenth century and eventually settled in Boston. As a result of these immigration laws, he could not bring the rest of his family to the United States. After working hard and supporting his family back home by repairing fishing nets and opening up a laundry in Boston, he died without being able to reunite his family in America. It wasn't until 1965 when Congress passed the Immigration and Nationality Act, which repealed the discriminatory immigration policies of 1924. This enabled the rest of my wife's family to immigrate to the United States, almost eighty years after her great-great-grandfather.

---

17. Curtis, "What Has Happened?," para. 17.

It is important to note that the civil rights movement played a major role in this repeal. "Preserving American homogeneity" is yet another expression of racial superiority that shaped immigration policies. Just as the civil rights movement sought to eliminate discriminatory attitudes and practices targeting African Americans, the Immigration Act of 1965 sought to eliminate racial quotas targeting those who were not seen as "American" enough.[18]

There are so many other examples in history that we may need to revisit or learn for the first time. In order to minister effectively in our ever-changing world, we need to reckon with our past and its continuing consequences. We need to continue to be lifelong learners and exegetes of the world we now inhabit, no matter how long you have called America your home.

Lament

As we take time to learn the stories of those in the margins, whether in history or in present time, it may be overwhelming. Feelings of anger, outrage, and despair might consume us. There's a temptation to run from it, but keep in mind that some do not have the luxury to do this. It's a daily reality they cannot escape. Another temptation is to try to fix it and attempt to be the hero. But rather than dismiss our feelings or offer superficial solutions, we as the North American church need to recover the biblical and liturgical practice of lament. The apostle Paul reminds us that, "If one part suffers, then every part suffers with it."

Unfortunately, the church has very little tolerance for melancholy, especially in worship. When was the last time you heard a sermon series in the book of Lamentations? Or an exposition on Psalm 88? The songs of lament put into words and give us vocabulary to express our deepest grief and longings. When we cannot utter words to express the dark night of our soul, lament validates our experiences. Practically, do your worship leaders, liturgists, or pastors mention in their prayers, reflections, and sermons the injustices that are occurring in your community and nation?

Although it is an incredible challenge to know what national events to mention or not on a given Sunday, it is important to prioritize the most vulnerable and invisible in our society, whether or not they are presently in your church. If they are in your worship service, your acknowledgement

---

18. Barber, "Civil Rights," para. 2–9.

is a signal to them that the church cares for people beyond themselves. Even a simple mention in prayer can provide a sense of solidarity that they are not alone.

As I reflect upon my parishioner's letter mentioned in the introduction, I wonder what difference it would have made in her experience in our church if we had taken time in our services to acknowledge and lament the deaths of Trayvon Martin, Michael Brown, and many others? What if we took time to address the specifics of these injustices in our sermons? What if we acknowledged the very real fears that many of our black brothers and sisters experience daily? If one part of the body suffers, shouldn't we also suffer with it? To do so is not political, it's biblical.

In your season of listening and learning about our community, perhaps you may have come across some unpleasant realities that have been buried in the history books. The church building that housed the Taiwanese immigrant church that I grew up in was an old historic Dutch Reformed Church that we rented from. There was a water fountain in the back stairwell that was rumored to be for "colored people." Later, I learned that there were deep connections between the Dutch Reformed Church and the slave trade. Even one of the pastors of the church, just six years before the Civil War, was still arguing on behalf of slavery as a biblical and permanent institution. This was not a sermon to his congregation, but in an address to the denomination's General Synod meeting.[19]

Many denominations and seminaries are coming to grips with their racist past. If the churches we serve have a long history, it's probably helpful to dig into the archives. Even if your church has a shorter history, it would still be instructive to understand how your church dealt with different social issues of their time. For example, how did your community respond during different waves of migration and immigration in your region? Did your community respond with hospitality by welcoming the stranger and foreigner among you? If a refugee population was resettled in your community, did your church engage, ignore, or even resist? Did your town or city participate in redlining in an effort to keep certain people groups out? You can find out through an online project called "Mapping Inequality,"[20] which details which areas in your region were deemed safe versus risky investments based on who was "infiltrating" your neighborhood.

---

19. Bruggink and Baker, *By Grace*, 101.
20. https://dsl.richmond.edu.

What we discover about our parishes may not be pleasant. But rather than bury history, it's important that we bring to the surface and face it as a community. It is biblical to lament and repent for not only your own sin, but the sins of our forefathers. This often goes against the ethos of American individualism, where we are only responsible for our own lives. The biblical practice of communal repentance reminds us that everything is interrelated and connected. To publicly acknowledge sins of commission and omission goes a long way towards healing. It's a proclamation that truth does matter. True healing cannot happen without truth telling.

Beyond worship services, churches need to integrate the work of truth telling and reconciliation as part of our discipleship. Thankfully there are currently more resources dedicated to helping churches work towards a more just future. One of many examples is the Repentance Project, which "exists to encourage racial healing by communicating the systemic legacies of slavery, building relationships, and creating opportunities—through formation, repentance, and repair—for a just future."[21] One of their resources is "an American Lent," which is a Lenten devotional that journeys through America's history of slavery, segregation, and racism. The aim is to guide individuals and groups into the dark valley of our nation's history into the hope of resurrection.

There may be organizations or ministries in your community that are already engaging on issues of racial injustice and equality. Rather than reinvent the wheel, why not join in on what God is already doing in your community? During the COVID-19 pandemic, many ministries moved online, which opened many new learning opportunities on race and culture in the form of online webinars, cohorts, and events. Even if there are no opportunities in your parish, there are certainly resources online that engage with these issues.

Lead

As you take time to listen, learn, and lament, at some point, you'll need to lead others to do the same. Change is slow and gradual, but it requires intentionality, resilience, and hope. Every context is different, but each has its own backstory to engage.

What you do during worship says a lot about your church's priorities and values. As noted earlier, create space in your prayers and worship for

---

21. https://repentanceproject.org/.

lament. Work with your worship leaders and musicians to make space for songs of lament. If you have a pastoral prayer or prayers of the people in your liturgy, make sure you are mindful of the vulnerable and invisible in your community. What and who you pray for speaks volumes on what your church cares about. Take time to evaluate who is up on stage. Those who are up front should represent the makeup of your community.

If there's not much diversity on your staff or in your community, then consider a pulpit exchange. A friend of mine invited me to preach at his church in rural Vermont as part of his "Community, Culture, and Civility" sermon series. It was the first time my family and I had ever set foot in Vermont, and it was the first time someone of Asian descent ever preached in his church. It was an eye-opening experience to listen and learn from rural, small-town America, and many of my misconceptions and stereotypes were challenged. I trust my family's presence did the same for others.

Perhaps the greatest challenge beyond your public worship practices is what happens behind the scenes in leadership. Every church has a particular culture that has become normative. That normativity may be stifling to other cultures. That is why it is important to be intentional in who you are discipling and raising up in leadership. You need the diversity of the body of Christ to be represented on your leadership team. Though it does not guarantee that your team won't have blind spots, the lack of diversity will almost guarantee that there will be.

Another indicator of your church's priorities is your operating budget. If there is commitment towards racial reconciliation and justice, is this reflected in your budget? Raising up minority leaders is an investment of time and money. Recruiting, training, and educating future leaders may be costly, but worth your investment. Budget planning might involve absorbing costs for the sake of another. You might live in a context where there is an influx of immigrant groups looking for a place to worship. Maybe there's a kingdom opportunity for your church to establish for a season a Bible study group or a new church plant for little or no cost. What if your space was like a greenhouse that allows for different immigrant groups to get their start? What if all the groups came together a few times a year to eat, celebrate, and worship together?

In the fight for racial justice, the church's public witness is also vital. Bringing churches together to show unity and solidarity is a start. Some local churches in Chicagoland organized a march, "Asian American Christians for Black Lives and Dignity," in response to the murder of

George Floyd. The march began at the Chinese Union Christian Church, a historic 105-year-old Chinese American church, and ended at Progressive Baptist Church, a historic 101-year-old African American Church. Along the way, there were different leaders of both the African American and Asian American communities offering prayers, songs, Scripture, and exhortation. Although the march was a powerful expression of unity and solidarity between two communities, the organizer, Ray Chang, acknowledged that the work is just beginning. He reflected: "The Asian American Christians for Black Lives and Dignity March was just one small step on the pathway towards racial justice and discipling followers of Jesus to embrace the whole counsel of God in their lives."[22]

Engaging our ever-changing, multiethnic, and multi-everything world is not easy. In fact, it's quite costly. This is not the fast track towards church growth. Including people who are different from you will slow things down as you to take the time to listen and truly empathize. That is why it goes without saying that Jesus has to be at the center of it all. The work of reconciliation and justice needs to be undergirded with the strength, resilience, and hope that can only come through the finished work of Christ. It is for Christ's sake that we attempt to live here on earth what will be so in heaven.

May the God of our multicolored kingdom grant us the faith, hope, and love we need to carry out his purposes here on earth as it is in heaven.

For Further Exploration

1. M. Daniel Carroll R. *Christians at the Border: Immigration, the Church, and the Bible*. Grand Rapids: Brazos, 2013.

2. William Frey. *Diversity Explosion: How Racial Demographics are Reshaping America*. Rev. and expanded ed. Washington, DC: Brookings Institution, 2018.

3. David P. Leong. *Race and Place: How Urban Geography Shapes the Journey to Reconciliation*. Downers Grove, IL: InterVarsity, 2017.

4. Soong-Chan Rah. *The Next Evangelicalism: Freeing the Church from Western Cultural Captivity*. Downers Grove, IL: InterVarsity, 2009.

---

22. Chang, "Asian American Christians," para. 16.

5. Sarah Shin. *Beyond Colorblind: Redeeming Our Ethnic Journey.* Downers Grove, IL: InterVarsity, 2017.

6. Bryan Stevenson. *Just Mercy: A Story of Justice and Reconciliation.* New York: Spiegel and Grau, 2014.

Engaging the Multiethnic Parish
Interview

REV. DEVLIN SCOTT MARRIED in June of 2009. Devlin and Katie started their lives together with the goal of serving God together. They met at Trinity International University, where Devlin was pursuing a bachelor of arts in communication and biblical studies and Katie was pursuing a bachelor of arts in English/communication. The day they had to work together on a school project interviewing one another sparked an interest in one another's stories that would forever link their stories together. Devlin went on to earn a master of divinity from Trinity Evangelical Divinity School and a master of arts in bioethics from Trinity Graduate School.

In 2012, God began to stir their hearts towards planting a church. They faithfully served and learned as staff pastors at Northwest Assembly of God in Mt. Prospect, Illinois for seven years, accepting increasing responsibilities and deepening a passion for the local church to serve God and the community.

On March 9, 2016, God confirmed his call to Devlin and Katie to plant a church and it was clear that the place they should start this church was in Newton, Massachusetts.

> **Q. Did you grow up in the church? If so, did your church play a role in shaping your understanding of race and culture?**
>
> I grew up in the Missionary Baptist Church tradition, which is predominantly black. I was born in Mississippi but raised in the suburbs of Chicago. My church shaped my understanding of being black. Blackness was affirmed and celebrated through worship, traditions, and life together. Since I grew up in a black neighborhood,

I wasn't exposed to different races and cultures until college and graduate school.

Q. Should all churches be ethnically diverse? Are there ever exceptions? In other words, what is the place of black, Asian, and Hispanic churches in God's kingdom?

If there is diversity in your community, I think all churches should try to reflect the makeup of their community. However, there is a place for ethnic churches, especially for first-generation immigrants whose first language is not English. Reaching the second and third generations, however, is a bit more complicated. Often, I've seen the second generation struggle between the world of their family and faith and the world of majority culture. There's an association that gets created between the faith and culture they grew up with, and often faith is the first casualty when trying to assimilate to "mainstream" white culture.

Contextualizing to the second and third generations will be critical. Where resources are slim, it might mean partnering with other youth ministries that can help youth make faith their own. But the challenge is to see how the gospel intersects with every aspect of their lives, including their own ethnicity and culture. The gospel doesn't eradicate culture, nor does it idolize it. Ideally, immigrant churches can reach both the first and second generations and are contextualized for both cultures.

There's also a place for churches to keep traditions and distinctions, recognizing they are a gift to the larger body of Christ. A good example of this in our community is Myrtle Baptist Church. In the 1880s there was a large influx of African Americans in Newton, many of them freed slaves and descendants feeling racial terror in the South after the Civil War. The neighborhood was called the "village," and the church was at the center of community life, providing a refuge for the African American community for generations. To this day, it is unapologetically black in its traditions and distinctions. But they are always trying to make their message accessible and intelligible. Every church needs a focus. But you can be focused and not exclusive.

Q. If a church wanted to be ethnically diverse, what should they be thinking about and what initial steps should they take?

It really depends on your context. In my city, there are already perceptions of what your church is like and it's hard to change that. Many assume already that your church might not be for them. That's not always in your control.

But you can shape the culture of your congregation. Since Sunday is the main gathering point, it's important to create an ethos that everyone is welcome to bring their experiences to the table. Are you making room for others to express themselves in worship that is uniquely them? We don't want to make certain forms prescriptive. But can we cultivate a culture where people are free to express themselves freely or not? Can there be freedom to be both celebratory and contemplative? We can all learn from each other. A little discomfort enables us to understand each other better and even appreciate what others bring to the table.

Not only does this apply to worship, but leadership as well. Are we inviting those with a different perspective and voice to the table? There's nothing more damaging than inviting POC to the table, but not trusting their instincts and insight.

8

A Passionate Plea for New Parish Ministry

Jason R. McConnell

> *"I look upon all the world as my parish..."*
>
> —JOHN WESLEY

WHEN MY CHURCH WAS in the process of planning a special service to honor and pray for our county legislators, an unconventional idea emerged in my mind. I called the office of former Vermont governor James H. Douglas (2002–2010) and invited him to come and share a testimony about how his Christian faith influenced his work in politics. Since he was serving as executive in residence at Middlebury College at the time, I expected to speak with an administrative assistant or leave a message on his voice mail. I was shocked when the Governor answered his own telephone and offered the humble greeting, "Good morning, Jim Douglas speaking!"

After stuttering over my first few words, I introduced myself and explained why I thought his personal testimony would be crucial to the success of our service. Not only would his presence guarantee attendance from our legislators, but he could encourage our church community from the unique perspective of a former governor. Even though I knew it was presumptuous (perhaps even provocative) to invite such a high-profile politician to speak at our little country church, I reckoned that the potential rewards outweighed the risks.

When I finally got up the courage to ask the governor if he would be willing to speak at our church, I heard a long silence on the other end of the line. As I braced myself for the rhetoric of rejection, he responded, "Jason, I'm intrigued by the idea, but as I sit here contemplating it, I'm honestly not sure how much my faith has influenced my politics." I did not anticipate my request striking such a nerve in the governor's soul. To minimize the momentary awkwardness, I quickly reframed the question and asked, "Well, could you come and speak about the importance of legislative work and inspire our county legislators? I can address the spiritual matters in my sermon." He uttered a sigh of relief and said, "I think I could do that! Let me check the date with my wife and I'll get back to you in a few days."

The governor not only confirmed the date, but by the time he arrived for the service, he had done some soul searching. He stepped into the pulpit and delivered a winsome speech about the importance of legislative work. But I was astonished when he unveiled how his faith had, in fact, influenced his work as a legislator and governor. During his testimony, he confessed that he had never really considered the impact his faith had on his politics, but after my request forced him to think about it, he realized how much his faith had, in fact, informed his legislative policies, ethical decisions, and the manner in which he dealt with people who didn't share his perspective.

Governor Douglas's address was nothing less than inspirational! Instead of reciting some canned political stump speech, he proclaimed a powerful message of faith that encouraged our legislators and blessed our whole church community. His testimony was the perfect setup for my sermon from 1 Timothy 2:1–7, titled "Of Prayer and Politics," and the climactic moment in the service came when our church leaders laid hands on all of the legislators and prayed for the Lord to guide their work at the statehouse. The entire service stirred everyone who attended: our church and community members, the legislators, and the governor himself.

After the service, my wife and I went to brunch with Governor Douglas and his wife. While we sipped coffee and savored eggs Benedict, we broke all the rules of civil etiquette—we talked about the taboo topics of politics and religion (and we did it without arguing). Amid a conversation filled with mutual respect and jovial laughter, the governor leaned in toward me and said, "Thank you for the opportunity to speak at your church today! You know, in almost forty years of public service, this was the first time anyone has ever invited me to church!"

Since that moment, I've spent significant time contemplating the gravitas of the governor's comment. Throughout his career, he had received countless invitations to speak at events ranging from political press conferences to military deployments, business grand openings, graduation ceremonies, medical meetings, and art exhibits, but he had never been invited to attend church, let alone speak at a church function. The church was one of the only institutions in the state that had never actively engaged the governor.

This fact caused me to ask a series of perplexing questions: Why hadn't anyone ever invited the governor to church? Do pastors consider their governor and other civic officials as a part of their parish? How about people from other sectors of the public square? What is the scope of this separation between pastoral and public life—why does it exist—and what can be done about it?

My conversation with the governor made me realize that pastors and other leaders in the public square are often like two ships passing in the night: they sail through the same waters, but they don't even know the other is there. Many people in the public square recognize the steeple, the cross, and the clerical collar as religious symbols, but they have no idea what actually happens inside the church. They drive by churches on their way to work every day, but they are unaware of the gospel's relevance for their lives. Likewise, many pastors are so focused on their work in the church that they become oblivious to the institutions and organizations in the community around them. Unfortunately, pastors tend to limit their parish to the people who affiliate with their particular church rather than the countless souls who constitute the broader community.

Reluctance to Engage the Public Square

There are many reasons why pastors are reluctant to engage the public square. Let me survey a few of the most significant ones. The first (and perhaps most important) reason is an anemic ecclesiology. By this, I mean a weak theology of the church that is inwardly fixated rather than outwardly focused—where the goal is to maintain the organization rather than fulfill the Great Commission to make disciples of Jesus Christ. Some pastors get so caught up in the inertia of preserving church programs that they have no energy or imagination for missional ministry in the broader parish outside the church. When pastors concentrate all of their efforts on the church, the membership is shaped by a ministry model that unintentionally diminishes the gospel in the public square. Even if internal church programs are thriving, the church may be isolated from its own community and have no gospel influence beyond its own walls.

Furthermore, some churches fall into the trap of a consumer ecclesiology, which reduces the role of the pastor to a parochial people-pleaser. In this pattern, the pastor functions as a "professional minister" who is hired to perform various ministries, and the church members become passive patrons rather than true disciples. Churches like this become so insular that they cannot envision ministry beyond themselves, especially if the pastor caves to this internal pressure rather than helping the congregation stay focused on the external mission.

Unfortunately, some pastors are particularly vulnerable to this pattern. The emotional codependence that forms from constantly fixing other people's problems feeds pastors' egos, and it establishes an unhealthy habit where pastors end up bearing the burden of most, if not all, of the ministries in the church. This pattern is contrary to the New Testament vision of pastors equipping church members to do the works of ministry (Eph 4:11–13) and being Jesus' witnesses to the ends of the earth (Acts 1:8). Anemic ecclesiology leads to an ineffective church.

The second reason pastors are reluctant to return to the parish is the all-consuming nature of church work. Even in churches that have a healthy ecclesiology, I have yet to meet a pastor who didn't feel busy. In addition to the pressure of preparing a weekly sermon and praying for the congregation, pastors have the constant responsibility of casting vision, training leaders, managing programs, attending committee meetings, counseling the discouraged, visiting the sick, and burying the dead. Most of these tasks are open-ended, which means they are never fully accomplished. More time can always be spent in prayer, sermon preparation, and pastoral visitation.

Moreover, most pastors are on call around the clock. They take crisis calls in the middle of the night and must conform their schedules to the needs of their congregation. If there aren't enough hours in the day for pastors to fulfill their core duties, how can they ever find time to engage the public square? Perhaps the pastor's role and expectations need to be redefined. Maybe churches could consider delegating ministry responsibilities to other members and freeing up more time for their pastors to pursue ministry in the public square.

A third reason pastors are reluctant to return to the parish is the fear of secular associations and spiritually contaminating influences. Some pastors and churches have embraced a sharp sacred/secular distinction and are thus suspicious of "worldly influences" that might pollute the purity of the church. The Christian church is called to uphold the highest standards of doctrinal purity and moral integrity, but it is hardy expected to cloister itself from the community and culture it inhabits. The monastic and fundamentalist movements have done the church a serious disservice by misapplying passages like 2 Corinthians 6:14-17:

> Do not be yoked together with unbelievers. For what do righteousness and wickedness have in common? Or what fellowship can light have with darkness? What harmony is there between Christ and Belial? What does a believer have in common with an unbeliever? What agreement is there between the temple of God and idols? For we are the temple of the living God. As God has said: "I will live with them and walk among them, and I will be their God, and they will be my people." "Therefore come out from them and be separate, says the Lord. Touch no unclean thing, and I will receive you."

While churches need to be wary of corrupting influences in the culture (which was certainly the case in Corinth), Paul does not advocate a wholesale withdrawal from the community. God desires Christians to be separate in character, not necessarily in association. Christians should be mindful of differences with unbelievers in worldview, spiritual values, and ethical conduct, but these differences should not impede the development of meaningful relationships or preclude all forms of partnership. After all, Jesus ate with "tax collectors and sinners" (Luke 15:1-2) and Paul proclaimed: "To the weak I became weak, to win the weak. I have become all things to all men so that by all possible means I might save some. I do all this for the sake of the gospel, that I may share in its blessings" (1 Cor 9:22-23). If Christians isolate themselves from the community and retreat from relationships with unbelievers, it will be impossible for them to fulfill the church's Great Commission. If it is approached winsomely, there is plenty of common ground to pursue the common good together.

A fourth reason pastors exhibit a reluctance to return to the parish is their lack of intellectual confidence to initiate a dialogue with leaders in the public square. Even though many pastors are well educated, they often feel intimidated by authorities outside their areas of expertise. Unless pastors have a liberal arts background or personal experience with a particular sector of the public square, they typically lack the necessary knowledge to engage in meaningful discourse.

In seminary, pastors receive training in biblical studies, systematic theology, church history, and homiletics, and all of these disciplines are essential for effective pastoral ministry. But since seminaries are often detached from larger universities, the theological curriculum doesn't provide the opportunities to inform or be informed by other disciplines, such as the sciences and humanities. This form of specialized education produces pastors with strong exegetical and leadership skills, but they have neither been equipped nor encouraged to contextualize their theology to public square issues that affect their local communities. Pastors may be able to parse Greek verbs and recite the latest church growth methodology, but they have seldom thought deeply about a theological framework for education reform or how the gospel should shape American economic systems, scientific research, technological advances, healthcare practices, artistic expression, and immigration policies.

This compartmentalized education has been a particular weakness in American evangelical circles. Notre Dame historian Mark Noll, in his landmark book *The Scandal of the Evangelical Mind*, offers a sobering indictment of the evangelical church's lack of intellectual engagement with the public square. Unlike its European and mainline counterparts, American evangelical institutions have focused on perpetuating their own perspectives rather than thoughtfully interacting with ideas from the so-called "secular" world. Noll counts the cost for the church and the public square:

> The price is a loss of first-level cross-fertilization between theological reflection in the arts and sciences . . . The existence of separate institutional structures preserves autonomy and may be safe socially. What is lost, however, is an ideal of Christian intellectual life in which theologians, biblical scholars, and scholars from other disciplines work in constant connection with each other. In such an ideal, scholars in Scripture would provide the others with the fruits of their labor in Bible study and theology. The others would offer biblical scholars interpretations of modern learning and creative ventures in applying the results of their labors to Christian teaching. Both together would reflect

on the foundational commitments and philosophical presuppositions that shape inquiry in every field of thought.[1]

When these intellectual ideals are neglected, pastors and leaders in the public square miss out on opportunities to learn from one another. Pastors end up feeling uninformed, ill-equipped, and ultimately too intimidated to initiate a conversation with other leaders. And this lack of engagement causes leaders in the public square to believe that the church has nothing to offer them. If pastors and business CEOs, scientists, healthcare professionals, civic officials, school superintendents, artists, and leaders from multiethnic networks all communicated and worked in conjunction with one another, the whole community would benefit from the fruits of their labor.

It is important for pastors to remember that many leaders in the public square display a similar timidity when conversing with a pastor. For someone who doesn't have theological education or a religious background, pastors can be daunting figures. But if pastors, in a spirit of humility and respect, are willing to initiate a conversation or relationship with a leader in the public square, the sentiment is usually reciprocated.

There are probably other reasons why pastors are reluctant to engage the public square, but these are some of the most obvious ones. Unfortunately, these have diminished the pastor's role in the community and curtailed the church's influence in the culture. If pastors continue to be paralyzed by an anemic ecclesiology, the all-consuming nature of church work, a fear of secular influences, and a lack of intellectual confidence, the Christian church will continue to be marginalized in American public life, and this lack of credibility will make it more difficult to fulfill the Great Commission. When pastors retreat from the public square, it has a negative impact on the church and the culture. But if pastors return to the parish and mobilize church members to do the same, the church and culture have a greater hope of flourishing together.

A New Parish Perspective: A Theology of the Pastor in the Public Square

Just as there are multiple reasons why pastors are reluctant to engage the public square, there are some theological imperatives that compel pastors to overcome their timidity and embrace a new parish perspective of

1. Noll, *Scandal*, 19–20.

ministry. The days of Reverend Manasseh Cutler, where the pastor was the most educated and esteemed member of the community, are surely gone. Over the past three hundred years, American culture has shifted so much that pastors will most likely never recover the once prestigious status they possessed in Puritan society. The parish is no longer defined by legal charters or strict geographical boundaries, but pastors and local churches still bear the responsibility to be Jesus' witnesses to the unsaved souls in their villages, towns, and cities. Many of these souls live and work in the public square.

A new parish perspective calls pastors to a ministry of presence and participation in the public square. But this new parish perspective isn't actually new; it is, in fact, quite old. It is embedded in the theological imperatives of the New Testament. For the scope of this chapter, let me focus on three: the incarnation imperative, the gospel imperative, and the credibility imperative.

Jesus' incarnation provides a theological imperative for the new parish perspective of ministry. Jesus Christ, the Son of God and the second person of the Holy Trinity, could have remained secluded in the unpolluted perfection of heaven, but instead he chose to take on the limitations of human flesh and live among a violent and vengeful people here on earth. He gave up the glory of golden streets and the ceaseless sounds of angel voices for a life of rejection and suffering, which culminated in his crucifixion. But he was willing to endure this darkness and death because he knew it would lead to redemption and the light of life. The apostle John famously testifies to this light that came into the world:

> In him was life, and that life was the light of men. The light shines in the darkness, but the darkness has not understood it . . . The true light that gives light to every man was coming into the world. He was in the world, and though the world was made through him, the world did not recognize him. He came to that which was his own, but his own did not receive him. Yet to all who received him, to those who believed in his name, he gave the right to become children of God—children born not of natural descent, nor of human decision or a husband's will, but born of God. The Word became flesh and made his dwelling among us. We have seen his glory, the glory of the One and Only, who came from the Father, full of grace and truth. (John 1:4–5; 9–14)

The doctrine of the incarnation establishes the pattern for new parish ministry—a ministry where pastors extend their presence beyond the safety of the church and the comfort of the Christian subculture by "taking on flesh" in the local community. The incarnation calls pastors to adjust their ecclesiological priorities and be present with nonbelievers on their turf, whether it be the chamber of commerce, science lab, hospital floor, statehouse, elementary school, art gallery, or a different ethnic neighborhood. The incarnation summons pastors to shine light into dark places and initiate relationships with people who don't share their Christian values. The incarnation implores pastors to face their fear of secular influences and overcome their lack of intellectual confidence. The incarnation entreats pastors to endure some degree of rejection and suffering from the very people they are trying to serve. The incarnation compels pastors to adopt a new parish perspective by becoming the hands and feet of Jesus in the public square and shining the light of Christ for people who would otherwise continue to walk in darkness.

In addition to the incarnational imperative, the gospel itself provides another theological imperative for the new parish perspective. The gospel can be simply defined as the good news that even though sin has separated humanity from God, God offers salvation through repentance and faith in the death and resurrection of his Son Jesus Christ. In Romans 1:16–17, the apostle Paul says:

> I am not ashamed of the gospel, because it is the power of God for the salvation of everyone who believes: first for the Jew, then for the Gentile. For in the gospel a righteousness from God is revealed, a righteousness that is by faith from first to last, just as it is written: 'The righteous will live by faith.'

Paul's definition of the gospel contains the imperative that this power of God for salvation must be made known to both Jews and Gentiles. It implies an outward looking mission that would surely include proclaiming the gospel beyond cultural comforts and social preferences. After all, Paul referred to himself as "the apostle to the Gentiles" (Rom 11:13) and he spent most of his adult life spreading the gospel throughout the Mediterranean world, which included various sectors of the public square: religious establishments (Acts 13:13–52), healthcare centers (Acts 14:8–18), business districts (Acts 16:11–15), prison facilities (Acts 16:16–34), intellectual organizations (Acts 17:16–34), art guilds (Acts

19:23–41), judicial assemblies (Acts 24–25) and political institutions (Acts 25:13–26:32).

How did the apostle to the Gentiles define his parish? It was certainly not restricted to any of the local churches he founded, but extended to the outside world where people had never heard the gospel of Jesus Christ. Paul was willing to engage any sector of the public square for the sake of the gospel. He embraced a new parish perspective that exemplified the Great Commission in Acts 1:8, when the resurrected Christ said to the apostles: "But you will receive power when the Holy Spirit comes on you; and you will be my witnesses in Jerusalem, and in all Judea and Samaria, and to the ends of the earth."

As one of the clearest instantiations of the church's gospel mission in the whole Bible, this mission was to begin in Jerusalem and then branch out into all of Judea and Samaria and eventually extend to all locations and peoples on earth. Judea was the region surrounding and encompassing Jerusalem. Samaria was the region to the north of Judea. This verse shows a strategic plan for the expansion of the church through witnessing about Jesus' death and resurrection. The gospel imperative implicit in the Great Commission prompts pastors to adopt a new parish perspective by engaging the public square.

As Jesus modeled a new parish perspective for ministry through his incarnation and the apostle Paul exemplified it through his commitment to fulfilling the Great Commission by preaching the gospel in various sectors of the public square, there is also a credibility imperative that undergirds the theological foundation of a new parish perspective. The apostle Paul knew that personal credibility was crucial for spreading the gospel. He understood that the believability of the message hinged on the trustworthiness of the messenger. In his final instructions to the church in Colossae, Paul admonished them to "Be wise in the way you act toward outsiders; make the most of every opportunity. Let your conversation be always full of grace, seasoned with salt, so that you may know how to answer everyone" (Col 4:5–6).

Paul knew that wise actions toward outsiders (nonbelievers) was essential for advancing the mission of the church. He understood that personal credibility directly impacts how a person receives the gospel message. He didn't want the church to be afraid of outsiders or be isolated from them. To the contrary, he wanted them to make the most of every opportunity to be good witnesses by earning credibility and cultivating authentic relationships. It is impossible to gain true credibility apart from a personal relationship, but the relationship must be built on trust, which requires strong character and high competence. This is why Paul emphasizes the importance of conversations that are filled with grace (character) and seasoned with salt (competence).

The credibility imperative is also expressed in Paul's words to Timothy about the qualifications for leadership in the church. In 1 Timothy 3:7, he said of the church elder, "He must also have a good reputation with outsiders, so that he will not fall into disgrace and into the devil's trap." If a church leader does not have a good reputation with unbelievers in the community, the church's gospel mission will be compromised.

If Paul thought the credibility imperative was important for ministry in a pre-Christian society (where most people had never heard about Jesus Christ or his gospel), how much more important is this principle in a post-Christian culture (where everyone has heard about Jesus and the gospel message carries baggage from the hypocrisy of Christians)? Here is where a new parish perspective can facilitate reestablishing credibility for the gospel. If pastors consistently practice what they preach—that is, maintain moral conduct, ethical practices, graceful speech, a peaceful presence, and faithful service—and if they do it in the public square, the gospel gains credibility in the whole culture. The New Testament imperatives of incarnation, gospel, and credibility should persuade pastors to look beyond their local churches and engage the public square.

A Practical Paradigm for New Parish Ministry

Now that we have considered some reasons why pastors may be reluctant to accept a new parish perspective of ministry and some theological imperatives that should persuade them otherwise, let us press on to the practice of new parish ministry. The previous chapters of this book have already explored how pastors can specifically engage the business, science, government, healthcare, education, arts, and multiethnic sectors of the public square. I do not want to rehearse those insights here. Rather, I would like to offer a broader paradigm for implementing new parish ministry. This simple paradigm emphasizes three increasing levels of pastoral engagement with the public square: presence, participation, and leadership.

Level 1– Presence in the Public Square

At some point in their career, most pastors learn about the importance of the ministry of presence. Whether it is forged during their seminary training or formed by some tragic event in the life of a church member, pastors eventually realize that a significant part of pastoral ministry is simply showing up. The ministry of presence means being there for someone, especially at critical times in a person's life. It implies moving in close to listen, laying down defensiveness and agendas, and lending an empathic ear and (on some occasions) an encouraging voice.

As a pastor myself, I believe in the power of presence, especially when people are feeling discouraged or disenfranchised. I have witnessed how a peaceful pastoral presence can reduce the anxiety in a room and provide a sense of hope in a seemingly hopeless situation. On many occasions, I have watched how a shepherd's presence can be a guiding light for people walking through the valley of the shadow of death. Although it is common for pastors to offer the ministry of presence during hospital visits, funeral services, and other difficult times, I've never heard a pastor or theologian suggest the ministry of presence with people in the public square.

A new parish paradigm of pastoral ministry recognizes the need for a ministry of presence in the public square. When pastors go out of their way to befriend business leaders, scientists, or artists in their community, they form personal relationships that could lead to a profound ministry of presence. If pastors would take time to build relationships with their local politicians, school superintendents, and leaders from the multiethnic community, they could earn enough credibility to be called on during times of personal or community crises. The ministry of presence begets opportunities for more presence. But where there is no presence, there is no relationship. Where there is no relationship, there is no ministry. And where there is no ministry, the gospel of Jesus Christ does not advance.

Therefore, a new parish perspective challenges pastors to establish a ministry of presence in the public square. This can be done in a multitude of ways. It can be as simple as inviting the mayor out for coffee, attending an art exhibit, or going to a school board meeting. A pastor could also take a local legislator or business leader to lunch and spend time getting to know each other on a professional and personal level. If the circumstances are conducive, a pastor's family could host multiethnic leaders and their families for a meal in their home. Regardless of the form, it is critical for pastors to reach beyond their own church members and form a ministry of presence and personal relationship with people in the public square.

Level 2– Participation in the Public Square

The second level of pastoral engagement in a new parish paradigm is participation in the public square. This level presents a greater opportunity for relational impact than mere presence, but it also requires a deeper commitment. It entails joining an organization, dedicating substantial time and energy, and consistently serving a cause. In the business sector, a pastor could become a member of the local business bureau or chamber of commerce. In the healthcare sector, a pastor could volunteer as a hospital chaplain or a hospice counselor. In the political sector, a pastor could become a regular contributor at legislative gatherings or lead prayers for the congressional assembly at the statehouse. In the education sector, a pastor could join the Parent Teacher Association or volunteer to coach a sport. Every sector of the public square offers a variety of ways for pastors to participate.

Throughout my tenure as a pastor, I have volunteered as a coach for the elementary school ski program. I became a certified emergency medical technician and assisted the local ambulance service. I joined the community restorative justice center and (among other things) participated in a program to help prisoners successfully reintegrate back into the community after they served their sentences. I was also elected to the regional school board, where I served as chairman and led multiple superintendent and principal search committees.

As I participated in each of these organizations and institutions, I met interesting people and formed wonderful friendships. I also learned about my local community and culture, earned credibility, solved problems, and gained countless opportunities to share the gospel of Jesus Christ, which may have never been heard otherwise. Over the years, many people I have met in the public square have repeated this refrain to me: "You are the only pastor I know." Though my participation in the public square, these people became a part of my parish, and in a sense, I became their pastor.

Level 3– Leadership in the Public Square

The third level of pastoral engagement in a new parish paradigm is assuming a leadership position in the public square. This level magnifies presence and participation, and it provides the pastor an opportunity to mobilize a group of people to achieve a common goal for the common good. Consequently, this level carries a higher ratio of risk and reward. On the risk side, a leadership position in the public square involves tremendous time and energy, which may make it difficult for pastors to fulfill their primary role of leading the church.

Leadership positions are also risky because they can be divisive; they sometimes demand decisions that affect people negatively, which could actually diminish a pastor's credibility in the church and community. When I served as chairman of the school board, I led labor contract negotiations that affected people in my church and community. This delicate dance demanded wisdom and discretion. If a pastor senses a call to a leadership position in the public square, he or she must be aware of the potential risks and do their best to minimize them.

On the reward end, leadership roles in the public square offer the pastor unparalleled visibility in the community. When a pastor serves well in a public leadership role, it builds a positive image of the Christian faith in general and pastoral ministry in particular. Leadership positions also create wider networks of relationships and new opportunities for churches to partner with other organizations in the public square.

Throughout church history, there are a number of positive examples of pastors assuming leadership positions in the public square. In the medieval church, St. Gregory the Great (540–604) spent his career with one foot in the church and the other foot in politics. He was well educated and possessed immense administrative acumen. He worked his way through the political ranks until he became the prefect (mayor) of Rome at the age of thirty. Among other things, his responsibilities included the supervision of local officials, food distribution, maintenance of the city infrastructure, as well as being the head of the military.

But Gregory could not resist the divine call of pastoral ministry. He left the position of the prefect and converted his family's villa in the Caelian Hill to the Monastery of St. Andrew, where he assumed the life of prayer and service as a monk. As Pope Pelagius became aware of Gregory's leadership abilities, he commissioned Gregory to be his papal ambassador in the important but turbulent city of Constantinople.

Gregory's pastoral and political roles eventually collided when he was elected pope in 590. For fourteen years until his death, he led the church through the pastoral practices of preaching sermons, quelling heresy, and developing worship music (Gregorian chant) and the political practices of administration, negotiation, and military protection. He was a "great" leader who ministered to the spiritual and physical needs of the people of Rome and beyond. Throughout his life, Gregory's parish continued to expand as a result of his leadership in the public square.[2]

Likewise, Abraham Kuyper (1837–1920) was able to walk the tightrope of pastoral ministry and public service successfully. After completing his theological studies, he accepted a call in 1863 to become a pastor in the Dutch Reformed Church. As his theology and ministry developed, he saw less and less distinction between sacred and secular pursuits. As he worked to reform the Dutch Reformed Church, he became interested in politics and was elected to parliament. He founded the Free University of Amsterdam and was made professor of theology there. He was eventually elected as the prime minister of the Netherlands and served in that prestigious role from 1901 to 1905. Michael R. Wagenman, in his book *Engaging the World with Abraham Kuyper*, offers this assessment of Kuyper's concern for and leadership in the public square:

> Abraham Kuyper was a pastor, journalist, theologian, institution founder, church reformer, and cultural critic. His peers regarded him as a theological genius. But it was his sustained concern for ordinary Christians and their public witness that animated his prodigious life ... Kuyper believed two things about the church. First, the church has a God given role to play in the civic marketplace of cultural institutions. And, second, this role cannot be carried out faithfully if the church retreats into the private sphere and develops a defensive posture against the world or accepts the sacred-secular dualism and engaged in a restricted ministry of only saving souls for heaven.[3]

Kuyper is a fine example of someone who regarded that the rewards outweighed the risks of pastors taking on leadership roles in the public square. His famous quote, "There is not a square inch in the whole domain of our human existence over which Christ, who is Sovereign over

---

2. Carole Straw provides an excellent introduction to Gregory the Great's life and thinking, with particular attention to his transitions between pastoral ministry and politics. See Straw, *Gregory the Great*, 1–27.

3. Wagenman, *Engaging the World*, 2.

all, does not cry, Mine!" is the perfect motto for a new parish perspective for pastoral ministry.

In modern times, Dr. Martin Luther King Jr. (1929–1968) is a clear and compelling exemplar of a pastor simultaneously shepherding a church and using a leadership position in the public square to promote the common good. King, who was born into a family of preachers, decided to enter the "family business" when he was just eighteen years old. He served as co-pastor while he carried on his mission of racial and social justice. He preached the wholistic gospel of Jesus Christ from pulpits inside the church, a prison cell in the Birmingham jail, and on the steps of the Lincoln Memorial in Washington, DC. It cost King his life, but he considered every oppressed person a part of his parish. He was a pastor who was willing assume the risks of a leadership position in the public square to achieve the reward of a better world.

Most pastors who aspire to leadership roles in the public square will never achieve the high-profile status of Gregory the Great, Abraham Kuyper, or Martin Luther King Jr. These are exceptional examples of how God used a few pastors to impact the world in profound ways. But when pastors implement a new parish perspective by daring to step into leadership roles in the public square, they have the opportunity to promote the gospel of Jesus Christ and the common good not only in their local communities but nationally and perhaps internationally.

Conclusion

As we plead with pastors to return to the parish by engaging the public square, we recognize that individual pastors have different leadership capacities and life circumstances that will determine their level of commitment to pastoral ministry in the public square. We wouldn't want any pastor to attempt engaging all of these sectors of the public square simultaneously. That would be a sure setup for pastoral burnout. Likewise, it would be foolish for pastors to sacrifice their families or churches on the altar of the public square. The pastor's stage of life, tenure at the church, leadership capacity, and personal interests should all factor into the decision to determine which sector of the public square and what level of pastoral engagement should be pursued. Although young pastors with a quiver full of children may not be able to provide the same level of leadership in the public square as empty nest pastors who have served their church for twenty years, they could volunteer at their children's elementary school or become a Little League coach.

Therefore, we recommend starting at level one by initiating the ministry of presence in a sector of the public square that captures the pastor's imagination. As pastors settle into the life of their church and community, they can consider expanding their pastoral presence into other areas of the public square or focusing on a higher level of participation or leadership in one specific sector of the public square.

If pastors return to the parish—that is, if they adopt the new parish perspective and the paradigm for pastoral ministry early in their careers—they will have decades to engage the public square for the sake of the gospel and the common good. And when new parish pastors come to the end of their lives, and their fellow community members read their obituary in the newspaper, may they join the Lord Jesus Christ by echoing the words, "Well done, good and faithful servant!"

Allow me to conclude by sharing an excerpt from the obituary of the Reverend Dr. Arthur L. Hilson of Portsmouth, New Hampshire. Listen to the legacy of this new parish pastor par excellence:

> The Reverend Dr. Arthur L. Hilson, 82, husband of Florine Hilson, of Portsmouth, entered the gates of heaven on Saturday, January 19, 2019. He was a loving brother, husband, father, pastor, friend, leader, teacher and mentor to many.
>
> Rev. Hilson was an educator at heart who had an unwavering faith in God. Pastor of New Hope Baptist Church for 28 years and a teacher and administrator for 40 years including University of Massachusetts—Amherst (Administrator, retiring 1991), the University of NH—Durham NH (Administrator & Adjunct Professor 1991–1995) and was the Associate Pastor at Bethlehem Community Baptist Church in Holyoke, MA (1979–1991). He loved to educate people on the word of God and the legacy of Africans in America. Over the last 18 years he became one of the most beloved teachers at Portsmouth High School and a sought-after educator all over the state.
>
> Not only was he an educator but he was a leader for his country and community. Arthur retired from the Navy in 1973 after 20 years of service. While in the state of NH he served on many boards in the community including: NH Commissioner of Human Rights, President American Baptist Churches of Vermont and New Hampshire, Advisory Board Aids Response Seacoast, Ethics Board Portsmouth Regional Hospital, Piscataqua Community Foundation's Diversity Advisory Committee,

Board of Directors Community Child Care Center, Board of Directors Portsmouth Rotary, Board American Bible Society, Portsmouth School Board, President NE Southern Christian Leadership Conference (SCLC), and President National Association for the Advancement of Colored People (Amherst, MA). He also served on the Portsmouth Police Commission; was a volunteer Chaplain at the Portsmouth Regional Hospital, served on the Board of Directors American Veterans Committee, was Chairman Board of Directors American Association Minority Veterans Programs Administrators, and Board of Directors National Association Veterans Program Administrators.

Recognition for his community involvement included the New Hampshire "Martin Luther King Award", the Ambassador of Peace Award, Seacoast MLK Coalition's "Citizen of The Year Award", Portsmouth Branch NAACP "Community Leader for Civil Rights", and the Congressional Black Caucus Special Recognition Award for Leadership.

For his many accomplishments Dr. Hilson is listed in "Who's Who Among African Americans," and "Who's Who Among American Educators."

When Arthur was not leading the masses, he enjoyed going to the movies with family, watching old westerns, adding to and enjoying his extensive collections of books and music, and playing a round of golf with friends and family.

Even the most ambitious pastors will rarely reach the level of leadership that Dr. Hilson achieved in a single sector of the public square, but if every pastor exhibited even a fraction of his presence in their own parishes, maybe the Christian church would eventually regain credibility in its local community and beyond. And maybe individual Christians would become the "salt of the earth" and "light of the world" (Matt 5:13–16) that Jesus hoped they would be. And parishioners inside and outside the church will see their good deeds and praise their Father in heaven.

Epilogue
The Making of Pastoral Learning Communities

David Horn and Jason McConnell

CERTAIN WORDS ARE PREGNANT with meaning. The word *kinship* is one of them. Puncture the tenor around this winsome little word and out flows a host of synonyms that head generally in the same direction, but branch out into multiple shades of meaning, words like *affinity, alliance, empathy, closeness, fellow-feeling, association, togetherness, similarity, agreement, sympathy,* and *harmony,* to name just a few. As an afterthought, the essential nature of this word, with all its meaning, is what we want to leave you with.

It is amazing what can be seen through the rearview mirror of a car. The landscape that has already passed us by most often reveals the greatest insights: signposts that offer direction after they have been passed in a blur, evidence of nature and commerce left behind us as they continue life after we hurl by, the world of the smallest events in our lives from the past that somehow gain new and deeper meaning upon further reflection.

Such has been the case in the writing of this book. We thought this book was about Christian community as we have attempted to describe it "out there" in our congregations and local communities. But, upon further reflection—in hindsight—we found in its making, that this book had as much to do with the community that has formed "in us," with the kinship that now wonderfully marks each of the eight of us who have lived and worked together for these past three years. Writing a multiauthor book has its challenges, but it has its delights as well. We didn't want this opportunity to pass without offering you some of what we took away in the process.

It took us three years and two one-week writing retreats to complete our writing task. Although we already knew one another on a surface level, our time together among the White Mountains of North Conway, New Hampshire, and a year later along the Atlantic seacoast in Gloucester, Massachusetts, was transformative in so many ways. Of course, central to each retreat and our communication in between, was the hard work of conceptualizing the tone and content of the book, writing and critiquing our chapters together, and editing our manuscript.

But something else happened during those times that was deeply moving for each of us as we communicated with one another, and in our retreats as we cooked meals together, sat around the table and ate and laughed together, shared personal and ministry concerns (some of them heartbreaking), and prayed together. In addition, on our two planned recreation days, we snowshoed Tuckerman's Ravine on a late winter bluebird morning and sea kayaked the Essex Sound on a brisk but beautiful autumn afternoon. In the midst of God's marvelous masterpiece, these experiences nurtured our souls and exercised our imaginations. Through it all, we became "kinsmen," fellow pastors who experienced something deep and abiding amongst ourselves that, upon further reflection, is the very thing we wish to pass on to our peers.

For those of you who are pastors, it this vision of kinship and community that we want to leave you with, in part because we feel that this commodity of the soul is so sorely lacking, certainly in the general population, but uniquely within the pastorate. By "unique," do we mean that it is exclusive only to this profession? Probably not. But there is plenty of evidence throughout the landscape of ministry that pastors live very parched, lonely lives.

A recent survey of one thousand pastors conducted by Lifeway Research suggests that, paradoxically, although 98 percent agree with the statement, "I feel privileged to be a pastor," with 93 percent strongly agreeing, more than half (55 percent) also agree with the statement, "I find that it is easy to get discouraged," and that pastoral ministry makes them feel lonely.[1] How can this be? How is it a profession that is admittedly so purposeful and that is entered into with such great delight, end up in a lifestyle of discouragement and loneliness? Is there something

---

1. Lifeway Research, "Pastors feel Privileged," para. 3–4.

in the structural drinking water of being a pastor that leads to such an anomaly?

Built into the warp and woof of the pastorate are at least three tendencies that seem to arise: the tyranny of place, time, and task. First, the tyranny of place. Both of us remember with fondness the moment we walked out of our places of formal theological education and headed into our first pastorates. For three and four years—while naïve visions of sugar plum pastorates were dancing in our idealistic little heads—we found ourselves steeped in the intense and artificially induced community of fellow students and faculty as we prepared ourselves for future ministry. What an amazing time of community building that was for us. And then we were called to our various places of ministry. For the two of us, it happened to be suburban Massachusetts and rural Vermont.

There is something about the centrifugal force that is generated at the end of our times as students together at seminary. All of us in pastoral training eventually get spun out in all directions and settle in locations around the country and globe—some urban places, others suburban, and still others rural. Many, but not all, of those places prove to be very lonely places. The latest statistics suggest that the medium-size church in America is seventy-five people. This means that the majority of us end up in single-staff settings and preach to congregations of twenty, fifty, or seventy-five people on a good Sunday, and that we end up walking into empty, quiet churches every Monday morning, very much alone.

But even if we are spun off into multi-staff contexts and lead positions in larger churches, the loneliness still persists—a loneliness bred by the responsibility and the isolation of leading complex and often conflict-vulnerable congregations. In the same article mentioned above, Ed Stetzer, vice president of research and ministry development of Lifeway, observes, "Pastors [of larger congregations] feel privileged, but clearly the reality of constant service can take its toll. There is discouragement and loneliness in ministry. It appears that the larger the church the more present the loneliness."[2] Of those in congregations with an average attendance of 250 or more, 17 percent strongly disagree that pastoral ministry makes them feel lonely at times. In comparison, 32 percent with churches of 0–49 and 27 percent with churches of 100–249 strongly disagree.

So it is, whether small or large, the proximity of our ministries enslaves us physically as well as mentally and emotionally to local and

---

2. Lifeway Research, "Pastors feel Privileged", para. 5.

often lonely places. Set apart from our peers, it takes time for loneliness to set in within our locations. Often times, loneliness is camouflaged as solitude, and what is wrong with solitude? Depending upon our personalities, relational intelligence, and basic need for others, solitude can very well be a desired steady state of mind for some. But chances are, in time, solitude begins to show itself for what it is. Ministry is a lonely place and we all desperately need people in our lives to affirm us and provide a much needed broader perspective.

So many novice pastors get caught up experimenting and enacting their own visions of ministry in their new churches that they fail to feel the beginning nagging tugs of this loneliness within their souls. It is only natural when the first natural tugs of isolation do occur, young pastors latch onto the relationships that are most readily available to them in their settings, their spouses and family members if they have them, or possibly, a well-regarded church member or two. But are these relationships adequate over the long haul? Perhaps, but time will tell as pastors' marriages and families are equally caught up into the pressures of ministry and eventually experience a similar loneliness.

The second tyranny in pastoral ministry is the tyranny of time. Is there a more unique distinctive of our vocation than in how we spend time? Our profession lives on the opposite side of the spectrum that characterizes many in our congregation who punch time clocks everyday—figuratively or literally. We live relatively nonstructured lives. With some exceptions, we are masters of our own calendar. Our lifestyles reflect significant latitude in how we plan our days. Consider what we are free to do often times, say, on Tuesday at 3:30 PM in comparison to others in our congregation. Watch us as we stand, yet again, on the sideline of another Little League game of our children. Who else has the ability to do that?

Of course, the opposite can be said. Who in our congregation do we find at the hospital room—once again—with a parishioner at 10:00 PM? Or, who else is out two or three evenings a week in meetings? What professions are required to be constantly on call for congregational crises that might come along at any time of the day or week?

And herein lies the tyranny. There is much talk about burnout in the pastorate. The drumbeat of pastors leaving ministry annually is approximately 250 per month, or 1 percent of the total, based upon Lifeway Research's findings. A good percentage of these claim burnout as the reason and often times the source of this burnout has fallen solely on the assumption that pastors are just working too hard. The discussion most often centers around the endless evening meetings and crises. In many cases, pastors are genuinely physically and emotionally exhausted.

But burnout has another side to it that deals equally with the tyranny of time. Much so-called burnout falls on the unstructured nature of the position. For many, burnout has more to do with the burden of maintaining and keeping a schedule. It is the problem of too much time in the church that needs to be structured—personally and for others—that always seems to fall on pastors' shoulders. It is the weight of managing large amounts of time well.

Frankly, there are two types of pastors relating to this issue, and both often claim to be victims of burnout. The first are those who have taken on the burden of time and become workaholics. They lack discipline in managing their work week well and overwork themselves to vocational death. But there are other pastors who err in the opposite way (and we all know them). Viewed from the outside, they lack a good work ethic. They are undisciplined pastors who lack the ability to effectively manage the large amount of time that fills the blank slate of their days and weeks. They burn out, not because of overwork, but underwork and a lack of accountability.

Look closely into the lives of many of these burned-out pastors and we find them entrenched in deep ruts. This leads us to the final tyranny, the tyranny of task. For a moment, retrace the footsteps of the average pastor through a typical week. What do we see? We see footprints deeply embedded in the minutiae and repetitiveness of daily life. Pastors' footprints run on well oiled (and not so well oiled) tracks. They are enslaved, often times, to the "habits of the heart" of multiple agendas and schedules of the congregation.

Now, follow the ruts of the wagon wheels of generations of wagon trains of countless pioneers as they traveled across the plains, over the Rocky Mountains, and along the Oregon Trail in the eighteenth and nineteenth centuries. Ruts can be a good thing. A well-worn rut was nothing short of a clear signpost that gave direction to weary travelers that followed. They acted as signs of encouragement that, if they persevered, others could follow the same tracks in the soil. And they gave evidence of travel-weary wisdom that helped others to not have to reinvent the wheel of their everyday lives along the way. Ruts can be a good thing. Perhaps we can even say that they are an inevitable part of everyone's life.

But ruts, too, can be a destructive force, and especially for pastors. It doesn't take long for pastors—even freshly minted pastors—to get caught up in the immediate and mundane details of day-to-day ministry. Finish one sermon on a Friday or Saturday night and you look around the corner and another one is looming the next Sunday. The necessary evil of church administration that all but a few actually enjoy, seems to invade every moment of our weeks. The latest suggestion that appears as a fresh insight from one parishioner has been heard countless other times in the weeks and months, even years prior.

The inevitable ruts of ministry can rob pastors of the freshness that once was a hallmark of their call to ministry. Where are the innovative ideas that captured their imaginations not too long ago? What happened to all of the personal motivation that is to be the fuel to motivate their congregations? We see this inertia toward complacency everywhere in our associations with other pastor colleagues. We see it embedded deep in their eyes. Maybe theirs is no different from other vocations, but the burden of leading congregations—a group of unpaid volunteers who have high expectations and often low aspirations—suggests that ministry is particularly vulnerable to complacency. Left unchecked, the ruts of ministry can lead pastors to the loss of motivation and creativity in their ministries.

To further punctuate the tyranny of task, pastoral ministry is one of the few occupations that lacks performance reviews and professional development requisites. While healthcare personnel, lawyers, educators, and many other professionals are subject to annual evaluations and continuing education credits to maintain their credentials, denominations and ecclesiastical governing bodies rarely require performance evaluations or pastoral development requirements to maintain their ordination status. Some pastors possess the sensibilities to ask their church leadership boards to inaugurate performance evaluations, but most are too insecure to initiate such a process. And as a result, they become perpetual victims of unfiltered pastoral criticism. If a buffet of disparaging comments is not tempered by systematic feedback and a steady diet of reassuring rhetoric, pastors will eventually suffer from discouragement and depression, which ultimately leads to disenchantment with ministry.

Likewise, some ministers maintain enough self-motivation to pursue advanced theological degrees, attend ministry conferences, join clergy clusters, and read books and periodicals for personal and professional growth, but many other pastors simply lack the impetus. And they are allowed (even enabled) to coast, sometimes for decades, without any formal development. Without ongoing spiritual/intellectual stimulation or practical skill improvement beyond performing their weekly duties, pastors remain vulnerable to tyranny of task and its twin consequences: boredom and burnout.

We speak of the above three tendencies in ministry as tyrannies because, for all of the wonderful things we can say about being a minister—and there are many—to be an effective pastor through time requires perspective to fight back the frequent oppression and arbitrariness that comes with the profession. What is it that keeps us mindful of the privileged nature of our high calling? All this brings us back to the doorstep of the eight of us pastors writing our book. Nothing new or profound here, but in looking back, what we shared together was a special kinship of place, time, and task.

First, the kinship of place. What is it about retreating from our normal lives that is so valuable for us? What is behind the impulse to get away on annual vacations, or to go camp in the summer, for example? Author and Franciscan friar Richard Rohr talks about the value of liminal space. He describes this space as:

> where we are betwixt and between the familiar and the completely unknown. There alone is our old world left behind, while we are not yet sure of the new existence. That's a good space where genuine newness can begin. Get there often and stay as long as you can by whatever means possible ... This is the sacred space where the old world is able to fall apart, and a bigger world is revealed. If we don't encounter liminal space in our lives, we start idealizing normalcy.[3]

Central to our time together as eight pastors was that we were physically separated from the routines and details and distractions in order to gain new perspective on our lives and ministry together. This can only happen in a "foreign" space, a "set apart" place. Again, place matters. From the vantage point of standing apart from the normal—the "betwixt and between" of liminal space in Rohr's words—we were able to gain new insight on what was otherwise routine.

Toward that end, as a preamble to beginning our writing, we spent significant time rehearsing our own stories with one another. We talked about the biographical details of our lives, our hopes and dreams, our conversions, our marriages, our successes but also our disappointments and failures, our plans for the future. In short, we talked about our private pilgrimages and how we got from "here to there." Because we were in a

---

3. Rohr, "Liminal Space," para. 3.

position to trust one another—we were becoming kinsmen—we felt safe to ask hard questions and make observations of one another. Even the simplest questions were asked. (Sometimes the most obvious and seemingly naïve question by another offers the greatest insight.) And, in sharing our stories with one another, we caught ourselves actually telling our stories to ourselves in fresh and new ways. Stepping back from what was most familiar in our lives, we were able to gain fresh insight into what was ordinary and consequently easily overlooked.

Second, the kinship of time: Everyone who enjoys a good cup of tea, knows that the quality of taste is intrinsically tied to how long the tea is steeped in the hot water. If you don't soak the tea bag long enough, you fail to extract the optimum flavor. Like a good cup of tea, we found that the quality of our experience was proportionate to the quantity of time we spent together. We valued "steeped" time. It was not enough to spend a few fleeting hours or a day or two together. We found that the kinship we shared required spending several weeks together.

This idea of quality time being directly equivalent to the quantity of time spent was reinforced over and over again by one of us who was responsible to oversee a program of continuing education for pastors for many years through a seminary. Year after year, he filled the plate with all manner of educational and inspirational programs for pastors—from one-day seminars to weekend retreats to online workshops to writing workshops to wilderness programs to sabbatical programs to extended programs that lasted sometimes fifteen and twenty years. What he found time and time again was, although all these programs had some value, the longer the program, the deeper the impact. What most pastors truly sought was "steeped time" together.

Finally, the task of kinship. Although the ultimate task that brought us together was the task of writing, we found increasingly the "real" task of our time together ran far deeper. It was the task of true brotherhood (and sisterhood). C. S. Lewis gives us a wonderful picture of authentic brotherhood on display in his own life in his description of the long walks through wood and dale he had with a few good companions. Inevitably they found themselves at the end of the day with feet propped up in an inn, a good port in hand, having great conversations. On the surface, he spoke of companionship as being between people who are doing something together—"hunting, studying, painting, or whatever you will." But, upon further reflection, the river that really ran through his relationship with his companions was far more than the sharing of activities. He said, these relationships "will still be doing something together, but something more inward, less widely shared and less easily defined.[4]" Shared activities were only an excuse to experience something far deeper.

Interestingly, we found the kinship we shared together as pastors had less to do with friendship, in the narrow sense of the word, than in something else. I suppose we would all call ourselves friends in a general way, but *friendship* is too sloppy a word to describe what we shared together.[5] Evidence of this is that few of us have remained in close contact with one another since we finished our writing. In hindsight, the true source of our kinship had more to do with the common sense of calling we shared together. It was a shared vision for ministry and commitment to learning from one another that occupied most of our time. And in this case, it was a common vision for returning to the parish and living out our pastoral task in the public square. Parish life and ministry was what we mulled over during our time together—comparing, testing, refining, and questioning our calling. In the end, this proved to be our task together as kinsmen.

These, then, are what we commend to you: A vision of "time set apart," "steeped time," and a "shared calling." We are convinced that, chief among all the things that pastors need to build into their lives in order to flourish over the long haul, is the "discipline" of kinship in a pastoral learning community. We intentionally speak of kinship as a "discipline," because the nurturing of true kinship doesn't just happen. Our experience is that it takes intentionality. Our time together as eight pastors is a prime example of this. We confess that, if it wasn't for the task of writing this book together, none of us would have found ourselves entering into the life-giving pastoral learning community we shared together. Sitting for those weeks around a common fireplace and dinner table together was an accident, an accident brought on by a common task. An accident, indeed, but given what we know now, it shouldn't have been. It is something that, for all persons in pastoral ministry, needs to be purposefully built into our lives.

---

4. Lewis, *Four Loves*, 89.

5. David Horn, in his book *Soulmates*, works through the classical literature of friendship in an effort to gain a deeper understanding of what is often meant by "Christian community," and makes what some would consider the surprising observation that friendship is not only not Christian fellowship as it is being describing in the New Testament; it is quite the opposite. Understanding this has significant implications for how community is nurtured within the church.

Bibliography

Abrams, M. H. *The Mirror and the Lamp: Romantic Theory and the Critical Tradition.* Oxford: Oxford University Press, 1953.
Anyabwile ,Thabiti. "Jonathan Edwards and American Racism: Can the Theology of a Slave Owner Be Trusted by Descendants of Slaves?" Lecture from Carl F. H. Henry Center, Deerfield, IL, February 1, 2012. https://henrycenter.tiu.edu/resource/jonathan-edwards-and-american-racism-can-the-theology-of-a-slave-owner-be-trusted-by-descendants-of-slaves/.
ASCD Committee on Platform of Beliefs. "What Is the Purpose of Education?" https://files.ascd.org/staticfiles/ascd/pdf/journals/ed_update/eu201207_infographic.pdf.
Banner, Joshua. "The Practitioner: Nurturing Artists in the Local Church." In *For the Beauty of the Church: Casting a Vision for the Arts*, edited by W. David O. Taylor, 123–44. Grand Rapids: Baker, 2010.
Barber, Rebekah. "How the Civil Rights Movement Opened the Door for Immigrants of Color." *Facing South* (February 3, 2017). https://www.facingsouth.org/2017/02/how-civil-rights-movement-opened-door-immigrants-color.
Bomback, Andrew. *Doctor.* New York: Bloomsbury, 2018.
Brown, Virginia. "The Gift of Time." *Thinking/Living Out Loud* blog (February 5, 2010). http://ginnysbrown.blogspot.com/2010/02/gift-of-time.html.
———. "Things equal are not the same." *Thinking/Living Out Loud* blog (November 12, 2009). http://ginnysbrown.blogspot.com/2009/11/blog-post.html.
Bruggink, Donald J., and Kim N. Baker. *By Grace Alone: Stories of the Reformed Church in America.* Grand Rapids: Faith Alive, 2004.
Bunyan, John. *The Pilgrim's Progress.* Uhrichsville, OH: Barbour, 1988.
Chang, Raymond, "The Asian American Christians for Black Lives and Dignity March." *Asian American Christian Collaborative* (July 1, 2020). https://www.asianamericanchristiancollaborative.com/article/the-asian-american-christians-for-black-lives-and-dignity-march-in-chicago.
Cho, Abraham. "Why Race Matters to God and What That Means For Us." Lecture hosted by Hope for New York City, January 14, 2016.
Collins, Francis. *The Language of God: A Scientist Presents Evidence For Belief.* New York: Simon and Schuster, 2006.
Curtis, Jesse. "What Has Happened To Evangelicalism? The History of Church Growth Offers A Clue." *Colorblind Christians* (September 15, 2019). https://

colorblindchristians.com/2019/09/15/what-has-happened-to-evangelicalism-the-history-of-church-growth-offers-a-clue/.

Daman, Steve. "What is the Quiet Revival?" Emmanuel Gospel Center (October 21, 2016). https://www.egc.org/blog-2/2016/10/13/understanding-bostons-quiet-revival.

Dewey, John. "Individual Psychology and Education." *The Philosopher*, 12, 1934. http://www.the-philosopher.co.uk/2016/08/individual-psychology-and-education-1934.html.

———. "My Pedagogic Creed." *School Journal* 54 (January 1897). http://dewey.pragmatism.org/creed.htm.

DiNatlae, Genevieve. "Ridding the world's oceans of plastic: Andover students' idea embraced by science community." *Andover Townsman* (February 20, 2020). https://www.andovertownsman.com/news/local_news/ridding-the-worlds-oceans-of-plastic/article_8a1e7d81-550-591b-afa0-f34d7b86e7e4.html.

The Eagle-Tribune, North Andover, MA. "Climate change." March 7, 2019.

Ecklund, Elaine Howard. *Why Science and Faith Need Each Other: Eight Shared Values that Move Beyond Fear.* Grand Rapids: Brazos, 2020.

Emmanuel Gospel Center Boston. "Boston Education Collaborative." https://www.youtube.com/watch?v=LzyuSG—0JA.

Farmer, Blake. "When Doctors Struggle With Suicide, Their Profession Often Fails Them." *NPR* (July 31, 2018). https://www.npr.org/sections/health-shots/2018/07/31/634217947/to-prevent-doctor-suicides-medical-industry-rethinks-how-doctors-work.

Foshay, Arthur W. "The Curriculum Matrix: Transcendence and Mathematics." *Journal of Curriculum and Supervision* 6 (Summer 1991) 277–93.

Franklin, Benjamin. "Proposals Relating to the Education of Youth in Pennsylvania." 1749. https://archives.upenn.edu/digitized-resources/docs-pubs/franklin-proposals.

Frey, William H. *Diversity Explosion: How New Racial Demographics Are Reshaping America.* Washington, DC: Brookings Institution, 2013.

Fujimura, Makoto. *Culture Care: Reconnecting with Beauty for Our Common Life.* Downers Grove, IL: InterVarsity, 2017.

Fujita, Akiko. "GPS Tracking Disaster: Japanese Tourists Drive Straight into the Pacific." *ABC News* (March 16, 2012). https://abcnews.go.com/blogs/headlines/2012/03/gps-tracking-disaster-japanese-tourists-drive-straight-into-the-pacific.

Garret, Elizabeth. "Becoming Lawyers: The Role of the Socratic Method in Modern Law Schools." The University of Chicago, 1998. https://www.law.uchicago.edu/socratic-method.

Gawande, Atul. *Being Mortal: Medicine and What Matters in the End.* New York: Metropolitan, 2014.

Gill, David W., "Commissioning Our People for the Workplace" Mockler Memo (January 2014). https://www.gordonconwell.edu/wpcontent/uploads/sites/19/2019/04/MM14.01CommissionYourWorkers.pdf.

Gilliss, Trent T. "Martin Luther King's Last Christmas Sermon." *On Being* (December 25, 2017). https://onbeing.org/blog/martin-luther-kings-last-christmas-sermon/.

Granberg-Michaelson, Wes. "Think Christianity Is Dying? No, Christianity Is Shifting Dramatically." *Washington Post* (May 20, 2015). www.washingtonpost.com/

news/acts-of-faith/wp/2015/05/20/think-christianity-is-dying-no-christianity-is-shifting-dramatically/.

Heinrich, Jill. "Ask the Expert: What Does Separation of Church and State Mean in America's Public Schools?" Cornell College News Center, 2019. https://news.cornellcollege.edu/2019/11/ask-expert-separation-church-state-mean-americas-public-schools-report/.

Horn, David. *Soulmates: Friendship, Fellowship, and the Making of Christian Community*. Carol Stream, IL: Hendrickson, 2017.

———. *A Story of God's Faithfulness: The History of the First Congregational Church of Hamilton*. Hamilton, MA: First Congregational Church, 2014.

Hunter, James Davison. *To Change the World: The Irony, Tragedy, and Possibility of Christianity in the Late Modern World*. Oxford: Oxford University Press, 2010.

Jefferson, Thomas. "Letter to George Whythe." 1786. https://founders.archives.gov/documents/Jefferson/01-10-02-162.

———. "Notes on the State of Virginia." 1781. https://search.lib.virginia.edu/sources/uva_library/items/u1768743.

Johnson, Todd. "Christianity in Asia." Gordon-Conwell (November 18, 2020). https://www.gordonconwell.edu/blog/christianity-in-asia/.

Kamrath, Angela E. *The Miracle of America: The Influence of the Bible on the Founding History and Principles of the United States of America for a People of Every Belief*. 2nd ed. Houston: American Heritage Education Foundation, 2015.

Keller, Timothy. "How Do Christians Fit into the Two-Party System? They Don't." *The New York Times* (September 29, 2018). https://www.nytimes.com/2018/09/29/opinion/sunday/christians-politics-belief.html.

Keller, Timothy, and Katherine Leary Alsdorf. *Every Good Endeavor: Connecting your Work to God's Work*. New York: Riverhead, 2012.

Kouzes, James M., and Barry Z. Posner. *Credibility: How Leaders Gain and Lose It, Why People Demand It*. San Francisco: Jossey-Bass, 1993.

Lewis, C. S. *The Four Loves*. San Diego: Harvest, 1960.

———. "The Weight of Glory." In *The Weight of Glory: And Other Addresses*. Grand Rapids: Eerdmans, 1965.

Lifeway Research. "Pastors feel Privileged and Positive, Though Discouragement Can Come." October 5, 2011. https://lifewayresearch.com/2011/10/05/pastors-feel-privileged-and-positive-though-discouragement-can-come/.

Littky, Dennis, and Samantha Grabelle. *The Big Picture: Education Is Everyone's Business*. Alexandria, VA: ASCD, 2004.

McCarthy, Niall. "America's Most Trusted Professions." *Forbes* (January 11, 2019). https://www.forbes.com/sites/niallmccarthy/2019/01/11/americas-most-least-trusted-professions-infographic/#1bb19a6f7e94.

McCaulley, Esau. *Reading While Black: African American Biblical Interpretation as an Exercise in Hope*. Downers Grove, IL: InterVarsity, 2020.

Meyer, Jason. "Jonathan Edwards And His Support Of Slavery: A Lament" *The Gospel Coalition*, 2019. https://www.thegospelcoalition.org/article/jonathan-edwards-support-slavery-lament/.

Morford, Doran. "Commencement Speech." Winnacunnet High School, Hampton, NH, June 2015.

NPR. "When Doctors Struggle With Suicide, Their Profession Often Fails Them." July 31, 2018. https://www.npr.org/sections/health-shots/2018/07/31/634217947/to-prevent-doctor-suicides-medical-industry-rethinks-how-doctors-work.

Nazianzus, Gregory. "Reflections on the Priesthood." http://www.newadvent.org/fathers/310202.htm.

Noll, Mark. *The Scandal of the Evangelical Mind*. Grand Rapids: Eerdmans, 1994.

Ozolins, Janis. *Education and the Pursuit of Wisdom: The Aims of Education Revisited*. New York: Routledge, 2018.

Picard, Rosalind. "I Got Smart and Took a Chance on God." *Christianity Today*, April 2019. https://www.christianitytoday.com/ct/2019/april/rosalind-picard-mit-professor-meets-author-knowledge.html.

Piper, John. "A Theology of Art in Five Minutes." 2013. http://www.desiringgod.org.

———. "We Are Makers—Lessons on Vocation from Dorothy Sayers." 2013. www.desiringgod.org (accessed March 1, 2020).

Postman, Neil. *Technopoly: The Surrender of Culture to Technology*. New York: Random House, 1992.

Rohr, Richard, "Liminal Space: Finding Life Between Chapters." https://inaliminalspace.org/about-us/what-is-a-liminal-space/.

Ryken, Leland. *Worldly Saints: The Puritans As They Really Were*. Grand Rapids: Zondervan, 1986.

Ryken, Philip. *Art for God's Sake: A Call to Recover the Arts*. Phillipsburg, NJ: P&R, 2006.

Scott, Donald M. *From the Office to Profession: The New England Ministry, 1750–1850*. Camden, NJ: University of Pennsylvania Press, 1978.

Semuels, Alana "Good School, Rich School; Bad School, Poor School." *The Atlantic* (August 25, 2016). https://www.theatlantic.com/business/archive/2016/08/property-taxes-and-unequal-schools/497333.

Shaughnessy, Andrew. "Expanding the Archive: How Art can Help Us Love Our Neighbor Better." *ByFaith* Q3. 2019. https://byfaithonline.com/expanding%E2%80%A8-the-archive.

Sherman, Amy. *Kingdom Calling: Vocational Stewardship for the Common Good*. Downers Grove, IL: InterVarsity, 2011.

Sproul, R. C. *Truths We Confess: A Systematic Exposition of the Westminster Confession of Faith*. Sanford, FL: Reformation Trust, 2019.

Stanglin, Doug, and Michael James. "Nearly 40 homes catch fire after natural gas tragedy north of Boston." *USA Today* (September 13, 2018). https://www.usatoday.com/story/news/2018/09/13/gas-explosions-massachusetts-leave-homes-fire/1295706002/.

Stevens, Mitchell. *Kingdom of Children: Culture and Controversy in the Homeschooling Movement*. Princeton Studies in Cultural Sociology. Princeton: Princeton University Press, 2009.

Strauss, Valerie. "What's the purpose of education in the 21st century?" *Washington Post* (February 12, 2015). https://www.washingtonpost.com/news/answer-sheet/wp/2015/02/12/whats-the-purpose-of-education-in-the-21st-century, emphasis original.

Straw, Carole. *Gregory the Great: Perfection in Imperfection*. Berkeley: University of California Press, 1988.

Stevenson, Bryan. *Just Mercy: The Story of Justice and Redemption.* New York: Spiegal and Grau, 2014.
Sweet, Leonard I. *Rings of Fire: Walking in Faith through a Volcanic Future.* Colorado Springs, CO: NavPress, 2019.
"Syrian, Lebanese and Other Arab Americans." *Global Boston*, Boston College Department of History. https://globalboston.bc.edu/index.php/home/ethnic-groups/syrianslebanese-and-arab-americans/.
Vanhoozer, Kevin, and Owen Strachan, *The Pastor As Public Theologian.* Grand Rapids: Baker, 2015.
Wagenman, Michael R. *Engaging the World with Abraham Kuyper.* Bellingham, WA: Lexham, 2019.
Walzer, Michael. *The Revolution of the Saints: A Study in the Origins of Radical Politics.* Cambridge: Harvard University Press, 1965.
Wang, K. "Indicator 10: Bullying at School and Electronic Bullying." *Indicators of School Crime and Safety,* National Center for Education Statistics (April 2019). https://nces.ed.gov/programs/crimeindicators/ind_10.asp.
Warner, Steve. "Immigrants And The Faith They Bring." *Religion Online*, 2020.https://www.religion-online.org/article/immigrants-and-the-faith-they-bring/.
"WHO guidelines on physical activity, sedentary behavior and sleep for children under 5 years of age." Geneva: World Health Organization, 2019. License: CC BY-NC-SA 3.0 IGO.
Wright, N. T. *Surprised by Hope: Rethinking Heaven, the Resurrection, and the Mission of the Church.* New York: HarperOne, 2008.
Yeh, Allen. *Polycentric Missiology: 21st Century Mission for Everyone Everywhere.* Downers Grove, IL: InterVarsity, 2016.
Yoshinaga, Kendra. "Babies of Color Are Now the Majority, Census Says." *NPR* (July 16, 2016). https://www.npr.org/sections/ed/2016/07/01/484325664/babies-of-color-are-now-the-majority-census-says.

www.ingramcontent.com/pod-product-compliance
Lightning Source LLC
Chambersburg PA
CBHW031401230426
43670CB00006B/604